# Managing Multilingual Workplaces

This book sets new trajectories for language-sensitive business and management research and pedagogy. The existence of language plurality characterises these. Empirical studies have been established as important and relevant for contemporary research. It has shifted language-sensitive research from the periphery to the centre of international management research. However, this field is rapidly changing, and new thematic approaches have begun to emerge. By addressing this, the book offers genuine and more nuanced insights into existing themes and comes with applications of emergent conceptual developments in different settings. The second part of the book covers methodologies and gives examples and cutting-edge insights into the role of translation in the execution of empirical research and theorising arising from it. Finally, the book draws together innovative ways of how to address the challenges of a multilingual teaching classroom and how to innovate in order to incorporate such diversity through pedagogic practice.

This book provides a source that unites insights from multilingual empirical research, methodological considerations and pedagogic practice in order to advance knowledge and debate. It will be a 'handy source' of information that offers direct access to the latest guidance on language-sensitive management challenges. It will, therefore, appeal to an internationally minded and mobile audience, including scholars, students and decision-makers.

**Sierk Horn** is Professor of International Management at the FH Vorarlberg, University of Applied Sciences, Austria. Until 2017 he held the Professorship of the Economy of Japan at Ludwig-Maximilian-University, Munich.

**Philippe Lecomte** is President and founding member of GEM&L. He has been Associate Professor at Toulouse Business School (TBS), France, for over 30 years. His current research interest is on language in international business and management education.

**Susanne Tietze** is Professor of Multilingual Management at Sheffield Hallam University, Sheffield Business School. She has a particular interest in translation as a method and concept to understand transformational process.

# Routledge Studies in International Business and the World Economy

# Managing Multilingual Workplaces

Methodological, Empirical and
Pedagogic Perspectives

Edited by
Sierk Horn, Philippe Lecomte,
and Susanne Tietze

Routledge
Taylor & Francis Group

NEW YORK AND LONDON

First published 2020
by Routledge
605 Third Avenue, New York, NY 10017

and by Routledge
2 Park Square, Milton Park, Abingdon, Oxon, OX14 4RN

First issued in paperback 2022

*Routledge is an imprint of the Taylor & Francis Group, an
informa business*

Publisher's Note
The publisher has gone to great lengths to ensure the quality of this
reprint but points out that some imperfections in the original copies may
be apparent.

*Library of Congress Cataloging-in-Publication Data*
Names: Horn, Sierk, editor. | Lecomte, Philippe, editor. | Tietze,
    Susanne, editor.
Title: Understanding multilingual workplaces : methodological,
    empirical and pedagogic perspectives / edited by Sierk Horn,
    Philippe Lecomte, Susanne Tietze.
Description: New York, NY : Routledge, 2020. |
    Series: Routledge studies in international business and the
    world economy | Includes bibliographical references and index.
Identifiers: LCCN 2020009769 (print) | LCCN 2020009770
    (ebook) | ISBN 9781138364790 (hardback) |
    ISBN 9780429431128 (ebook)
Subjects: LCSH: Communication in management—Cross-cultural
    studies. | Multilingual communication. | Intercultural
    communication. | International business enterprises—
    Management—Cross-cultural studies.
Classification: LCC HD30.3 .U53 2020 (print) | LCC HD30.3
    (ebook) | DDC 302.3/5072—dc23
LC record available at https://lccn.loc.gov/2020009769
LC ebook record available at https://lccn.loc.gov/2020009770

ISBN: 978-0-367-52161-5 (pbk)
ISBN: 978-1-138-36479-0 (hbk)
ISBN: 978-0-429-43112-8 (ebk)

DOI: 10.4324/9780429431128

Typeset in Sabon
by Apex CoVantage, LLC

This book is dedicated to Nigel Holden, a true pioneer and advocate of language-sensitive research.

# Contents

## SECTION 1
## Methods and Methodologies in Multilingual Research     1

### New Perspectives and Approaches to Language-Based Research     3
SUSANNE TIETZE

# Figures

# Tables

# Editors

**Sierk Horn** is Professor of International Management at FH Vorarlberg, Austria. Previously, he was Professor of the Economy of Japan at the Munich School of Management, Ludwig-Maximilians-Universität, Germany. He holds a PhD in Modern Languages and a Habilitation on Cross-Cultural Management from Freie Universität, Berlin, Germany. Much of his work takes the perspective of resilience of individuals and organisations and sits at the juncture of language and international management. He is a regular commentator on how organisations tackle fragile environments.

**Philippe Lecomte,** PhD, is President and founding member of GEM&L, an international research group on management and language. He has been Associate Professor at Toulouse Business School (TBS), France, for over 30 years. He was head of the Language Department of TBS and co-director of the Major in International Management at TBS. He has co-edited two special issues on language and management in leading international management journals. His current research interest is on language in international business and management education.

**Susanne Tietze,** MA, MBA, International Teaching Diploma (IMD), PhD, is Professor of International Management at Sheffield Hallam University. She has researched and published about the role of English as a lingua franca in management research and how it is used as a knowledge-shaping practice. She has published five books about language and international management, and she is currently the Principal Investigator of a UK Research Council grant which explores language and translation work in multilingual business communities. Her contemporary research focuses on the exploration of translator agency in international knowledge transfer.

# Contributors

**Wilhelm Barner-Rasmussen** is Professor in Business Administration at Åbo Akademi University School of Business and Economics. His work on language, multilingualism and boundary spanners is rooted in a longstanding interest in knowledge sharing and social capital in internationally active organisations. He has published on these issues in leading international business journals such as *Journal of International Business Studies* and *Journal of World Business*.

**Linda Cohen** is a specialist in managing cultural and linguistic diversity in organisations. She chaired the Department of Language and Culture at ESCP Europe, Paris campus and has taught in French universities and business schools. Her current research areas include the use of English as a working language in international business, managing language diversity in organisations and teaching and learning in multicultural/multilingual contexts. She is a founding member of GEM&L, an international research group on management and language, and is currently a consultant in managing diversity in organisations.

**Dominic Detzen** is Associate Professor in the Department of Accounting at the Vrije Universiteit Amsterdam. He completed his PhD in 2013 at HHL Leipzig Graduate School of Management. His research centres on the audit profession, where he has investigated issues on professional socialisation, identity work and language.

**Shea Fan** is Senior Lecturer of International Business at RMIT University, Australia. She holds a PhD from the University of Melbourne. Shea's key research interests include cross-cultural management, multinational corporation management, expatriate management and immigrants with a special focus on an identity perspective. Shea has published in *Human Resource Management*, the *Journal of World Business*, *Applied Psychology: An International Review* and the *International Journal of Human Resource Management*.

**Claudine Gaibrois** is Lecturer in Culture, Society and Language at the Zurich University of Applied Sciences and an External Lecturer on

Managing Multilingual Companies at St. Gallen University and at EM Strasbourg Business School. She received her PhD from St. Gallen University for her thesis on the discursive construction of power relations in multilingual organisations. Her research interests include linguistic and cultural diversity, communication in organisational contexts, intercultural communication and power relations. Her work has been published in journals such as the *Journal of World Business*, the *International Journal of Cross-Cultural Management* and the *European Journal of International Management*. Claudine Gaibrois has conceived and taught lectures on the management of language diversity in different educational contexts and in different formats. She is a board member of the GEM&L (Groupe d'Etudes Management et Langage) and has joined its scientific committee.

**Arkadiusz Gut** is Associate Professor (PhD in Philosophy and Psychology) in the Department of Cognitive Science at the Nicolaus Copernicus University in Toruń, Poland, and Visiting Professor in the Huazhong University of Science and Technology, China and the City University of New York, the USA. He is a recipient of scholarships and fellowships from the Polish Foundation for Science, the Fulbright Foundation and the Stefan Batory Foundation. His main research interests include cognitive science, cross-cultural studies, cognitive developmental psychology, language as a tool for thinking and philosophy of mind. He has published in *Multilingua: Journal of Cross-Cultural and Interlanguage Communication, Synthese, Journal of Intercultural Communication, Studies in Logic, Grammar and Rhetoric, Brentano Studien, Philosophy of Science* and *Polish Journal of Philosophy*.

**Anne-Wil Harzing** is Professor of International Management at Middlesex University, London, a Visiting Professor at the Tilburg Institute of Governance and a Fellow of the Academy of International Business. Her research interests include international HRM, expatriate management, HQ–subsidiary relationships, the role of language in international business and the international research process. She has published more than 120 journal articles and book chapters on these topics and has been listed on the Web of Knowledge Essential Science Indicators top 1% most cited academics in Economics & Business worldwide since 2007. Anne-Wil also blogs regularly about all things academia and runs CYGNA, a network for female academics.

**Jane Kassis-Henderson** is Emeritus Professor at ESCP Europe Business School, Paris campus. Her research interests focus on language-related factors in international management and academic contexts, particularly the consequences of the use of English as a working language in multicultural/multilingual settings. Her publications include studies of language diversity in international management teams and of the implications of language boundaries on the development of trust in teams. She is a founding member of GEM&L, an international research group on management and language.

**Kaisa Koskinen** is Full Professor of Translation Studies and Head of Languages at Tampere University, Finland. Professor Koskinen's publications include the monographs *Beyond Ambivalence. Postmodernity and the Ethics of Translation* (PhD, 2000) and *Translating Institutions. An Ethnographic Study of EU Translation* (Routledge 2008). Her current research interests include the concept of translatorial action from contemporary and historical perspectives, ethics of translation, as well as translation, user experience and affect, and her forthcoming publications include *Translation and Affect* (Benjamins, 2020) as well as edited volumes *Translating in Town* (Bloomsbury, 2020) and *Routledge Handbook of Translation and Ethics* (2020). Koskinen is actively involved in PhD training. She is an inaugural member of the steering committee of the DOTTSS Translation Studies Doctoral and Teacher Training Summer School (2012–) and the director of DOTTSS Tampere in June 2018. She is also the secretary of the international doctorate in translation studies network ID-TS (2017–).

**Hélène Langinier** is Associate Professor at EM Strasbourg—University of Strasbourg, France. She is member of the Research Lab Humanis. She teaches and conducts research in the field of intercultural management, linguistic diversity and expatriates' adjustment. She manages personal and professional development for international students. She started her career in human resources in an international audit and advisory firm in Luxembourg and Berlin where she recruited and managed international mobility.

**Lukas Löhlein** is Assistant Professor at the Institute of Management Accounting and Control at WHU—Otto Beisheim School of Management. Before joining WHU, Lukas was a Postdoctoral Researcher at the London School of Economics and Political Sciences (LSE) from 2015 to 2017. Lukas earned his PhD from the University of Luxembourg.

**Irina Mihailova** is Senior Researcher in International Business and Sales Faculty at University of Eastern Finland and a Researcher in International Business Faculty at Aalto University, School of Business. Dr. Mihailova has conducted research in a number of areas including competitiveness and institutional development in emerging markets, internationalisation strategies of Russian firms and learning through IJVs. Currently, her work is focusing on topics belonging to internationalisation in digital sectors and emergence of new business models. Her work has appeared in *Academy of Management Review*, *Journal of World Business*, *Management and Organization Review*,

*Management International Review, Thunderbird International Business Review* and *Critical Perspectives in International Business* among others.

**Terry Mughan** is Associate Professor of International Business at Royal Roads, University, Canada and formerly Professor of International Management at Anglia Ruskin University, UK. He has conducted numerous studies of business internationalisation for, among others, the OECD, the European Commission and UK Trade and Investment. His first degree was in foreign languages and they have always featured as an important variable alongside culture, strategy and practice in his inquiries. In recent years he has been developing innovative approaches to language in business centring on a language-general approach for non-specialist linguists.

**Virpi Outila** is Lecturer in International Business at Leeds University Business School. Her research interests include international HRM, headquarter-subsidiary relationship, practice/knowledge transfer and cultural issues with the focus on emerging economies, particularly Russia. Prior to joining academia she worked as a business executive in HRM for several years in various Finnish MNCs. Her expertise covers all areas of HRM with a special focus on international HRM and business with Russia.

**Rebecca Piekkari** is Markus Wallenberg Professor of International Business at the Aalto University, School of Business. She has a long-standing interest in language diversity as a critical management challenge for international organisations and as a methodological challenge for organisational research. Over the years she has taught many multilingual groups of PhD, MSc and BSc students in various programmes around the world. Her work has been published in journals such as the *Academy of Management Review*, *Journal of Management Studies* and *Journal of International Business Studies* as well as in several handbooks in the area. Her current research interests focus on the role of translation and translators in international business. She is a Fellow of the Academy of International Business and European International Business Academy.

**Markus Pudelko** is Professor of International Business at the University of Tübingen, Germany. He has earned master's degrees in Business Studies (University of Cologne), Economics (Sorbonne University) and International Management (Community of European Management Schools) and a PhD (University of Cologne). His current research is on multinational teams, the impact of language on international business, headquarters–subsidiary relationships and Japanese HRM. His work has been published in journals such as the *Academy of Management Journal*, *Journal of International Business Studies*, *Human Resource Management*, *Leadership Quarterly* and *Journal of World Business*.

**Anne-Marie Søderberg** is Professor at Copenhagen Business School, Denmark. With a research focus on cultures, communication and learning processes, she has created a bridge between her background in the humanities and her present position as an international business scholar. She has published extensively in international handbooks, edited volumes as well as journals such as *International Journal of Cross Cultural Management, International Journal of Human Resource Management, Journal of International Business Studies, Journal of International Management* and *Management International Review*.

**Helene Tenzer** is Associate Professor of International Business at the University of Tübingen, Germany. She has earned a master's degree in International Cultural and Business Studies and a PhD at the University of Passau. Her current research focuses on language in international business, multinational teams, leadership in multinational enterprises, organisational behaviour and the management of foreign subsidiaries. Her work has been published in journals such as the *Journal of International Business Studies, Leadership Quarterly, Journal of World Business* and *Management International Review*.

**Denice Welch** is Honorary Professor at the University of Melbourne, recently retired from Melbourne Business School. Her research interests are in international management, including the effects of language on a range of organisational areas. She has researched and published about multilingualism as a challenge for the multinational enterprise. One of her areas is international human resource management and global careers. Her latest research addresses the relation between internationalisation and language strategy.

**Lawrence Welch** is Honorary Professor at the University of Melbourne, recently retired from Melbourne Business School. His research focuses on the internationalisation of business firms including the role of language differences. He has recently published a book chapter about risk and uncertainty of firms in the international context. He has also published about translation behaviour in international companies.

**Michał Wilczewski** is Assistant Professor at the University of Warsaw, Poland, where he directs Business Communication Research Center, and Visiting Researcher in Copenhagen Business School, Denmark. He maintains an active research agenda, with particular focus on intercultural communication in MNCs and intercultural experiences of business expats, missionaries, and international students. He has published in *Multilingua – Journal of Cross-Cultural and Interlanguage Communication* and *Learning, Culture, and Social Interaction*, among others. His latest book *Intercultural Experience in Narrative* (2019) offers new insights into intercultural experiences, communication, and cultural challenges faced by Polish professionals in China.

**Huiping Xian** is Lecturer in the Work, Employment and Organisation Division at Sheffield University School of Management. She received her doctorate from Manchester Metropolitan University, UK. Her research interests are women's careers, HRM issues in Chinese organisations, qualitative research methods, and cross-cultural and translation issues in international research. Her book (with Meng-Lewis) titled *Business Research Methods for Chinese Students: A Practical Guide to your Research Project* was published in 2018. She has also published papers in *Human Resource Management* and *International Journal of Human Resource Management*.

# Foreword to Managing Multilingual Workplaces

Given the relevance of language issues to international business, it has been somewhat surprising that it has taken academics working in the field so long to take a serious account of language. This was evident when we started our work in the mid-1990s with Rebecca Piekkari. Literature searches at the time revealed that language in the IB context was not viewed as a primary theme, hence the title of our first publication used the word 'forgotten.' The word 'neglected' would have been just as apt. This impression was borne out when we began to present our early ideas to colleagues at conferences. A common reaction was: "Of course language is important but so what?"

In answering such comments, an important step was to recognise the need to separate language from the composite constructs of culture and psychic distance. We termed this as opening the 'black box' to expose language as a construct in its own right. As we pointed out, this bundling had tended to mask the role of language. It was assumed, and often mentioned to us initially, that it was empirically difficult and even inappropriate to separate out one component from the composite of culture.

However, focusing on language separately has facilitated the investigation of its role in multilingual workplaces, particularly the multinational. Over the course of our research, we have been able to expose the pervasive way language infiltrates a wide range of international business processes—such as interunit communication, employment practices, networks, knowledge transfer, international marketing and strategy, selection of new markets, coordination and control, and organisational design. Our findings illustrated how language had important consequences, affecting the way international firms operate and ultimately their performance. For example, we concluded that if multinationals are to function as knowledge entities, they need to act as language entities. We were able to drill down into the organisation to explore how language can facilitate or impede processes in more ways than just person-to-person communication. Language was shown to be more than a technical issue that machine translation can readily fix.

Considering language separately also facilitated its consideration as a resource that could provide the MNC with specific competences and therefore competitive advantage. Over the past three decades, IB scholars have shown the important role of knowledge and knowledge transfer in effective performance. Importantly though, language was missing as a factor in this line of research. However, language was shown to have an important impact. It is an active agent in the international knowledge transfer process. The challenge was not only to recognise this important role, but to appreciate that language is a resource that needs to be built and nurtured. This comes at a cost to the individual and international firm. We conceptualised language resources as deriving from human, social and organisational capital, resulting in what we termed language operative capacity (LOC). But possessing language resources does not ensure readiness for use. First, language needs to be recognised as a resource—identified and deployed in place and in time when required. For this to happen, though, management needs to be 'language aware.' Second, language resources and their use need to be actively managed. This is being reflected in some international firms in the development of coherent language strategies.

One of the satisfying results of the burgeoning attention has been acceptance of the legitimacy of language-related research—attested by the growing volume of work by a diverse group of researchers from various countries and disciplines, the wide range of journals accepting language-oriented articles, the number of special journal issues and dedicated conferences. These developments have assisted in 'selling' the role and importance of language to some dismissive international business colleagues.

Lately, we have seen the benefits of inter-disciplinary research. Work by international business scholars has influenced and been influenced by colleagues from linguistics, communication and language teaching. This collaboration has been the result of the building of common interest areas rather than traditional territory protection. We have come a long way since our first seminar presentation to a joint gathering where those from linguistics were openly hostile to the idea that IB scholars were 'talking about language,' which they saw was their domain alone. This book is testament to the benefits of open and receptive collaboration.

What's next? We don't need to convince the audience that language matters. That is now well established. The question is *how* does language matter? In what ways? In what processes? And how does language affect outcomes for businesses in the international arena? Can we assume that the factors we identified in the multinational context are equally applicable to other ways of operating internationally, such as through agents, licensing, franchising and alliance partners? Whereas the multinational has been the focus of much language research, we should not lose sight of the fact that many, if not the bulk of, language exchanges occur on the ground in foreign markets.

What we see as a potential negative for future research is that we can allow the debate about the dominance of English to become *the issue*. The English-based business weekly *The Economist* has often pointed to the prominent role of English in international business activities. Its coverage includes attempts to preserve other languages from the inroads made by English. Articles also concede that the power of English is driven partly by international business education frequently conducted in English, and partly by the spread of social media and the Internet. In this debate, a question posed by many is whether the power of English will be extended or curtailed by technological developments in the area of machine translation. One could argue that with easier translation the importance of a common language such as English will be diminished. As a result, we may enter an era of 'language deglobalisation'. Of course, how more convenient and accessible machine translation will be used in normal discourse and social situations remains questionable. But one should not rule out surprising developments. We cannot predict, but it is reasonable to assume that more of the translation work will be taken out of the hands of humans.

Much of the early research into the importance of language in international business used qualitative methodologies. This stage was important in building an understanding of how language permeated processes such as communication within organisations. Later work has developed also through more broad-scale quantitative studies, with some utilising a mixed-method approach. Perhaps the more difficult but important work has been at the theoretical level which can be said remains to be extended.

Denice Welch
Melbourne Business School,
University of Melbourne

Lawrence Welch
Melbourne Business School,
University of Melbourne

# Managing Multilingual Workplaces: Empirical, Methodological and Pedagogic Perspectives

Over the last 20 years, work at the juncture of language and international business was of great vibrancy. The central proposition of this body of literature was the need to disentangle 'language' from 'culture.' Language gives meaning to experiences at work. The intensive research on language use in organisations, thus, helped to make the implicitness of cultural differences (and their impact on experiences when managing across cultures) more explicit. In other words, the great insight of this line of research was to give voice to the true diversity of otherwise 'invisible' assumptions about 'how things are done' in organisations.

Language influences what happens inside organisations. It also invades engagement with the outside world. Sharing knowledge, networking and building relationship are central challenges for most companies. And they all have to do with the way language is used (Holden, 2002). This makes language a key resource for achieving competitive advantages. By extension, this recognition has spurned research activities in the field of individual behaviour in organisational and managerial contexts. Over time the spotlight shifted from how people go about their tasks within these contexts to the dynamics that shape interactions with each other to the inside (including intra- and inter-group behaviour) and to the outside (e.g. customers, suppliers). In short, our knowledge about the way people make use of language in organising and managing in an internationalising world is relatively advanced.

A deep understanding about the role language in international business pays off in many situations: be it in the decision-making to enter foreign markets, in competing (or cooperating) with firms from around the world or in executive roles in multi-cultural teams (to name just a few examples). Those in the know can only profit from the close engagement with the reality that the language-sensitive research agenda pursued. The topics tackled by the researchers offer an unclouded view of the interplay of language, culture and competing interests. Now that, after a period of high vibrancy, research on language has gained maturity in the domain of international business, a sincere and intelligent discussion of what lies ahead seems timely. Contributing to the future development of this field is the primary concern of this volume.

Languages and language-based research have by now been established as legitimate topics and approaches in international business and management, despite the dominance of English as the language of pedagogy and publication. However, there is still a shortage of knowledge and practical guidance on how language plurality informs research protocols and pedagogic interventions. Despite the topicality of the 'languages' topic, not only for business and management, but also in the light of significant changes in the political policy landscape (e.g. Brexit) as well as shifts in the composition of mobile labour forces (Hogan-Brun, 2017; Kelly, 2018), there is no comprehensive source that draws together methodological, empirical and pedagogic insights.

This book brings together influential thinkers on languages in organisations. Together, we address how language-sensitive approaches are relevant across different domains of academic work, i.e. in terms of research work (methodological questions and empirical settings) and also in terms of pedagogic practice. In particular, in the light of contemporary and future challenges 'for languages,' we wish to stimulate, provoke and inform research, policy and pedagogic practices.

The book is divided into three interlinked parts, where each part presents a distinct perspective on language plurality.

- The methodological part of the book challenges the notion that the methods of social sciences can readily and unproblematically be appropriated by language-sensitive international management scholars; it is shown that issues of translation, incommensurable meanings of different languages and the notion of lack of equivalence need to be established as important supplements to existing (social science) research designs;
- The empirical part of the book takes forward and deepens existing research streams. Its innovation lies in its contribution to adding nuance to current debates (e.g. multilingual global teams) by establishing vocabulary (e.g. translanguaging) in line with capturing the complexities of languages-in-use and by deepening our understanding of the complex interplay between languages and cultures;
- The pedagogic part offers insights into the 'what's next' of multifaceted pedagogic approaches. The contributions ask critical questions of the integration of language into specifically international business education and making multilingual classroom central to management education. By drawing together innovative ways of how to address the challenges of a multilingual teaching classroom, we offer insights into pedagogic practice and highlight why we should bother with language in international business and management education.

This book is an edited collection of contributions about a multilingual world, and it is concerned with how, when and why languages are used at work, in education and research. The chapters of this book, the editorials, the foreword and the concluding discussion are all written in English: a fact that may seem hardly noteworthy—yet is it not interesting that neither of the three editors is a native speaker of English; that they communicated during the genesis of this book in English despite German being potentially a more obvious language for them to use (two are native speakers of German; one has native speaker competence); that of the 21 authors only three are native speakers of English; and that Scandinavian, Central European and some Eastern European geographies, as well as China, are represented? Whereas some of the represented languages and nation-states and cultures reflect the networks of the editors, it is likely that all authors have received part of their education at English-language based universities or have had excellent access to English learning resources and structures. Knowledge work is utterly dependent on having a 'shared code,' a meaning system and communicative practices which enable knowledge to be created and shared. In contemporary times, this code, system and practice is the English language.

The treatment of English is, therefore, a central aspect of this book, across all three sections. Lillis and Curry (2010) point to the importance of English as a literary practice of academic writers, which is useful as well as political because it is imbued with "values and ideologies" (p. 18) which underpin the politics of academic knowledge production: in other words, only knowledge expressed and published in English is considered useful and valid (cf. Steyaert & Janssens, 2013; Tietze & Dick, 2013).

The position in this book is, however, not to reject English—a practical impossibility if one wants to reach a global audience—but we encourage all to use it more reflectively, always with an eye towards languages' power to enable as well as to constrain, to liberate as well as to imprison and to create as well as to suppress. We return to the theme of reflexivity in the discussion at the end of this book.

There is another argument as to why research into the use of English in global processes continues to matter. Philosophically, this goes back to linguistic anthropology and in particular to linguistic relativity, which proposes that one's native language shapes the way one perceives and enacts the world. This means that English—like any other language—provides categories for segmenting, coding and understanding the world, both social and material, that we inhabit and that each cultural/language group has a different perspective on what constitutes reality: "The real world is to a large extent unconsciously built on the language habits of the group" (Sapir, 1949, p. 161). Without such ordering of what we see and experience, life would be chaotic as all meaning, inference, association and labels fall away.

Therefore, to speak of management, business education and research exclusively in and through English is a helpful, necessary and important way to communicate and to share knowledge; however, it is also restrictive to the extent as not all possible knowledge and understanding about global contexts, encounters and how to understand them can be expressed in English only. Yet, English as the lingua franca of business and management is successful—it works unproblematically in a practical sense and within a pragmatic approach to language. If one is 'good enough' in the language, it is considered 'useful.' It simply works. However, misunderstandings and marginalising effects of weak English non-native speakers are still a reality in the business world. Another issue is the illusion created when using English as a foreign language for cross-border communication. In her recently published book about communication strategies with Chinese and North American people Tréguer-Felten (2018) draws on discourse analysis (in the French sense of this methodology i.e. content analysis) in order to demonstrate that speakers using 'good' English fail to communicate correctly because their communication strategies are embedded in their own culture. English is then only a kind of artificial wrapping of these culturally driven communication acts. The result is the illusion that they communicate properly. The use of English as lingua franca (ELF) only hides the communication failure. In this sense, ELF appears to be more a dangerous illusion than a true success. To what extent and depth subtleties of meaning, differences in meaning, understanding and communication strategies can all and always be expressed and reflected in English is a key theme of this book. The linguist Anna Wierzbicka (2014) proposes that language is a contingency of how the world is perceived, one's spectacles so to speak, and that English words such as "reality, fact, evidence, mind, emotions, anger, self-esteem, fairness, reasonable, rights, privacy and so on" (Wierzbicka, 2005, p. 217) are not innocent or neutral and absolute concepts. Instead, they are loaded with (usually) unexamined meanings and worldviews.

Thus, all chapters concern themselves with the role of English in relation to 'other' languages and how they are used together, in parallel or in challenge to each other. Some chapters follow a foreignisation strategy of writing in English, which means that some words and meanings from other languages and cultures are left visible in the published text in order to signal to the reader that language and cultural differences continue to exist, even if English is used as a global lingua franca to communicate findings of research projects, to teach in classroom and to engage with practice and businesses.

The collection of 11 chapters together with three editorials for each part of the book and a discussion, which points to the emerging big themes which unite methodology/research, empirics and pedagogy, provide in our view a comprehensive resource to inform research, pedagogy and quite possibly also policy. Thus, the scope of this book arguably goes beyond the topicality of languages for business and management. There are significant changes in the broader political policy landscape (e.g. Brexit, unrest in Hong Kong) where the use of language shapes our understanding of discourse, public and otherwise. Let's not forget the role of new media here, as they fundamentally change the way we make sense of evidence and unfolding events. In short, there are still many aspects relating to language plurality, translation and education which remain unaddressed. Although it is of course not possible to address every single aspect in detail, this volume offers new ways of thinking about how to teach and understand languages in the context of business and management research, education and, by extension, the uncertain environment firms operate in. We have divided the book into three related fields of applications (methodological challenges; empirical perspectives and pedagogic innovations) which are characterised by the existence of language plurality. Furthermore, in the discussion, we draw some emergent themes taken from these parts together in such a way as to point to future trajectories for research, pedagogy and practice.

Thus, the aims of this book are:

- To provide a source that unites insights from multilingual empirical research, methodological considerations and pedagogic practice: The ideas we distilled from the individual chapters point to the big themes of reflexivity, translation as an as yet not fully explored communication 'tool' in global epoch; the role of flexibility and mobility in terms of workforces and interactions at the workplace, but also within classroom scenarios);
- To advance knowledge and debate about each of these: Each part offers advances which have not been established in the extant literatures. For example, in the methodological part, innovative research designs and the role of multi-agentic translation are discussed; in the empirical part new insights into the relationship between language and culture are offered; contributions of the pedagogy part offer novel conceptualisation of learning and teaching;
- To consolidate the standing of the language-sensitive body of works in order to deepen the role it plays in international management across research and pedagogy;
- To provide a 'handy source' of information which offers direct access and guidance about language-sensitive management challenges, which appeals to an internationally minded and mobile audience.

The strong emphasis of providing conceptual insights based on empirical findings, together with thorough investigations of questions of methodology and pedagogic practice, herald the consolidation of the language-sensitive field, and we hope that this volume will be helpful in grounding 'languages' even more firmly into approaches within international management teaching and research. Taken together, we suggest that the way forward for research on language use in organisations is a more reflective use of English as a shared language, knowledge code and system of practices.

## References

Hogan-Brun, G. (2017). *Linguaonomics*. London: Bloomsbury.

Holden, N. (2002). *Cross-cultural management: A knowledge management perspective*. Harlow: Pearson Education.

Kelly, M. (Ed.). (2018). *Languages after Brexit: How the UK speaks to the world*. London: Palgrave Macmillan.

Lillis, T., & Curry, M. J. (2010). *Academic writing in a global context: The politics and practices of publishing in English*. London and New York: Routledge.

Sapir, E. (1949). *Selected writings* (D. G. Mandelbaum, Ed.). Berkeley and Los Angeles: University of California Press.

Steyaert, C., & Janssens, M. (2013). Multilingual scholarship and the paradox of translation and language in management and organization studies. *Organization*, 20(1), 131–142.

Tietze, S., & Dick, P. (2013). The victorious English language: Hegemonic practices in the management academy. *Journal of Management Inquiry*, 22(1), 122–134.

Tréguer-Felten, G. (2018). *Langue commune, cultures distinctes: Les illusions du globish*. Québec: Presses Universitaires de Laval.

Wierzbicka, A. (2005). There are no "colour universals", but there are universals of visual semantics. *Anthropological Linguistics*, 47(2), 217–244.

Wierzbicka, A. (2014). *Imprisoned in English: The hazards of using English as a default language*. Oxford: Oxford University Press.

# Section 1

# Methods and Methodologies in Multilingual Research

*Editor: Susanne Tietze*

# New Perspectives and Approaches to Language-Based Research

*Susanne Tietze*

Language-based themes as a legitimate area of inquiry within international management research have been propelled forward by researchers interested in the use of languages in multilingual work contexts. By now, these themes have consolidated into a recognized research stream, which is developing its own networks and philosophies. Tietze and Piekkari (2020) put forward the notion that language-based research continues to develop as a field of inquiry and is currently characterized by 'increasing institutionalization of networks as well as by the beginnings of interdisciplinary work between international business, institutional scholarship, organisational studies, and translation studies' (ibid., in press, p. 8). Thus language-based research has achieved a degree of maturity and such maturity is expressed, amongst others, by debates and questions about research philosophy, research methods and research designs. This compilation of four book chapters is, to the best of our knowledge, the first collection of academics' considerations of such questions. The intellectual stimulation offered by this part lies in its authors' competence in shedding light on a neglected method (experiments) (Chapter 1); the role of translation as an integral and central act of data analysis and researcher sense making (Chapter 2); the role of translation of Western research philosophies from a Chinese perspective (Chapter 3); and a novel conceptualization of the multilingual organization as a translatory space with translatorial linguistic ethnography offered as a methodological avenue to understand multilingual work places as spaces of translation (Chapter 4).

Therefore, this part offers innovative insights into alternate research designs (experiments; translatorial linguistic ethnography); it demonstrates how interlingual translation is part of data analysis; how translation is an ongoing, multi-agentic act. It offers a conceptual take on multilingual work places which transcends current understanding of these workplaces being multilingual and predominantly located in multinational corporations (Frederikson, Barner-Rasmussen, & Piekkari, 2006).

## Researching Multilingual Workplaces: Language Practices

Multilingual workplaces have been investigated for almost three decades (Tietze & Piekkari, 2020) and the early emphasis on the location of research within multinational enterprises and focusing on the role of the common corporate language (frequently, but not always English) and its respective constellation with 'other languages' has yielded fruitful knowledge about how and to which consequence languages are deployed in multilingual work organizations. This body of work has been analyzed by two recent literature reviews. Tenzer, Terjesen, and Harzing (2017) reviewed 264 journal articles and showed that the conceptualization of language within business studies is divided as languages are either seen as static, discrete entities or hybrid and situational codes. This divide is to an extent reflected in the four chapters as Chapter 1 is showcasing experimental approaches, with a view to 'test whether theory . . . is plausible' and to provide evidence of causality (p. 1); whereas Chapter 2 is based on a more interpretive approach, where meaning is seen as shifting, ambiguous and grounded in historical-political context. Perhaps, as Tenzer et al. (2017) propose, the requirement is to find complementarities between these different 'takes on language'; with experiments yielding clarity and in particular in-depth case studies or ethnographies yielding insights into complexities. Karhunen, Kankaanranta, Louhiala-Salminen, and Piekkari (2018) have reviewed recent studies located in multinational corporations and for these authors, the most promising take on language-based research is informed by a social practice view of language. In general, this view is that meaning is created through taking actions in the world and analysis needs to focus on how such actions are enabled or constrained (in multilingual contexts) by using languages in particular ways, with particular groups and with particular intents.

The different philosophical approaches adopted in the four chapters reflect different understandings of languages either as language use in situated contexts—Chapter 2 is perhaps the most prominent example of this approach—or as language as being a code 'to be cracked' within a more realist approach. Whether or not the two can be aligned and be used in a complementary fashion as envisaged by Tenzer et al. will remain open for now. From the perspective of a committed interpretivist (i.e. the perspective of the author of this introduction, Susanne Tietze), I find one study published in 2010 by Akkermans, Harzing and Witteloostuijn intriguing. Using a quasi-experiment the authors demonstrate that a foreign language is a strong primer for behaviour by a research design within which participating Dutch students play a business game, and that when this game is played in English, their behaviour becomes less cooperative and more competitive. I do not know of a case study or interview-based study that has yielded such clear findings about the influence of language on behaviour (or practice)—a key argument in the debate on why languages matter in understanding behaviour in multilingual contexts.

## Researching Multilingual Workplaces: Translatorial Practices

It may well be a sign of a conceptual shift in language-based research communities that three chapters engage with translation as part of a multilingual research project, with translation as an integral and central aspect of research philosophies and with translation as a conceptual take on multilingual work places. The inherent logic of this translation perspective is that if different languages co-exist in one form or other, there are two basic means to enable communication: the use of a bridge language like English or translation between languages (see Feeley & Harzing, 2003 for an overview over how to manage language diversity). English as such a bridge language, and how it is used and to what consequence has been thoroughly investigated by 'language-sensitive international business research' (Piekkari & Tietze, 2011), and the contemporary field is turning to translation to explore 'the other' means, i.e. translation.

The turn to translation is currently gaining momentum based on the notion that there is no absolute equivalence of meaning between languages, and this provides indeed opportunities for research designs and execution. Chapter 2 is a case in point as its focal concept, empowerment, did not exist at all on the level of the word/concept or on the level of experience in the researched setting. This raises the question of how one does research something that does not exist neither conceptually or experientially. The research team turns to the use of proverbs as a means to explore empowerment at the Russia subsidiary and also details the translation process that occurred during data analysis. It is shown, how meaning emerged, was changed and rethought during the interlingual translation process and that 'translators' included agents outside the research project itself, in this case an editor. Thus, data analysis is multi-agentic and unfolds from the interlingual act of translation (see also Xian, 2008). In a similar vein, Chapter 3 states that reflexivity of researchers in multilingual research relates to their 'own role in the translation process' (Chapter 3, p. XXX) and their potential influence on the outcomes. Providing an insider account of the author's experience of translating Western research methodologies into Chinese, it is shown that translation is cultural practice and that it involves the 'recreation of meaning and knowledge that make sense to the target audience' (Chapter 3, p. XXX). Xian uses her own past confusion when as a doctoral student she was being confronted with terms such as 'grounded theory' or 'critical realism' and how difficult it was for her to make sense of these terms—despite being a competent user of English in oral and written forms. From my own experience, the providers of research methods training in the UK (and in some European universities I am familiar with) care little about whether these traditions and philosophies make sense to 'other' audiences. Efforts are only expended to make such training more sophisticated and effective, instead of questioning the taken-for-granted use of Western philosophical paradigms.

Chapter 4 by Koskinen offers a conceptual innovation by framing multilingual workplaces as translatorial spaces: as spaces of translation where translation needs to happen for mutual comprehensibility and where multilingual repertories meet and mix. Additionally, she proposes that such workplaces feature ongoing translator activity that transgresses the boundaries of equivalence-based research. This chapter therefore offers language-based research communities a different way of framing future research, perhaps offering a way away from the identifying language practices or barriers to identifying translatory practices. The empirical example in this chapter is based on a translatorial linguistic ethnography—and provides a detailed description of what is entailed in this approach in terms of layers of contextualization and translator agency (with translators being either professional translators or other organizational agents also). To the best of our knowledge, language-sensitive research in (international) management is yet to produce such ethnographic studies that document how organizations are translated into being.

## What Next?

Karhunen et al. (2018), Tenzer et al. (2017) and Tietze and Piekkari (2020) purport that language-sensitive research has got a bright future, that it will feature more interdisciplinary approaches and research located in other localities than the MNC. In this regard getting access to organizations is vital to ensure that empirical and conceptual exploration provide trajectories for theoretical deepening as well as for practical application of research findings. Here, perhaps, experimental designs may provide findings clarity and preciseness may convince business audiences that language research matter.

Taken together, the four contributions of this part may herald more variety in the use of research designs, more interdisciplinary projects in terms of employing methods from the social sciences, but also the arts and the humanities and last not least in engaging with translation as expressive and constitutive of multilingual workplaces and research practices.

In terms of advancing the research practices and approaches within language-based management research, I propose that useful starting points are:

a)  to develop protocols for reporting the translation process in written research accounts, which transcend the back translation approach favoured by international business research (Chidlow et al., 2014)—Chapter 2 provides some ideas of how this could be achieved;

b)  to deepen and broaden the use of methodologies and research designs by expanding the methodological reach of research designs and advocate and use methods less frequently employed—Chapters 1 and 4 provide detailed accounts of available designs; by combining multiple methods to assess their potential to yield innovative findings and theorizations; by starting a tradition in which reflexivity plays a more prominent role;

c)  to leave 'other' language data visible, i.e. to foreignize writing strategies in order to disrupt the palatable presentation of one's finding and to acknowledge the existence of other languages, concepts and perspectives—Chapters 2, 3 and 4 have such inbuilt reminders of 'other languages', while remaining intelligible to an English speaking international readership;

d)  to find creative and effective ways to work with organizations, practitioners and language users and to inform their practices and policies.

Language-based research has been, sometimes inadvertently, quite 'radical' in challenging the notion that English is a universal language of all (management) knowledge and that its use is unproblematic. Some accounts point directly to the hegemonic assumptions which underpin the monolingual worldview of much of the management academy (Steyaert & Janssens, 2013; Tietze, 2018). Engaging in language-based research is inevitably asking questions about 'the other'—whether it is the other language or the other language user or other meanings. The research methods and concepts offered in the four chapters of this part provide techniques and concepts of how to engage in language-based research. All of these techniques, their applications and their underpinning episteme are offering the field something new, innovative and challenging. More importantly, they offer food for thought on how to engage with 'the other' which language-sensitive researchers invariably meet in research encounters, whether in the field or in the laboratory or while sitting at the desk.

## References

Akkerman, D., Harzing, A. W., & Van Witteloostuijn, A. (2010). Cultural accommodation and language priming. Competitive versus cooperative behaviour in a prisoner's dilemma game. *Management International Review, 50*, 559–583.

Chidlow, A., Plakayiannaki, E., & Welch, C. (2014). Translation in cross-language international business research. Beyond equivalence. *Journal of International Business Studies, 45*, 562–582.

Feeley, A. J., & Harzing, A. W. (2003). Language management in multinational companies. *Cross-Cultural Management: An International Journal, 10*(2), 37–52.

Frederikson, R., Barner-Rasmussen, W., & Piekkari, R. (2006). The multinational corporation as a multilingual organization. The notion of a common corporate language. *Corporate Communications: An International Journal*, *11*(1), 406–423.

Karhunen, P., Kankaanranta, A., Louhiala-Salminen, L., & Piekkari, R. (2018). Let's talk about language: A review of language-sensitive research in international management. *Journal of Management Studies*, *55*(6), 980–1013.

Piekkari, P., & Tietze, S. (Eds.). (2011). A world of languages: Implications for international management research and practice. *Journal of World Business*, *46*(3), 267–268.

Steyaert, C., & Janssens, M. (2013). Multilingual scholarship and the practice of translation and language research in organization studies. *Organization*, *20*(1), 131–142.

Tenzer, H., Terjesen, S., & Harzing, A. W. (2017). Language in international business: A review and agenda for future research. *Management International Review*, *57*(6), 815–854.

Tietze, S. (2018). Multilingual research, monolingual publication: Management scholarship in English only? *European Journal of International Management*, *12*(1–2), 28–45.

Tietze, S., & Piekkari, R. (2020). Languages and cross-cultural management. In B. Szkudlarek, L. Romani, J. Osland, & D. Caprar (Eds.), *The Sage handbook of contemporary cross-cultural management* (pp. xxx–xxx). London: Sage.

Xian, H. (2008). Lost in translation? Language, culture and the roles of the translator in cross-cultural management research. *Qualitative Research in Organizations and Management: An International Journal*, *3*(3), 231–245.

# 1 Moving Beyond the Baseline

## Exploring the Potential of Experiments in Language Research

*Shea Fan and Anne-Wil Harzing*

In the last 30 years, language research in International Management has changed from being a niche topic to occupying the centre stage. Researchers are, thus, starting to look back at what has been achieved and to consider how to move this stream of research forward (see e.g. Karhunen, Kankaanranta, Louhiala-Salminen, & Piekkari, 2018; Tenzer, Terjesen, & Harzing, 2017). This chapter also contributes to this goal, but with a narrower focus, i.e. analyzing the use of experimental designs in language research in International Management. In the rest of this chapter, we use the term language research to mean language research in International Management.

One of the key purposes of research is developing a theory and using it to make predictions. Theory is "about the connections among phenomena, a story about why acts, events, structure, and thoughts occur" (Sutton & Staw, 1995, p. 378). To test whether or not the theory we have developed is plausible, we need evidence of causality, specifically 1. covariation between cause and effect, 2. temporal precedence of the cause and 3. elimination of alternative explanations for the causal relationship (Cook & Campbell, 1979). Compared with surveys and case studies, an obvious advantage of experimental design is its ability to establish causality through a process called randomization. By randomly assigning participants to treatment and control groups, an experimental design can ensure that no unmeasured variables are systemically associated with the dependent variable; thus, plausible alternative causes can be eliminated (Colquitt, 2008). Researchers are then able to claim that the dependent variable is caused by the independent variable and that alternative causes can be ruled out. Consequently, experimental design provides a strong test of how robust a theory is (Zellmer-Bruhn, Caligiuri, & Thomas, 2016). If what is developed is an organizational theory, evidence of causality enables us to advise managers to implement practices grounded in theory with confidence, knowing that the intended outcomes can be expected to materialize (Tung & Stahl, 2018).

Over the last 10 years, the use of experimental methods has received an increasing level of attention in the field of Management and International Business. Editors of major journals have encouraged its use (see e.g. Colquitt, 2008; Reeb, Sakakibara, & Mahmood, 2012; van Witteloostuijn, 2015; Zellmer-Bruhn et al., 2016). However, experimental research is still under-represented in the field of International Management and is even rarer in language research. Having said this, the topic of language has been studied in cross-cultural psychology, psycho-linguistics, international marketing and cognitive science, where experiments are used frequently. The current experimental language research in International Management has been influenced by these disciplines.

The objective of this chapter is not to explain how to design experimental research *per se*. Readers can identify many books and articles that offer detailed explanations on how to conduct experimental research. Instead, we first review the present use of experimental design in language research and then provide some explanations as to why experiments are rarely used. Using this information as the *baseline* for the present application of experimental methods in language research, we then illustrate how this method can be applied more broadly to advance research in the field.

## Exploring the Baseline: Experimental Design in Current Language Research

To establish the *baseline* for the present use of experiments in language research, we reviewed all papers included in two recent review articles (Karhunen et al., 2018; Tenzer et al., 2017). We found that although language researchers have used a large variety of research methods, including case studies, interviews, ethnographic studies, surveys and conceptual research, only seven articles used an experimental design. We subsequently identified a further article, published in 2017, that had used experimental methods. All eight articles are summarized in Table 1.1.

Using these eight articles as our baseline, we have identified a number of key characteristics of experimental research in the extant language in International Management literature.

1. *Outcome variables*. All eight articles focus on the same language effect, namely how the use of language (foreign vs. native language) affects people's attitudes (Harzing & Maznevski, 2002; Harzing et al., 2005; Harzing et al., 2009), decisions (Zander et al., 2011), individual behaviors, (Akkermans et al., 2010; Urbig et al., 2016; Gargalianou et al., 2017) and team behaviors (Comu et al., 2010). Researchers typically contextualized this language effect in the setting of corporate language use and language differences in culturally

*Table 1.1* A list of articles using the experimental design in language research

| Authors, year and journals | Research questions | Theories | Manipulations | Sample |
|---|---|---|---|---|
| 1. Harzing and Maznevski (2002), in *Language and Intercultural Communication* | Do respondents adjust their responses in a way that reflects the cultural values associated with the language of the questionnaire? | Cultural accommodation | Language of questionnaires (native vs. English) | Undergraduate students in 7 countries |
| 2. Harzing et al. (2005), in *International Journal of Crosscultural Management* | Does the use of English-language questionnaires lead to homogenization of responses? | Cultural accommodation | Language of questionnaires (native vs. English) | Undergraduate students in 24 countries [includes the 7 countries in #1] |
| 3. Harzing et al. (2009), in *International Business Review* | How does language and culture affect survey response styles (in both rating and ranking options)? | Cultural accommodation, Linguistic confidence | Language of questionnaires and scenarios (native vs. English) | a) Undergraduate students in 24 countries [as in #2]; b) MBA students in 16 countries |
| 4. Akkermans, Harzing, and van Witteloostuijn (2010), in *Management International Review* | How does language (English vs. native) and cultural experience affect cooperative vs. competitive behavior? | Cultural accommodation | Language used in the games (native vs. English) | Undergraduate students in the Netherlands |
| 5. Comu, Unsal, and Taylor (2010), in *Journal of Management in Engineering* | How do cultural differences and language skills affect project network performance? | Cultural diversity and linguistic competence, Transaction cost analysis | Monocultural teams (native English) vs. multicultural teams (English as 2nd language) | University students [UG and PG] in USA |

(Continued)

Table 1.1 (Continued)

| Authors, year and journals | Research questions | Theories | Manipulations | Sample |
|---|---|---|---|---|
| 6. Zander et al. (2011), in *Journal of World Business* | How do language (English vs. native) and culture affect managers' decisions (leadership related decisions) | Cultural accommodation | Language of scenarios and questionnaire (native vs. English) | MBA students in 17 countries [as in #3] |
| 7. Urbig, Terjesen, Procher, Muehlfeld, and van Witteloostuijn (2016), in *Academy of Management Learning & Education* | Does the use of a native or a foreign language in the classroom impact students' propensity to free ride? | Dual process theory of higher cognition | Language used in the games (native vs. English) | Undergraduate students in the Netherlands |
| 8. Gargalianou, Urbig, and van Witteloostuijn (2017), in *Cross Cultural & Strategic Management* | How does using foreign languages affect cooperative behaviors in a prisoner's dilemma setting? | Cultural accommodation | Language used in the games (native vs. foreign) | Undergraduate students in Belgium |

diverse teams and organizations. Furthermore, some researchers not only tested the language effect in isolation, but also investigated its interaction with culture (e.g. Zander et al., 2011).

2. *External validity.* A strong finding should have both internal validity (the effect can be attributed to the cause instead of other factors) and external validity (the effect can be generalized). Following the International Business research tradition, these articles demonstrate an international focus through their sample choices and the scale of their research. Four articles conducted large-scale cross-national studies in seven to 24 countries (see Table 1.1). This multi-country sampling strategy enabled the researchers to test their focal language effects in different national and cultural contexts and using different languages. This enhanced the generalizability (i.e. external validity) of their findings.

3. *Experimental design and manipulation techniques.* Research design and manipulation techniques are essential elements of experimental research. Although the total number of articles using experimental designs is small, they have applied quite different types of designs with settings including lab environments (e.g. Urbig et al., 2016), the participants' natural environment (e.g. Harzing et al., 2009) and games (e.g. Gargalianou et al., 2017). Additionally, these papers have explored a selection of manipulation techniques, including priming (e.g. Harzing & Maznevski, 2002) and vignettes (e.g. Zander et al., 2011).

4. *The use of student samples.* All eight studies used undergraduate students as their research sample, except for Zander et al. (2011), which used MBA students. Student research samples are very common in experimental design, especially in economics and psychology. It is a convenient and practical sample design choice. First, when the design includes computer simulation or other lab-based manipulations, students are much more accessible; it is difficult to recruit employees to participate in lab-based research. Further, in cross-country research, student samples are relatively homogenous compared with employee samples, so it is easier to ensure the comparability of results. Of course, student samples raise a potential challenge to internal validity. In the later part of the chapter, we discuss the pros and cons of using students as a sample and its implications for International Management and language research.

The low incidence of experimental research demonstrates that the baseline of experiments in language research is rather low. Moreover, in spite of the earlier-mentioned achievements, we have also identified considerable limitations in current experimental research in this field. First, only a very small number of researchers have engaged with this research method, with five out the eight articles co-authored by Harzing and three co-authored by van Witteloostuijn, who has been advocating the use of experiments in International Business (van Witteloostuijn, 2015). Second, most of the articles were published between 2002 and 2011 and there has been a relative lack of activity in recent years. Finally, the majority of studies tested the cultural accommodation effect, which— building on the psycho-linguistics literature—tries to establish the extent to which using a foreign language leads participants to accommodate their attitudes and behaviors to the values of the culture associated with the foreign language in question. However, language research in IM has made considerable progress in recent years and many more language phenomena, effects, concepts and mechanisms have been identified. Fur- thermore, psycho-linguistics is only one of the related research streams that we can draw upon; other research streams, such as cross-cultural psychology, general management and international marketing are also good sources of theories, mechanisms and research design techniques. Therefore, there are still considerable unexplored opportunities for the use of experimental methods in the IM context. In the next sections, we discuss why we believe experimental research has not been widely used in the IB/IM field to date and illustrate how this research method could be explored further by language researchers.

## Why Are Experimental Designs Rarely Used?

The limited number of publications using experiments in language research does not necessarily imply that researchers are not interested in this method. However, they face a number of challenges that might make them reluctant to adopt experimental methods.

### IB/IM Research Tradition Favors Survey Research

Survey research is the dominant research method used in the IB/IM field at large. Survey research enables the researcher to test models with mul- tiple antecedents, mediators, moderators and dependent variables in one study. This allows the researcher to capture the inherent complexity of IB/IM phenomena. In contrast, the majority of experimental research tests the effect of a small number of factors, normally one to three, in a smaller model. As a result, authors conducting experimental research might encounter reviewer concerns that other factors that might affect the dependent variable were not included in the model, making it poten- tially more difficult to publish experimental research.

We argue that this tradition might, in fact, be detrimental to the field of IB/IM. Although survey research has made significant contributions to our understanding of IB phenomena, like any research method it has its limitations. Survey research only generates evidence for correlational relationships between multiple antecedences and outcomes. It is also unable to rule out the possibility that the outcomes might be caused by unmeasured factors. As a result, although multiple factors can be included in a model, researchers cannot be entirely sure that the outcomes were indeed caused by these factors. In contrast, well-designed experiments display high levels of internal validity and can establish causality (Aguinis & Bradley, 2014). Although one experiment cannot identify all possible causes of a phenomenon, multiple studies can achieve this goal incrementally and, thus, ensure external validity. Both surveys and experiments have their strengths and weakness, but in order to understand IB/IM phenomena we need the contribution of both these research methods.

### Lack of Rigorous Training and Experience in Experimental Design

Many IB/IM researchers have considerable knowledge of and experience of conducting survey research but are unfamiliar with experiments. They might be reluctant to change their research trajectory and use a research method with which they are not familiar. Good experiments require a rigorous research design. A flawed design can easily be picked up in the review process and these flaws are difficult to fix.

Moreover, experiments often test a single, clearly defined, relationship in one study. If an experiment is unsuccessful or produces null results, which may happen quite often, the data are unlikely to be publishable. This means that the time and resources that researchers have invested do not lead to a tangible outcome. In contrast, researchers have more flexibility when using survey methods, because they can test multiple hypotheses in one and the same study. Even if some of the hypotheses are not supported, it is still possible to publish a paper. Facing institutional pressures for publication, IB/IM researchers may, thus, be inclined to stay with the safer option of survey research.

### The Developmental Stage of Language Research

Language research in the IB/IM field is a relatively new area of research. Researchers have identified many theoretical mechanisms through interviews, case studies and ethnographic research, as well as conceptual work in the past two decades. To further theorize some situated, context-sensitive theories that have been developed through inductive research, the next step is to conduct deductive research to test specific hypotheses. Evidence of internal validity is needed so that the causal relationships within these theories can be conclusively demonstrated. Evidence of external validity is also needed so that the generalizability of these theories across contexts can be established. Quantitative research can, thus, enhance the current, predominantly qualitative, language research.

Experimental research in particular can make a valuable contribution in this respect. However, experiments are situated within a positivist philosophical research tradition, assuming the existence of an objective truth. They also involve a deductive approach. Its key research concerns are to test and refine existing theories through evidence of causality and generalizability (Corley & Gioia, 2011). To achieve these goals, the theories and mechanisms to be tested in experiments need to be conceptually well-established and empirically operationalized (or measured). However, many findings in language research have yet to be maturely operationalized; this raises challenges for experimental design. As a result, current experimental research has only used a narrow range of theories, in particular theories that have been well-operationalized in other disciplines such as psycho-linguistics and cognitive science.

## Moving Beyond the Baseline: Attitudes, Design Choices and Illustrations for Language Research

### *Thinking Experimentally*

To facilitate the use of experimental designs, the first step is to develop a positive attitude toward experiments. Researchers need to be prepared to follow the call from the editors of *Journal of International Business Studies* to start "thinking experimentally" (Zellmer-Bruhn et al., 2016, p. 404). Thinking experimentally means that we prepare ourselves to use this research method effectively. It involves accumulating knowledge about experimental methods, actively following the development of experimental research in IB and general management research, and searching for mechanisms, theories and manipulations in related disciplines that can be introduced into our context. Furthermore, thinking experimentally means that when planning a new language research project, we give experiments the same consideration as other research methods. This requires researchers to develop the ability to identify phenomena suitable for experiments, to formulate research questions that are appropriate to experiments, and to build a team that has the relevant expertise.

Experiments are, in fact, a very suitable research method for language research. A large amount of language research involves micro-level phenomena. Some key topics include: corporate language policies, individuals' use of a foreign language, the influence of one person's language ability on other employees or team members and language-related discrimination or stereotypes. The dependent variables are usually individuals' cognition, perceptions, attitudes, behaviors or decisions. Experimental design is appropriate to test the causal factors influencing these types of variables and might, thus, help us to advance current language research (van Witteloostuijn, 2015).

The remainder of this chapter outlines the key choices that need to be made in experimental design: student samples vs. mixed samples, between-subject vs. within-subject design, single vs. multiple studies and manipulation techniques. Due to a lack of examples in existing language research, we have selected popular topics in language research and illustrate how experimental designs can be applied for each choice.

### Design Choice 1: Student Samples vs. Mixed Sample Designs

Experimental research is often criticized by Management scholars for its use of undergraduate student samples (Tung & Stahl, 2018), whereas in psychology and behavioral economics student samples are perfectly acceptable. The key issue, however, is the extent to which students are representative of the target population. If the study in question investigates fundamental human processes, such as how native language vs. foreign language use affects people's cognition, using a student sample is legitimate, because students are a representative sample of the target population. Hence, the findings based on student data can be generalized across populations (Bello, Leung, Radebaugh, Tung, & Van Witteloostuijn, 2009).

In the IB field, however, the mechanisms of interest often reflect specific work contexts rather than basic human processes (Bello et al., 2009). As a result, students who have not worked in these specific work environments are unlikely to have the features of the target population that researchers want to investigate (Harrison & List, 2004). Some examples of these specific contexts could be working overseas as expatriates or being subject to language policy decisions. If students do not have this type of experience, the manipulation might not trigger the hypothesized effect among student participants or trigger a response different from what was hypothesized. As a result, findings based on student samples might not be generalizable to the population of employees.

### Illustration

In the context of language research, using a student sample could still have its merits. Although many students do not have work experience, they can have language experiences that resemble those of employees. For instance, in non-English speaking countries, an increasing number of universities have adopted an English-only policy. This policy might affect the university's entry criteria, students' performance assessment and students' interactions with each other. This situation is similar to a corporate policy of using English as a corporate language and the consequences that may have within an organization. To some extent, students in these universities might, thus, have very similar experiences to employees working in organizations that use their non-native language as the corporate language, such as anxiety when using the language or being undervalued or marginalized due to low corporate language proficiency. Students could, therefore, be an appropriate example to study some of these basic psychological mechanisms in language research. However, students might not be a representative sample for certain interpersonal dynamics, because the interactions between students are different from those between employees who have defined roles and contractual relationships with the organization. In this situation, researchers can use a multi-sample design. For example, study 1 could use a student sample to test the hypothesis as a pilot study. If the hypothesis is supported, study 2 could replicate the result using real employees. Many web-based surveys (e.g. Qualtrics) and crowdsourcing tools (e.g. Amazon Mechanical Turk) can now help to reach target samples with specific characteristics (van Witteloostuijn, 2015). An ideal situation would be to then test the hypothesis in a real organizational setting in study 3 to eliminate possible self-selection bias in the web-based sample.

### Design Choice 2: Between-Subject vs. Within-Subject Design

The use of between-subject or within-subject design is an important choice when conducting experiments. Between-subject design requires different participants in the treatment and control groups. Each participant only receives *one* treatment. Normally, each group is advised to have a minimum of 20 cases (Simmons, Nelson, & Simonsohn, 2011). Thus, this type of design can be costly, as it requires different participants for treatment and control groups. Furthermore, in between-subject designs it is important to ensure that the experimental and control groups are comparable on any factors that might impact the dependent variable such as demographic characteristics. This can be achieved through randomization, i.e. randomly allocating participants to the treatment or control groups, and can be checked using statistical procedures to compare groups. If these requirements are not met, then plausible alternatives cannot be ruled out. For example, if the randomization principle was not executed effectively, the mean age of the experimental group might be significantly different from that of the control group; thus, the observed effect could be caused by the age difference rather than the experimental manipulation.

A within-subject design asks participants to react to all treatments. Compared with between-subject design, this type of design requires a smaller number of participants. However, because every participant needs to react to multiple treatments, this design faces the risk of a carry over effect, meaning participants' reactions to a subsequent treatment might be affected by their prior treatments. This can be manifested through very different or very similar responses to conditions (Hsu, Simmons, & Wieland, 2017). If a strong carry over effect cannot be counterbalanced in the design, then a within-subject design may not be a suitable choice. The carry over effect can be counterbalanced to some extent by randomizing the order of the treatments when presented to the participants. This is easily achieved through a computerized survey. In an article included in Table 1.1, Zander et al. (2011) used a within-subject design. All participants were asked to respond to six different managerial decision-related scenarios (i.e. 1. rewarding individuals or teams, 2. CEO's decision-making, 3. manager's goal-setting, 4. face-saving, 5. conflict-resolution, 6. empathizing). The carry over effect was not an issue in this study because rather than focusing on the issues *per se*, the objective of the study was to identify whether the respondents' choices in these situations reflected patterns of the influence of their national cultural norms.

*Illustration*

The level of English language fluency and accents have been popular topics in language research. One research angle could be accent-based discrimination. Researchers have found that a foreign language accent can affect the results of employment-related decisions (Hosoda & Stone-Romero, 2010) and evaluative judgments can be affected by people's foreign language accent (Hansen, Rakić, & Steffens, 2014). This phenomenon can also be examined in the context of MNCs, such as how accent affects interactions between expatriates and host country employees. Using a between-subject design, researchers could prepare two audio clips, one with an expatriate speaking English without accent (the control condition) and the other with an expatriate speaking English with an accent, such as an Indian accent (the treatment condition). We could then randomly allocate employees (e.g. employees in the headquarters of an American MNC) to listen to one of the audio clips, and ask them to evaluate the ability of the speaker based purely on the audio information. This design could reveal how an English accent might bias people's evaluation of expatriates' ability. Of course, depending on the choice of accent and the nationality of expatriates and host country employees, the results may differ. Researchers can decide which choice to make based on their focal phenomenon and research question. A within-subject design is not suitable for this example because the two audio clips only vary in the accent and the content is kept constant. If participants are asked to listen to both clips, the carry over effect is likely to be strong. Additionally, after listening to both versions of the audio clip, participants are likely to guess the researcher's intention, and this understanding is likely to affect their subsequent evaluations.

### Design Choice 3: Single vs. Multi-study Design

Although a single-study design can demonstrate the effect of the key mechanism, it cannot claim that the results are conclusive, whereas in a multi-study design, researchers can provide evidence with stronger internal and/or external validity. For example, researchers can test the main effect in one study, and then introduce a new variable (e.g. a moderator) in a follow-up study. In this way the design can test the main effect as well as its boundary conditions. Researchers could also test the effects of the focal variable on different dependent variables or its effect across different samples. Moreover, when testing the effect of a new variable, researchers can use different ways to operationalize the same variable, such as by manipulating it in one study and measuring it using a scale in another study. In Fan and Harzing (2017), the researchers tested the effect of ethnic identity confirmation, a perceptual agreement between two people regarding the importance of their shared ethnicity. In one study, the focal concept was measured using a Likert scale; in another study it was manipulated using vignettes. The combination of the two approaches measuring the same construct—and providing very similar results—strengthened the internal validity of the research (Fan & Harzing, 2017). Finally, a multi-study design can also be a hybrid research design, such as mixing a lab experiment with field research (e.g. surveys). Lab experiments provide greater control and precision and provide evidence for causality. Survey research using real employees can contribute to generalizability (McGrath, 1981). Hence, a combination of both methods would create a much stronger study.

### Illustration

Language researchers have revealed that using a corporate language policy affects the perceived status of employees in MNCs (Neeley & Dumas, 2016). To further test the relationship between language policy and perceived status, a multi-study experimental design can be deployed. The first study can be designed to establish the main effect of the introduction of a corporate language policy on employees' perceived status within the organization; the second study can replicate the effect using a different dependent variable such as perceived career advancement or intention to leave the organization; the third study could introduce another variable, such as employees' personal characteristics (e.g. language proficiency or nationality) and test how these variables affect the relationship between corporate language policy and perceived status. Furthermore, a survey study could be used to test whether the language policy influences actual or perceived status.

### Design Choice 4: Manipulation Techniques

As illustrated in our discussion of current experimental research in the language in the IM field earlier, different manipulation techniques can be used. Here we discuss three key options: language priming, vignettes and naturally-occurring events.

## Option 1: Language Priming

According to social cognition research, our stored knowledge, such as stereotypes, goals or implicit theories, can be activated by contextual cues. Priming involves using specific information to activate this knowledge and examine how it influences subsequent social judgments and behaviors (Molden, 2014). For example, bicultural individuals are believed to have two sets of cultural knowledge, which can be activated by contextual cues (Hong, Morris, Chiu, & Benet-Martínez, 2000). When studying American-Chinese biculturals, researchers used culturally prototypical images (e.g. Chinese flag and historical images vs. American flag and images) to activate the Chinese or American cultural knowledge set in participants' minds and tested whether participants' attitudes, judgments and behaviors were affected by the cultural knowledge thus activated (Cheng, Lee, & Benet-Martínez, 2006; Hong, Wan, No, & Chiu, 2007).

### Illustration

Language can be used as a prime. It can activate cultural knowledge or country-related stereotypes, which can subsequently affect people's attitudes, judgments or behaviors. In some of the studies presented in Table 1.1, researchers used the survey language as a prime in traditional survey-based research, randomly distributing different language versions of the survey to participants. A comparison of the results under the two different conditions revealed the effect of language on participants' attitudes and behaviors. Similarly, researchers can also embed a language prime in well-established experimental games, such as the prisoner's dilemma game (Keysar, Hayakawa, & An, 2012) or simulated tasks (e.g. Comu et al., 2010).

## Option 2: Vignettes

Vignettes are "carefully constructed and realistic scenarios to assess dependent variables including intentions, attitudes, and behaviours" (Aguinis & Bradley, 2014, p. 352). A well-designed vignette can realistically present organizational reality and helps participants put themselves in this situation, even if they might not have personally experienced it. This type of manipulation enhances experimental realism and subsequently external validity (Aguinis & Bradley, 2014). By presenting vignettes to participants, researchers can solicit participants' responses to hypothetical situations. Vignettes can take different forms. In addition to a written format, researchers can also use pictures, audio or video vignettes. When audio or video is used, it is advisable to hire professionals with trained voices and trained performing skills in the production, so that the highest quality can be ensured. Vignettes are especially suitable for the study of sensitive topics (Aguinis & Bradley, 2014). Some topics might be unethical to study in a survey and/or could invite responses that reflect social desirability. In contrast, participants might feel more comfortable to provide honest responses when reacting to a hypothetical situation.

*Illustration*

A written vignette is relatively easy to develop and use. Among the eight papers we discussed previously, the design by Zander and her colleagues (2011) used a combination of language manipulation (English vs. native) and scenarios of managerial decisions. They created scenarios for six aspects of leadership, namely rewarding individuals or teams, decision-making, goal-setting, face-saving, conflict-resolving and empathizing. Within each scenario, six to eight potential actions were provided and respondents were asked to rank their top three of preferred actions. We present the texts used in the scenario "rewarding individual or teams" next as an example (p. 301):

## Scenario 1: Rewarding

You are a manager of a product division that includes several workplace teams. In your opinion what would be the best way to reward high performing employees in this division?

S1–1. Individual financial incentive based on each employee's individual performance (individual reward)

S1–2. A group-based financial incentive based on the results of the team (group reward)

S1–3. A profit-sharing scheme for all employees based on the performance of the entire company (profit sharing)

S1–4. Non-financial individual incentives (individual non-financial)

S1–5. Public recognition of the best performing employees (individual recognition)

S1–6. Public recognition of the best performing teams (team recognition)

S1–7. Faster promotion of high performing individuals (individual promotion)

They first gave participants a new identity, such as "a manager of a product division" and a brief description of the organizational context, i.e. "a product division that includes several workplace teams". This information set the parameters for the hypothetical situation. They then solicited participants' decisions on the "best way to reward higher performing employees in this division". Because the research instruments were distributed in multiple countries, they were able to compare if the responses were affected by national cultures or language.

Furthermore, with regard to language research, audio vignettes could be a very good choice. For example, researchers can manipulate accents or language proficiency through audio. If researchers plan to introduce the literature on leadership or emotions to language research, videos would be appropriate to manipulate leadership styles or emotions (e.g. anger). Finally, vignettes can be developed when researchers aim to investigate sensitive topics in language research. For example, asking employees to report their behaviors related to discrimination and stereotyping against employees with lower corporate language ability in a survey could be too sensitive. However, asking them to report what they are likely to do based on a hypothetical situation might be more acceptable.

### Option 3: Naturally Occurring Events

Another type of manipulation (or treatment) is using natural events. Of course, we cannot actually manipulate a natural event. This type of experiment uses a naturally occurring event in the field as an experimental treatment and compares selected variables before and after the event (Harrison & List, 2004). We present two examples illustrating how these experiments can be designed. Example 1 used an unexpected event as a treatment, whereas Example 2 is a good example of how to turn a planned event into an experimental treatment.

Example 1: Olivas-Lujan, Harzing, and McCoy (2011) tested whether the September 11 terrorist attacks, an unexpected event, changed the norms and values of American university students by combining two datasets originally collected for other projects. Data used in study 1 of this article were collected from two American universities, namely the University of Virginia and the University of Pittsburgh. Although this was not part of the original design, the data in Virginia happened to be collected before September 11 (in April 2001), whereas data in Pittsburgh were collected after September 11 (in December 2001). Another wave of data from the same universities was collected late March/early April 2002. This unexpected event might have changed students' responses; thus, it created an opportunity for researchers to compare the data before and after the event. The authors found that the terrorist attacks on September 11 decreased the level of cosmopolitanism displayed by American students and increased their perceived importance of relationship hierarchy (Kluckhohn & Strodtbeck, 1961). In addition, they found that students' ideal type of job had changed, with security of employment and having a job that allows one to serve one's country becoming significantly more important. These findings were supported for both the immediate effect and the delayed effect (Olivas-Luján et al., 2011). This article used a second—completely unrelated—study to independently verify the results of the first study. Data for the pilot in study 2 were collected before September 11 (in March 2001), whereas data for the main study were collected after September 11 (in October 2001). A comparison of the data before and after the event supported the fact that September 11 increased the perceived importance of hierarchy, measured in this study by Hofstede's Power Distance dimension.

Example 2: Cheng and her colleagues (2011) conducted research to test whether the 2008 Beijing Olympics increased mainland Chinese' perceptions of Chinese and Western cultural differences. Thus, they investigated whether instead of promoting "One World one dream", holding the Olympics actually increased perceived inter-group differences. Study 1 of this research used a 2 (Time: before Olympics vs. after Olympics) X 2 (the Olympic salience: symbol exposure by adding a small Beijing Olympic symbol at the bottom right corner of each page of the questionnaire. vs. No symbol exposure) between subject design. The results revealed that Olympic salience had no effect on the perceived cultural differences in either type of set of values *before* the Olympics, but it increased the perceived cultural difference in values three months *after* the Games (Cheng et al., 2011). Study 2 of this research tested the effects of intercultural competitiveness priming through the Olympics experience in mainland China. This was a 3-factor between subject design with two manipulations: 2 (Time: before Olympics vs. after Olympics) X 2 (Brands: Chinese vs. American) and a measured factor (cultural identification). Different from study 1, this study included a control group. Student participants were asked to rate how strongly each Chinese (vs. American) brand evoked positive and negative inter-group emotions and how strongly they felt about each brand. Hong Kong students were used as a comparison group because although a part of China, Hong Kong enjoyed a high level of political autonomy and many Hong Kong Chinese do not perceive mainland Chinese as an ingroup. The study revealed that mainland participants expressed more positive emotions and had more positive perceptions towards the mainland Chinese (vs. American) brand at the end of the Olympics, regardless of cultural identification. This result indicates that the Olympic experience strengthened ingroup favoring emotions and perceptions. In contrast, these patterns were not observed among participants from Hong Kong.

Because the experimental treatments used in these articles were real events (the September 11 attacks and the Beijing Olympics), they were able to offer greater realism than designs using artificial manipulations. Both examples described previously used a pre-test and post-test design, so that the changes in the target variables could be observed. Example 1 used longitudinal data, making it possible to test if the effects of the event endured. If the natural event is a training program or a pilot launch of a new policy in an organizational context, evidence of a lasting effect can give organizations more confidence to implement the training program or new policy (Zellmer-Bruhn et al., 2016). Example 2 included a control group that was not affected by the event using the same time points as the experimental group. By using a control group as a comparator, such as a "no-training" group or a unit of the organization not subjected to the new policy, an experimental design can eliminate plausible alternatives and increase robustness (Reeb et al., 2012).

*Illustration*

Many language-related events that occur in MNCs could be used as "natural events", such as the implementation of a language-training program, the launch of a new language policy, or the arrival of a group of expatriates from the parent company of the MNC which changes the mono-lingual environment in the subsidiary. The key is to obtain information about planned events and make sure that key variables are measured before and after the event. It is also necessary to identify a control group that does not receive the treatment and measure key variables in the control group roughly at the same time that they are measured in the treatment group. An example would be an organization launching a new language-training program. Researchers can measure target variables three months before and after the training program. They can also select employees who will not receive the training program as the control group. Understandably, it is not always possible for researchers to plan for naturally occurring events. However, when an event happens, prepared researchers who "think experimentally" will be able to capture it and identify how an ad-hoc design can be implemented.

## Conclusion

In this chapter, we have reviewed the current status of experimental research in language research in the international management literature. In its three decades of development, language research has mainly benefited from qualitative research and survey methods. To further advance our knowledge in this field, we need to test the causality of relationships and mechanisms that have been identified; this is where experimental designs can make a significant contribution. In this chapter, we have provided language researchers with many suggestions on designing effective experiments, such as using mixed samples (e.g. combining student and employee samples), mixed designs (e.g. combining experiments and surveys), vignettes and naturally occurring events. Given the current scarcity of experiments in the language research literature, there are ample opportunities for novel research with the use of experimental designs. We, therefore, issue a call to researchers to realize the tremendous potential of experiments in language research.

# References

Aguinis, H., & Bradley, K. J. (2014). Best practice recommendations for designing and implementing experimental vignette methodology studies. *Organizational Research Methods*, 17(4), 351–371.

Akkermans, D., Harzing, A.-W., & van Witteloostuijn, A. (2010). Cultural accommodation and language priming. *Management International Review*, 50(5), 559–583.

Bello, D., Leung, K., Radebaugh, L., Tung, R. L., & van Witteloostuijn, A. (2009). From the editors: Student samples in international business research. *Journal of International Business Studies*, 40(3), 361–364.

Cheng, C.-Y., Lee, F., & Benet-Martínez, V. (2006). Assimilation and contrast effects in cultural frame switching: Bicultural identity integration and valence of cultural cues. *Journal of Cross-Cultural Psychology*, 37(6), 742–760.

Cheng, S. Y., Rosner, J. L., Chao, M. M., Peng, S., Chen, X., Li, Y., & Chiu, C. Y. (2011). One world, one dream? Intergroup consequences of the 2008 Beijing Olympics. *International Journal of Intercultural Relations*, 35(3), 296–306.

Colquitt, J. A. (2008). From the editors publishing laboratory research in AMJ: A question of when, not if. *Academy of Management Journal*, 51(4), 616–620.

Comu, S., Unsal, H. I., & Taylor, J. E. (2010). Dual impact of cultural and linguistic diversity on project network performance. *Journal of Management in Engineering*, 27(3), 179–187.

Cook, T. D., & Campbell, D. T. (1979). *Quasi-experimentation: Design and analysis issues for field settings*. Chicago: Rand McNally.

Corley, K. G., & Gioia, D. A. (2011). Building theory about theory building: What constitutes a theoretical contribution? *Academy of Management Review*, 36(1), 12–32.

Fan, S. X., & Harzing, A.-W. (2017). Host country employees' ethnic identity confirmation: Evidence from interactions with ethnically similar expatriates. *Journal of World Business*, 52(5), 640–652.

Gargalianou, V., Urbig, D., & Witteloostuijn, A. V. (2017). Cooperating or competing in three languages: Cultural accommodation or alienation? *Cross Cultural & Strategic Management*, 24(1), 167–191.

Hansen, K., Rakić, T., & Steffens, M. C. (2014). When actions speak louder than words: Preventing discrimination of nonstandard speakers. *Journal of Language and Social Psychology*, 33(1), 68–77.

Harrison, G. W., & List, J. A. (2004). Field experiments. *Journal of Economic Literature*, 42(4), 1009–1005.

Harzing, A.-W., Baldueza, J., Barner-Rasmussen, W., Barzantny, C., Canabal, A., Gustavo Dávila, A. P., . . . Zander, L. (2005). Does the use of English-language questionnaires in cross-national research obscure national differences? *International Journal of Cross Cultural Management*, 5(2), 213–224.

Harzing, A.-W., Baldueza, J., Barner-Rasmussen, W., Barzantny, C., Canabal, A., Gustavo Dávila, A. P., . . . Zander, L. (2009). Rating versus ranking: What is the best way to reduce response and language bias in cross-national research? *International Business Review*, 18(4), 417–432.

Harzing, A.-W., & Maznevski, M. (2002). The Interaction between language and culture: A test of the cultural accommodation hypothesis in seven countries. *Language and Intercultural Communication*, 2(2), 120–139.

Hong, Y.-Y., Morris, M. W., Chiu, C.-Y., & Benet-Martínez, V. (2000). Multicultural minds: A dynamic constructivist approach to culture and cognition. *American Psychologist, 55*(7), 709–720.

Hong, Y.-Y., Wan, C., No, S., & Chiu, C.-Y. (2007). Multicultural identities. In S. Kitayama & D. Cohen (Eds.), *Handbook of cultural psychology* (pp. 323–346). New York: Guilford Press.

Hosoda, M., & Stone-Romero, E. (2010). The effects of foreign accents on employment-related decisions. *Journal of Managerial Psychology, 25*(2), 113–132.

Hsu, D. K., Simmons, S. A., & Wieland, A. M. (2017). Designing entrepreneurship experiments. *Organizational Research Methods, 20*(3), 379–412.

Karhunen, P., Kankaanranta, A., Louhiala-Salminen, L., & Piekkari, R. (2018). Let's talk about language: A review of language-sensitive research in international management. *Journal of Management Studies, 55*(6), 980–1031.

Keysar, B., Hayakawa, S. L., & An, S. G. (2012). The foreign-language effect: Thinking in a foreign tongue reduces decision biases. *Psychological Science, 23*(6), 661–668.

Kluckhohn, F. R., & Strodtbeck, F. L. (1961). *Variations in value orientations.* Westport, Conn.: Greenwood Press.

McGrath, J. E. (1981). Dilemmatics: The study of research choices and dilemmas. *American Behavioral Scientist, 25*(2), 179–210.

Molden, D. C. (2014). Understanding priming effects in social psychology: What is "social priming" and how does it occur? *Social Cognition, 32*(Supplement), 1–11.

Neeley, T. B., & Dumas, T. L. (2016). Unearned status gain: Evidence from a global language mandate. *Academy of Management Journal, 59*(1), 14–43.

Olivas-Luján, M. R., Harzing, A. W., & McCoy, S. (2011). September 11, 2001: Two quasi-experiments on the influence of threats on cultural values and cosmopolitanism. *International Journal of Cross Cultural Management, 4*(2), 211–228.

Reeb, D., Sakakibara, M., & Mahmood, I. P. (2012). From the editors: Endogeneity in international business research. *Journal of International Business Studies, 43*, 211–218.

Simmons, J. P., Nelson, L. D., & Simonsohn, U. (2011). False-positive psychology: Undisclosed flexibility in data collection and analysis allows presenting anything as significant. *Psychological Science, 22*(11), 1359–1366.

Sutton, R., & Staw, B. (1995). What theory is not. *Administrative Science Quarterly, 40*(3), 211–218.

Tenzer, H., Terjesen, S., & Harzing, A.-W. (2017). Language in international business: A review and agenda for future research. *Management International Review, 57*(6), 815–854.

Tung, R. L., & Stahl, G. K. (2018). The tortuous evolution of the role of culture in IB research: What we know, what we don't know, and where we are headed. *Journal of International Business Studies, 49*(9), 1167–1189.

Urbig, D., Terjesen, S., Procher, V., Muehlfeld, K., & van Witteloostuijn, A. (2016). Come on and take a free ride: Contributing to public goods in native and foreign language settings. *Academy of Management Learning & Education, 15*(2), 268–286.

van Witteloostuijn, A. (2015). Toward experimental international business. *Cross Cultural Management, 22*(4), 530–544.

Zander, L., Mockatis, A. I., Harzing, A.-W., Baldueza, J., Barner-Rasmussen, W., Barzantny, C., . . . Viswat, L. (2011). Standardization and contextualization: A study of language and leadership across 17 countries. *Journal of World Business*, 46(3), 296–304.

Zellmer-Bruhn, M., Caligiuri, P. M., & Thomas, D. C. (2016). From the editors: Experimental designs in international business research. *Journal of International Business Studies*, 47(4), 399–407.

# 2 How to Research 'Empowerment' in Russia

## Absence, Equivalence and Method

*Virpi Outila, Rebecca Piekkari and Irina Mihailova*

### Translating Employee Empowerment into Russia through Proverbs

The movement of management ideas and practices across diverse organisational and geographical contexts within multinational corporations (MNCs) has been a recurrent theme in organisation studies and international business (IB) literature. Extant research in IB has traditionally framed this phenomenon as practice transfer investigating whether the transferred practices in subsidiaries resemble those of the parent, or which factors impact the success of transfer process (Kostova & Roth, 2002; Rosenzweig & Nohria, 1994; Zaheer, 1995). However, this body of research has provided limited insight into how local actors in the receiving country make sense of these 'imported' practices on the micro level. In this methodological chapter we argue that the notion of translation is particularly appropriate for understanding the metaphorical and interlingual transformation that a practice undergoes when it is moved to a new organisational context. Moreover, we show how local actors use proverbs to translate and make sense of one organisational practice, employee empowerment.

The study is set in the context of a Finland-based MNC that introduced employee empowerment as an organisation practice in its Russian subsidiaries. Empowerment is a particularly intriguing concept to study in the Russian context, because there are no equivalent terms for it in the Russian language. Hence, we pose the following research question: *How can we study translation of empowerment as a foreign practice by Russian subsidiary managers and employees of a Finnish MNC?*

This cross-language study makes several contributions to the methodological literature. First, we identify proverbs as a means through which actors attach local meanings to empowerment, an 'imported' management practice. Proverbs are "traditional, pithy, often formulaic and/or figurative, fairly stable and generally recognizable linguistic units used to form a complete utterance, make a complete conversational contribution and/or to perform a speech act in a speech event" (Norrick, 2014, p. 7). Proverbs capture the cultural, historical and institutional characteristics of a nation and provide an emic understanding of the context. Second, we explain how we worked with our data set to interpret local meanings across language boundaries. In particular, we explain the collective efforts behind translating and analysing proverbs from Russian to English. Proverbs are particularly challenging to translate as linguistic resources and such methodological details are rarely found in published research accounts (Chidlow, Plakoyiannaki, & Welch, 2014). Third, we uncover how local actors translate a Western management practice in a metaphorical and interlingual sense into a non-Western context. As Cassell and Lee (2016, p. 3) explain, little is known about how translators 'do translation in practice'.

The rest of the paper is structured as follows. We first discuss the literature on translation of organisational practices across societal, institutional and cultural boundaries and introduce the notion of employee empowerment. We then describe our qualitative cross-border study and document the ways through which we worked across language boundaries to interpret the data set collected in Russian but reported in English. Finally, we discuss our findings and offer implications for scholars interested in conducting cross-language research.

## Literature Review

The study draws on the translation approach developed in Scandinavian institutionalism, a form of new institutionalism that highlights translation and sensemaking when practices travel across borders (Czarniawska & Joerges, 1996). Whereas new institutionalism emphasises processes of isomorphism and standardisation in explaining the similarity of organizational practices (DiMaggio & Powell, 1983), Scandinavian institutionalism "highlights organisational variation and distinctiveness" (Boxenbaum & Strandgaard Pedersen, 2009, p. 179). The notion of translation is at the heart of this school of thought, referring to the modification that a practice undergoes when it is made sense of in a new organisational context (Boxenbaum & Strandgaard Pedersen, 2009). However, Scandinavian institutionalism uses translation in a metaphorical sense and explicitly distances itself from literal, interlingual translation (Czarniawska & Joerges, 1996, p. 24).

Studies conducted in this tradition emphasise how local actors make sense of newly introduced practices and ideas and attach local meanings to them (Czarniawska & Joerges, 1996). A sensemaking approach suggests that organisations are talked into existence (Weick, Sutcliffe, & Obstfeld, 2005) and that narratives, metaphors and discursive practices are important resources for sensemaking (Brown, Stacey, & Nandhakumar, 2008; Cornelissen, 2005; Maitlis & Lawrence, 2007). Hence organisational actors are not passive receivers but active translators, interpreting and editing ideas and management models (Czarniawska & Sevón, 2005).

HRM represents a new functional area in Russia and therefore an established terminology and vocabulary of human behaviour does not exist in the country. As Holden, Kuznetsova, and Fink (2008) state, terms such as coach, mentor and empowerment are "virtually untranslatable" in the Russian context (Holden et al., 2008, p. 122), because they lack a corresponding meaning system in Russia as well as other post-communist countries. Empowerment originates from the United States: its roots are in the human relations movement of the 1920s, when there was a shift in focus from technological to human aspects in management (Wilkinson, 1998). Management scholars appropriated empowerment in the mid-1980s to refer to employee participation in decision-making and the subsequent increase in employees' knowledge, information and resources. It was also used in connection with the perceived ownership of their work (Bartunek & Spreitzer, 2006). Because the meaning of employee empowerment is less established and familiar to research participants in Russia than in market economies, this research setting is particularly suitable for a translation approach.

## A Qualitative Cross-Border Study

The research approach of this study is interpretive, emphasising the sensemaking of empowerment in terms of the meanings people bring to it (Denzin & Lincoln, 2005). We conducted a qualitative cross-language study in order to obtain an in-depth understanding of how employees in Russia make sense of empowerment.

The case company is a Finnish MNC that has been in the Russian market for over 50 years. Since 1997, the company, which we call Genro for the sake of confidentiality, has established subsidiaries in six cities in Russia. As mentioned earlier, our empirical research revealed that there is no word for employee empowerment in either Russian or Finnish. Empowerment was, however, embedded in the Finnish parent company's values and leadership principles, emphasising giving and taking responsibility, trust and employee independence, which are considered core elements in empowerment.

The first author of this chapter had a dual role in the field, as she was both a researcher and a manager helping the company to understand the challenges it faced when moving its core values and practices, one of which was employee empowerment, to the Russian operations. Whereas the insider status of the first author assured access to rich data, her position also influenced the narratives of the research participants and called for particular sensitivity and reflexivity. We consider such a situation an inherent part of research projects in which a researcher studies her own organisation (see e.g. Alvesson, 2009).

## Constructing and Analysing Data Across Language Boundaries

During and after her employment in this company, the first author conducted altogether 86 in-depth, semi-structured personal interviews with Russian managers and employees between May 2013 and April 2014. The first author's ability to interview in Russian was of critical importance, as the majority of the research participants did not speak English. The interviews were carried out with top managers, middle managers and white-collars. The first author did not talk to blue-collars, because the majority of them were outsourced migrant workers. This group was not directly affected by Genro's empowerment efforts, as they were usually employed by subcontractors. The interviews were conversational in nature and lasted from 1 to 1.5 hours. All of them were recorded with the exception of one upon the interviewee's request.

As there is no equivalent word for empowerment in Russian, the researcher and the local actors participating in this study had to interpret the meaning of empowerment in a metaphorical and interlingual sense. The researcher posed indirect questions about empowerment in the form of participation in decision-making, opportunities to influence, the role of trust between the manager and employees, goal-setting and taking the initiative. The first author's familiarity with the participants made them feel comfortable and enabled rapport and a sense of connection.

Our data set was primarily in Russian and did not contain any English loan words. We coded selected parts of the interviews in English because it was the reporting language of the study and the dominant language of our sources. However, we frequently returned to Russian for the raw data in order to stay as close as possible to the meanings expressed in the interview language. The data set was transcribed and analysed in Russian. This was enabled by the fact that the entire co-author team is fluent in Russian and one of us is a native speaker. We have a deep understanding of the Russian context and have been trained both in the West and in Russia. The first author, who is Finnish by birth, has spent a considerable amount of time working and studying in Russia. Hence, we had the collective expertise to interpret the data through the lenses of native Russian and Western backgrounds.

We started analyzing the data set by transcribing the interviews verbatim. This stage of the study was followed by a content analysis which refers to identifying, coding and categorising the raw data (Patton, 2002). In analysing the data we used Atlas.ti computer-assisted qualitative data analysis software.

## Collective Translation and Analysis of Proverbs

In the course of the data analysis we noticed that proverbs played an important role in interviewees' talk. Proverbs are a linguistically challenging methodological tool for researchers, because they often contain archaic words or unusual word order and are difficult to translate. When faced with such a translation task, the researcher needs to decide whether to translate the proverb literally or use idiomatic expressions. Let's take the proverb 'доверяй, но проверяй' as an example. The literal translation of the proverb is 'trust but verify', whereas the idiomatic translation reads 'trust is good, control is better'. In this case we decided to use the literal translation of the proverb 'trust but verify', because we felt that it better conveyed the commanding tone of the Russian proverb. In some other cases, we opted for a non-literal translation strategy that would still preserve the proverb-sounding character of the text. We did not try to find exactly the same proverbs in both Russian and English, as some proverbs were only local, but others were regional or even global, i.e. identical across many languages. The co-author team discussed all translations and agreed upon the final translated versions of the proverbs.

We addressed the translation task through a collective effort of several rounds of translation. Initially, the first author translated the proverbs from Russian to English and the native author verified it. In the next round, we involved external, professional interpreters and a professional proof reader to check our translation. The external interpreters were employed by the case company (one of them was a native Russian speaker), and the proof reader was a native English speaker with an understanding of Russia and the Russian language. He provided suggestions regarding the English translation of the proverbs.

The translation process of proverbs was open-ended and extended itself over a considerable period of time. In the course of presenting our findings, we have received comments and suggestions from colleagues such as journal reviewers and conference participants about how to translate and interpret the meaning of the proverbs. For example, the proverb concerning initiatives, 'инициатива наказуема', could be literally translated as 'initiative is punished'. However, the proof reader commented that this translation might be confusing for the English-speaking audience. Therefore, he suggested translating the proverb as 'taking the initiative is a punishable offence'. The words 'punishable' and 'offence' form a common phrase and therefore would be more understandable for our English-speaking readership.

Another example is the translation of the proverb 'я начальник—ты дурак; ты начальник—я дурак'. The literal, word-for-word, translation of the proverb would be 'I'm the manager, you're the fool; you're the manager, I'm the fool', which we used in one of our manuscripts submitted to a journal. However, our reviewer challenged the translation and suggested that we use the word 'boss' instead of 'manager'. We agreed as it better conveys the harsh tone of the Russian proverb and hence changed the translation of the proverb. Thus, various parties challenged and engaged in the translation of the proverbs, thus highlighting the collective character of our translation effort.

In addition, the importance of context in translating and interpreting the meaning of proverbs became evident in our study (e.g. Gabriel, 2015). Even within a single national context, individuals read proverbs differently depending on their age, professional background and regional origin which are likely to shape the interpretation. Therefore, data sets containing proverbs can only be understood in context.

## Local Translation of Empowerment

We identified three ways how the interviewees used proverbs in the process of translation: 1) using a proverb to support one's own opinion, 2) using a proverb to contrast its meaning with one's own opinion and 3) using a proverb to emphasise an important element associated with empowerment. In addition, the analysis of proverbs allowed us to decipher the local translation of empowerment in the Russian context. In the following, we have organised our findings according to the proverbs used spontaneously by the interviewees. These proverbs dealt with the following themes related to the empowerment: the relationship between manager and subordinate, decision-making, trust, initiatives and attitudes towards mistakes.

The relationship between manager and subordinates plays a key role in empowerment. Sharing power and assigning responsibility and autonomy to employees is at the core of empowerment. Responsibility is also included in Genro's values and leadership principles. Some interviewees described the relationship between manager and employee in Russia with the proverb 'I am the boss, you are the fool; you are the boss, I am the fool', (Я начальник—ты дурак; ты начальник—я дурак) as the following quotation from a middle manager illustrates:

> In Russia there is a principle, 'I'm the boss, you're the fool; you're the boss, I'm the fool'. This principle always works everywhere Russia, it is like national wisdom. We cannot achieve democracy and friendly relations like in the Scandinavian countries. It is not our mentality.

This excerpt is an example of the first way to use proverbs to support one's own opinion. This particular proverb emphasises the superiority of the manager and illustrates the traditional Russian thinking about a strong, autocratic leader who makes all the decisions. *Nachal'nik*, the Russian word for boss in the proverb, was initially used in the army to mean a leader (Izbarekov, 2011). It has since spread all over society and been used to describe Russian management in general. The proverb includes the views of both the manager and the employee with the employee accepting the superior position of the manager. As mentioned by the interviewee, this also reflects the strong difference between Scandinavian, or Western, cultures and values, in our case empowerment, and Russian cultures and values.

The core of empowerment lies in encouraging employees to make decisions regarding their own work, because it means taking responsibility. As managers feel that they bear the ultimate responsibility for the work of their department, they need to practice control in order to prevent employees from making wrong decisions. The following quotation illustrates these views:

> Employees should participate in business operations and in discussions of decisions. In Russia the tradition is naturally that 'I'm the boss, you're the fool'. This system works in Russia, but I don't support it.

Here the interviewee uses the proverb to contrast its meaning with his own opinion. This reflects the tension under which the subsidiary operates: the Russian cultural legacy builds on the superiority of the manager, but the Western headquarters expects local subsidiary employees to participate in decision-making. The ideals of autocratic leadership have been a recurrent theme in leadership studies regarding Russia. People in Russia have been accustomed to authoritative figures through centuries: the Russian Orthodox Church, tsars, landowners and the communist party elite (Elenkov, 1998). It has also been argued that Russians have a need for powerful leaders, who should always know more than their employees (Kets de Vries, 2001; McCarthy, Mary, Puffer, Ledgerwood, & Steward, 2008). Our data show that these ideas are still prevalent in Russia.

Empowerment entails granting employees an increased level of autonomy over their own work. This reduces the degree of manager's control while at the same time inviting more trust on the part of the manager. However, the findings show that the Russian managers interviewed constantly sought to verify and control the performance of their subordinates. The proverb 'trust but verify' (Доверяй, но проверяй) was used by many managerial interviewees, as the following quotation shows:

> No matter if you trust, you need to periodically verify, because everybody makes mistakes. 'Trust but verify!'

This is another example of using the proverb to support one's own opinion. The interviewee seems to resort to the proverb to justify his views and behaviour. The proverb conveys that in Russia control and trust are not mutually exclusive but exist simultaneously. In other words, the manager may both control and trust the employee. Hence it seems that trust as a corporate value translated differently into the Russian context than at headquarters in Finland. Russia has been generally characterised as a low-trust society (Inglehart et al., 2014). A strong Russian cultural tendency is to distrust individuals, groups and organisations that are outside personal relationships. Within in-groups of family members, friends and colleagues there are trusting relationships, whereas out-groups are typically not trusted (McCarthy & Puffer, 2008). As Russia is a low-trust society, the degree of trust is unlikely to be so great that no control would be needed. Our findings, however, emphasise that although control is important in Russian workplaces, without trust there would be no working relationships at all. Hence trust and control complement each other (Outila, Mihailova, Reiche, & Piekkari, 2018).

Previous research suggests that empowerment and initiatives are related to each other in that empowered employees are inclined to show initiative (Spreitzer, 1995). In Russia, however, taking initiatives is not a tradition; everyone knows the saying 'taking the initiative is a punishable offence' (инициатива наказуема), which was popular in the Soviet time. Interviewees in the local subsidiaries were also aware of this saying, as the following quotation illustrates:

RESEARCHER: Do you think that you can take initiatives?
RESEARCH PARTICIPANT: Well, as we say, 'taking the initiative is a punishable offence'. If you take an initiative, then [you need to] implement your suggestion. But in principle, if there is a reasonable suggestion that can be implemented, of course you can take initiatives, but first of course discuss it with your manager.

Here again the interviewee uses the proverb to get support to her own opinion. The interviewee starts her reply to the question posed by the interviewer with the proverb and then explains its meaning. The interviewee emphasises how initiatives may result in punishment, because the presenter of the initiatives may end up implementing them. Also, the interviewee points out that only 'reasonable' initiatives are welcomed and the rest are punishable. Whether an initiative is reasonable is determined by the manager, and therefore all initiatives need to be cleared by the manager first. Hence, the attitudes towards suggestions reflected in the proverb can be seen to demonstrate an authoritative approach and lack of support for empowerment in Russia. The unwillingness of Russians to show initiative has been explained by historical features in the literature. Traditionally individuals who tried to be better than the group were looked on with suspicion (Elenkov, 1998), and it has been safer not to draw too much attention to oneself (May, Puffer, & McCarthy, 2005).

The topic of mistakes has not been much discussed in relation to empowerment in previous research. However, our interviewees used many proverbs that referred to mistakes on several occasions, revealing that mistakes play a major role in the daily working life of Russian subsidiary employees. Hence our interviewees used the proverb to emphasise an important element—mistakes—that they associated with empowerment. This represents a third way of using proverbs. The following quotation illustrates this approach:

'All mistakes are different'. First, you need to talk about the mistake. Depending on the level of harmfulness for the company there can be different consequences, either tough decisions or soft advice. In general, I understand if a person makes mistakes. If the mistake concerns something new, that's normal. If there are many mistakes about something that is familiar, then your reaction should be more severe. There are different approaches to mistakes.

The proverb 'all mistakes are different' (ошибка ошибке рознь) describes varying attitudes towards mistakes. The quotation suggests that managers are used to analyse mistakes thoroughly in terms of their nature, frequency and consequences, and explore the possible reasons for them. The proverb also underscores the importance of ensuring that the person learns from mistakes as well as the harshness of punishment in the Russian work environment in general. It should be noted that the largest number of proverbs in our data set were associated with mistakes and their role in empowerment, which indicates the significance of this theme in Russian context. Hence the proverbs provided a more nuanced view of the local meanings of empowerment. Traditionally mistakes have been severely punished in Russia. Fey and Shekshnia (2011, p. 61) even state that "it is hard to find companies in Russia where employees are not punished for honest mistakes". Fear of making mistakes and the possibility of being punished decreases willingness to take responsibility for one's own work and show initiative, which are important elements of empowerment in the West.

The research findings are summarised in Table 2.1, which compares the local translation of empowerment in the Russian subsidiaries with the headquarters' intended meaning. As Table 2.1 shows, control, mistakes, punishments and lack of encouragement for initiatives are local

*Table 2.1* Summary of the translation of empowerment in the subsidiaries, based on the HQ intended meaning

| Element of empowerment | Western understanding | Eastern translation |
| --- | --- | --- |
| **Decision-making** | Employees take responsibility, and managers trust them. | Employees take limited responsibility under managerial control. |
| **Initiatives** | Initiatives are part of everyday work. | Initiatives need to be agreed with managers and carried out by proposers. |
| **Trust/control** | Managers trust employees to take responsibility and complete their tasks independently. | Managers trust employees to a certain degree but control their work constantly. |
| **Attitudes to mistakes** | Learning takes place from mistakes. | Learning from one's own mistakes and those of others takes place through punishment. |

Source: Research data

meanings associated by the interviewees with the empowerment practice. The local translation of employee empowerment in Russia is characterised by the control of the manager in order to support the employee and prevent possible mistakes, learning of which takes place through punishments. Hence, although the practices were implemented according to the headquarters' guidelines, the underlying values of the practice were not transmitted in the form intended by headquarters.

## Discussion

This methodological chapter contributes to research on translation of organisational practices from a Western to a non-Western context both in a metaphorical and interlingual sense. We uncovered how Russian managers and employees used proverbs to translate empowerment—a Western practice—in order to make it locally meaningful. As proverbs are inherited from generation to generation (Hrisztova-Gotthardt & Varga, 2014), they preserve values that reflect the historical, institutional and cultural features of the nation. Proverbs help identify underlying values that drive behaviour. We argue that proverbs can be viewed as an innovative way to theorise about the context-specific nature of empowerment in Russia (Outila, Piekkari, & Mihailova, 2019).

In Russia proverbs are commonly used in everyday speak. Permyakov (1989), a Russian paremiologist, has stated that every adult Russian language speaker knows more than 800 proverbs, proverbial expressions, popular literary quotations and other forms of cliché. Even though proverbs are useful in conveying contextual features, proverbs have been rarely used in organisational research or in international business. This lacuna of research is surprising considering the increase in work exploring the role of language and discourse in organisational life (Phillips & Oswick, 2012) and the overall dominance of discourse-based approaches to translation (Doolin, Grant, & Thomas, 2013). Metaphors, another type of linguistic device, have instead received a significant amount of scholarly attention (Cornelissen, 2005; Cornelissen & Kafouros, 2008). Like metaphors, proverbs also guide perceptions and interpretation of reality and advance the understanding and sensemaking of the world.

We have discussed elsewhere (Outila et al., 2019) various opportunities as well as risks and limitations in relation to the use of proverbs (see Table 2.2). We argue that by using proverbs the researcher is able to decipher deep and nuanced cultural meanings that could be debated even by locals as discussed earlier. Hence, they can be used as a tool to reach a connection with research participants on a deeper and more trustful level. Proverbs are also a means for the participants to express themselves explicitly in their native tongue. Moreover, proverbs provide the speaker with the possibility of not taking full responsibility for the argument and instead lend authority to national wisdom. We further note that the use

*Table 2.2* Opportunities and limitations related to the use of proverbs

| Opportunities | Risks and limitations |
| --- | --- |
| Proverbs assist the researcher in gaining insight into deep cultural meaning and tacit knowledge. | The use of proverbs requires in-depth mastery of the local language and culture. |
| Proverbs allow the researcher to engage with participants on a deeper and more trustful level (almost as an insider). | Proverbs may run the risk of being ignored or overlooked by the researcher. |
| Proverbs allow the participants to express themselves meaningfully in their native tongue. | Proverbs may mislead the researcher by conveying stereotypical meanings. |
| Proverbs allow conversion of tacit knowledge into explicit knowledge. | Proverbs may create the risk of distortive reflection of politically sensitive messages. |
| Proverbs enable the participants to proffer opinions without taking full responsibility for the meanings conveyed. | Proverbs may create the risk of micropolitical manipulation of meaning. |
| Proverbs lend authority to national wisdom. | |

Source: Research Data

of proverbs requires that the researcher possess in-depth knowledge of the local language and culture, otherwise these linguistic resources may be overlooked or ignored. Proverbs may also convey stereotypical meanings and create the risk of micropolitical manipulation of meaning and hence mislead the researcher.

Furthermore, we contribute to the literature by providing methodological details about how we interpreted local meanings from our data across language boundaries. We explain how we as researchers collectively interpreted and analysed proverbs from Russian to English. These translation efforts were complemented by a journal reviewer and Russian conference participants who challenged our translation of proverbs. We highlight the collective effort of the translation which provided new insights of employee empowerment in Russia.

In our study the role of local actors as users and consumers of proverbs was crucial in translating empowerment as an organisational practice. For the interviewees, proverbs seemed to be a widely shared way to express similarities, differences and tensions between the Western and Russian understanding of empowerment. The interviewees used proverbs intuitively when they wanted to explain why a certain type of behaviour was (not) appropriate in Russia. Many of the Russian proverbs used by the interviewees conveyed opposite meanings to the Western view of empowerment: for example, 'I'm the boss, you're the fool' emphasises the superiority of the manager, whereas in the Western understanding of empowerment the manager shares power and gives autonomy to

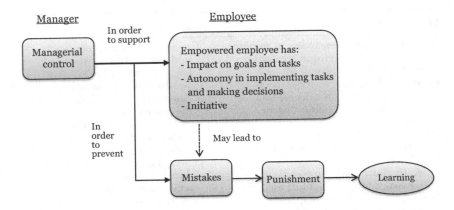

*Figure 2.1* Reconceptualisation of employee empowerment in Russia

employee; 'trust but verify' underlines control, whereas empowerment in the West calls for trust; 'taking the initiative is a punishable offence' advises one to refrain from showing initiative, whereas the Western view of empowerment encourages initiative-taking; 'all mistakes are different' highlights the importance of analysing mistakes thoroughly in order to punish employees so that they learn, whereas based on the Western understanding employees learn from their mistakes. Hence, these proverbs reveal the tension between the sending context in the West (i.e. the origin of the foreign practice) and the receiving non-Western context. Figure 2.1 illustrates the local translation of empowerment.

## Conclusion

The goal of this methodological chapter was to show how to study the translation of employee empowerment, a Western management practice, into a non-Western context. Russian subsidiary managers and employees engaged in metaphorical and interlingual translation when making sense of employee empowerment through the use of proverbs. We also described in detail how our collective acts of translating proverbs from Russian to English shaped the meaning of empowerment. Our study shows that translation is not just a mechanistic task but an important part of the analysis.

Our study provides several implications for researchers. When researchers create open and trustful relationships with research participants, the latter may be encouraged to use vivid expressions, such as proverbs. At best, this can provide rich and context-sensitive insights into the research phenomenon. In order to pay attention to such expressions, we emphasise the importance of researchers' local language skills and cultural sensitivity. Our study also highlights the value of giving participants space for their own sensemaking during fieldwork, as it enables various interpretations of concepts to emerge. Proverbs are challenging linguistic resources which may require collective translation efforts in order to decipher their meaning. We acknowledge that collective translation may be an open-ended process extending itself well beyond exiting the field (Michailova et al., 2014).

Finally, this study provides a number of avenues for future research. Proverbs can be powerful tools for understanding different contexts as they carry historical, institutional and cultural features over time. For example, in China proverbs are often used in company documents (e.g. Tréguer-Felten, 2018) and everyday speech. They signal the speaker's high level of education and experience (Fiedler, 2014), offering valuable information about Chinese cultural and institutional features. Previous research has shown that features related to empowerment found in our study, such as the employee's need for support and fear of mistakes, as well as employees' need for detailed instructions have been identified in India (Gertsen & Zølner, 2012) and China (Søderberg, 2015). This indicates that our findings could be applicable in other non-Western contexts as well.

Whereas we analysed the use of proverbs in interview settings, which are performances co-constructed for and with the researcher, it would be interesting to know more about how local actors use proverbs in naturally occurring everyday talk. Besides proverbs, antonyms, synonyms, jargon and other discursive resources could also be studied to shed light on various phenomena. In addition, 'key words', i.e. words that are particularly common and important for a certain culture, might offer valuable insights about it (Wierzbicka, 1997). As Wierzbicka argues, in Russian sudba ('fate'), dusha ('soul') and toska ('melancholy-cum-yearning') serve as such 'key words'.

In conclusion, we join the group of scholars who have started to develop a degree of sensitivity to the multiplicity of languages in research methodology and have opened their minds to new meanings and understandings of established concepts.

# References

Alvesson, M. (2009). At-home ethnography: Struggling with closeness and closure. In S. Ybema, D. Yanow, H. Wells, & F. Kamsteeg (Eds.), *Organizational ethnography: Studying the complexities of everyday life* (pp. 156–174). London: Sage.

Bartunek, J. M., & Spreitzer, G. M. (2006). The interdisciplinary career of a popular construct used in management: Empowerment in the late 20th century. *Journal of Management Inquiry, 15*, 225–273.

Boxenbaum, E., & Strandgaar Pedersen, J. (2009). Scandinavian institutionalism—A case of institutional work. In T. B. Lawrence, R. Suddaby, & B. Leca (Eds.),

*Institutional work—Actors and agency in institutional studies of organizations* (pp. 178–204). New York: Cambridge University Press.

Brown, A. D., Stacey, P., & Nandhakumar, J. (2008). Making sense of sensemaking narratives. *Human Relations, 61,* 1035–1062.

Cassell, C., & Lee, B. (2016). Understanding translation work: The evolving interpretation of a trade union idea. *Organization Studies, 1,* 1–22.

Chidlow, A., Plakoyiannaki, E., & Welch, C. (2014). Translation in cross-language international business research: Beyond equivalence. *Journal of International Business Studies, 45,* 562–582.

Cornelissen, J. P. (2005). Beyond compare: Metaphor in organization theory. *Academy of Management Review, 30,* 751–764.

Cornelissen, J. P., & Kafouros, M. (2008). Metaphors and theory building in organization theory: What determines the impact of a metaphor on theory? *British Journal of Management, 19,* 365–379.

Czarniawska, B., & Joerges, B. (1996). Travels of ideas. In B. Czarniawska & G. Sevón (Eds.), *Translating organizational change* (pp. 1–17). Berlin: de Gruyter.

Czarniawska, B., & Sevón, G. (2005). *Global ideas: How ideas, objects and practices travel in a global economy.* Malmö: Liber & Copenhagen Business School Press.

Denzin, N. K., & Lincoln, Y. S. (2005). *The Sage handbook of qualitative research.* Thousand Oaks, CA: Sage.

DiMaggio, P. J., & Powell, W. W. (1983). The iron cage revisited: Institutional isomorphism and collective rationality in organizational fields. *American Sociological Review, 48,* 147–160.

Doolin, B., Grant, D., & Thomas, R. (2013). Translating translation and change: Discourse-based approaches. *Journal of Change Management, 13,* 251–265.

Elenkov, D. (1998). Can American management concepts work in Russia? *California Management Review, 40,* 133–156.

Fey, C. F., & Shekshnia, S. (2011). The key commandments for doing business in Russia. *Organizational Dynamics, 40,* 57–66.

Fiedler, S. (2014). Proverbs and foreign language teaching. In H. Hrisztova-Gotthardt & M. A. Varga (Eds.), *Introduction to paremiology: A comprehensive guide to proverb studies* (pp. 294–325). Warsaw and Berlin: DeGruyter Open Ltd.

Gabriel, Y. (2015). Reflexivity and beyond—A plea for imagination in qualitative research methodology. *Qualitative Research in Organizations and Management: An International Journal, 10,* 332–336.

Gertsen, M. C., & Zølner, M. (2012). Recontextualization of the corporate values of a Danish MNC in a subsidiary in Bangalore. *Group & Organization Management, 37,* 101–132.

Holden, N. J., Kuznetsova, O., & Fink, G. (2008). Russia's long struggle with Western terms of management and the concepts behind them. In S. Tietze (Ed.), *International management and language* (pp. 198–213). London: Routledge.

Hrisztova-Gotthardt, H., & Varga, M. A. (2014). *Introduction to paremiology: A comprehensive guide to proverb studies.* Warsaw and Berlin: DeGruyter Open Ltd.

Inglehart, R., Haerpfer, C., Moreno, A., Welzel, C., Kizilova, K., Diez-Medrano, J., . . . Puranen, B. (Eds.). (2014). *World values survey: Round six—Country-pooled datafile version.* Madrid: JD Systems Institute. Retrieved March 10, 2015, from www.worldvaluessurvey.org/WVSDocumentationWV6.jsp

Izbarekov, V. (2011). *Svyataya sila slova: ne predat rodnoy yazyk.* Danilov: Danilov muzhkoi monastyr.

Kets De Vries, M. F. R. (2001). The anarchist within: Clinical reflections on Russian character and leadership style. *Human Relations, 54,* 585–627.

Kostova, T., & Roth, K. (2002). Adoption of organizational practice by subsidiaries of multinational corporations: Institutional and relational effects. *Academy of Management Journal, 45,* 215–233.

Maitlis, S., & Lawrence, T. B. (2007). Triggers and enablers of sensegiving in organizations. *Academy of Management Journal, 50*(1), 57–84.

May, R., Puffer, S., & McCarthy, D. (2005). Transferring management knowledge to Russia: A culturally based approach. *Academy of Management Executive, 19,* 24–35.

McCarthy, D. J., Mary, R. C., Puffer, S. M., Ledgerwood, D. E., & Steward, W. H., Jr. (2008). The legacy of transactional leadership. *Organizational Dynamics, 37,* 221–235.

McCarthy, D. J., & Puffer, S. (2008). Interpreting the ethicality of corporate governance decisions in Russia: Utilizing integrative social contracts theory to evaluate the relevance of agency theory norms. *Academy of Management Review, 33,* 11–31.

Michailova, S., Piekkari, R., Plakoyiannaki, E., Ritvala, T., Mihailova, I., & Salmi, A. (2014). Breaking the silence about exiting fieldwork: A relational approach and its implications for theorizing. *Academy of Management Review, 39,* 138–161.

Norrick, N. R. (2014). Subject area, terminology, proverb definitions, proverb features. In H. Hrisztova Gotthardt & M. A. Varga (Eds.), *Introduction to paremiology: A comprehensive guide to proverb studies* (pp. 7–27). Berlin: DeGruyter Open Ltd.

Outila, V., Mihailova, I., Reiche, B. S., & Piekkari, R. (2018). A communicative perspective on the trust-control link in Russia. *Journal of World Business.* doi:10.1016/j.jwb.2018.11.001

Outila, V., Piekkari, R., & Mihailova, I. (2019). A discursive void in a cross-language study on Russia: Strategies for negotiating shared meaning. *Management and Organization Review, 15,* 403–427.

Patton, M. Q. (2002). *Qualitative research and evaluation methods.* Thousand Oaks, CA: Sage.

Permyakov, G. (1989). On the question of a Russian paremiological minimum. *Proverbium, 6,* 91–102.

Phillips, N., & Oswick, C. (2012). Organizational discourse: Domains, debates and directions. *Academy of Management Annals, 6,* 435–481.

Rosenzweig, P. M., & Nohria, N. (1994). Influences on human resource management practices in multinational corporations. *Journal of International Business Studies, 25,* 229–251.

Søderberg, A.-M. (2015). Recontextualising a strategic concept within a globalizing company: A case study on Carlsberg's 'winning behaviours' strategy. *International Journal of Human Resource Management, 26,* 231–257.

Spreitzer, G. M. (1995). Psychological empowerment in the workplace: Dimensions, measurement, and validation. *Academy of Management Journal, 38,* 1442–1465.

Tréguer-Felten, G. (2018). *Language Commune, culture distinctes: Les Illusions du "Globish"*. Québec: Les Presses de l'Université Laval.

Weick, K. E., Sutcliffe, K. M., & Obstfeld, D. (2005). Organizing and the process of sensemaking. *Organization Science, 16*(4), 409–421.

Wierzbicka, A. (1997). *Understanding cultures through their key words: English, Russian, Polish, German, and Japanese*. New York: Oxford University Press.

Wilkinson, A. (1998). Empowerment: Theory and practice. *Personnel Review, 27*(1), 40–56.

Zaheer, S. (1995). Overcoming the liability of foreignness. *Academy of Management Journal, 38*, 341–363.

# 3 Translating Western Research Methodology Into Chinese

## A Contextualised Approach in Practice

*Huiping Xian*

Whereas researchers' reflexivity has been acknowledged and, to some extent, promoted within business and management research, the notion of how international scholars (here broadly referring to scholars who use English as a second language) deal with language, culture and translation is rarely addressed. International researchers, who are often translators themselves, have to overcome a language and culture divide in the translation process (Piekkari & Tietze, 2011; Xian, 2008). Currently, these challenges and researchers' reflexivity remain largely unknown. A number of authors have conceptualised "reflexivity" in a range of different epistemological stances. Reflexivity in this chapter refers to researchers' awareness of their own role in the translation process and their potential influence on the outcomes (Cassell, Bishop, Symon, Johnson, & Buehring, 2009). It can be achieved through critical engagement with and amendment of one's practice (Reissner, 2018). The purpose of this chapter is to provide an "insider" account of my own experience of translating Western research methodology into Chinese with a specific focus on issues related to translating research philosophy. Here, I challenge the dominant view that language is a passive tool for communication and translation is an objective process that transfers meaning between languages without changes. Using examples of translating philosophical concepts into Chinese, I argue that translation is a cultural practice, and it entails the recreation of meaning and knowledge that make sense to the target audience. I propose a contextualised approach, in which a foreign concept is interpreted, supplemented with local knowledge specially to the target language and reconstructed in a comprehensible domestic style.

This chapter aims to combine abstract theoretical discussions with the actual experience of translation. In doing so, this chapter contributes to current debates about languages and methodologies in international business and management research (Chidlow, Plakoyiannaki, & Welch, 2014; Gawlewicz, 2016; Xian, 2008) and researcher reflexivity (Alvesson & Sköldberg, 2018; Reissner, 2018). The rest of the chapter is organised around four sections. The first section will discuss my motivations for translating Western research methodologies into Chinese, for both research and teaching purposes. The second section will engage in current debates on language, culture and translation within business and management research and argue for a contextualised approach to translation. In the third section, I will reflect on my experience and show how Western philosophical terminologies can be recontextualised into Chinese language and culture through translation. This chapter will then conclude by considering the implications of the contextualised approach and reflexivity of the translator's role in business and management research.

## Motivations for Translating Western Research Methodology

I have translated Western research methodologies into Chinese for both research and teaching purposes. Western research methodologies in the present chapter refer to the vast body of literature that has emerged since the 1970s from an English-American tradition under the name of "Social Studies of Science". This field explores "gnoseological, epistemological and methodological interpretations of nature and morphology of the manufactured scientific knowledge, methods for obtaining and explaining this knowledge, interpreting ideals of scientificity, and mechanisms regulating this activity" (Kornienko, 2015, p. 388).

My first motivation for translation stems from the limitations of Chinese researchers' preferred methods, which are largely quantitative. International researchers often find Western methodology challenging, not least because of marked differences between philosophical perspectives. It has been long recognised that ontological and epistemological positions could be culturally-specific. Easterby-Smith and Malina (1999) reflect on their experience of a UK-China collaborative research project and note that Chinese researchers were striving to obtain accurate data and factual information in interviews, whereas their UK counterparts focused more on people's perception and interpretation of events. These scholars also observe that Chinese researchers expect agreed-upon answers to each question and look for similarities and patterns between cases, whereas British researchers are deliberately looking for different accounts and contradictions among various stakeholders within the same organisation. Thus, they suggest that Chinese researchers are more likely to take a realist and objectivist ontological stance, whereas British researchers tend to adopt a constructionist and interpretivist view. Not surprisingly, this different philosophical stance can lead to a different methodological approach. The deductive approach has been reported to be highly popular among Chinese scholars. For example, Quer and colleagues' review of 180 empirical papers in leading international journals in the broad areas of business and management in China show that overwhelmingly 82.2% of these papers adopted a deductive/quantitative approach (Quer, Claver, & Rienda, 2007). Similarly, Cooke (2009) comes to the same conclusion after analysing 230 China-related papers relating specifically to Human Resource Management and suggests that quantitative research designs, typically in the form of questionnaire survey, dominate data collection. This type of research starts with Western theories and models and incorporates contextual factors of China, such as collectivism or *guanxi*, with an attempt to modify or extend existing theoretical predictions relating to the dependent variables.

However, researchers quickly realise that general knowledge developed in the West provides only limited explanations of local concepts that are deeply embedded in Chinese culture and society, both of which are fundamentally different to that of the United States or Europe (Lau, 2002; Tsui, 2004). A search for a theoretical framework to research phenomena unique to the Chinese context (such as guanxi, Confucius ethics, yin-yang, job allocation in state-own enterprises, etc.) in Western literature has often proven to be fruitless. Reflecting on methodological challenges of researching in China, Stening and Zhang (2007) point out that "Western conceptualisations and measurements of Chinese culture are inadequate and flawed insofar as they take, among other things, a rational perspective rather than one based on contradictions and process" (p. 123). Consequently, both Cooke (2009) and Tsui (2004) note that although the amount of China-related articles is large in quantity, there seems to be a lack of quality in many empirical studies, which tend to be simple and descriptive. Subsequently, only a small percentage of them find their way into top-ranking international journals. Broader discussions of the difficulties of non-English speaking scholars' publishing in top journals often include a critique on socio-political and economic powers, which allow some countries to colonise others (Jack & Westwood, 2006), and the dominance of the English language in the production and dissemination of scientific outputs (Tietze & Dick, 2013). Lau (2002) highlights several barriers that Asian scholars face when publishing in international journals. One such barrier is that Asian scholars and students (including those from China) traditionally receive little training in Western research methodology and academic writing. Thus, it seems useful for many international scholars to broaden their research designs and embrace a variety of sophisticated philosophical and methodological approaches.

My second motivation comes from the increasing number of Chinese students studying in English-taught and research programmes. Statistics from China's Ministry of Education show more than 600,000 Chinese students left the country to pursue overseas studies in 2017, representing an 11.74% increase from 2016 (MOE, 2018). From the receiving end, data from the Higher Education Statistics Agency reveal that a total of 106,530 Chinese students enrolled in UK universities during the 2017–2018 academic year (HESA, 2019). A study conducted by the Chartered Association of Business Schools (2016) reports that 86% of responding schools identified China as being their largest source of international students. The same study further finds a 26% increase of non-EU students registered in doctoral programmes. Elsewhere, institutions in other English-speaking countries such as the United States, Canada, Australia and New Zealand have seen similar increases. For example, Chinese students account for 30% of enrolments in Australian universities (Department of Education and Training, 2019).

Whereas the landscape of international education has changed, there has been little discussion about the needs of, and support for, international students studying Western research methodologies. From my experience (first as student, now as supervisor), Chinese students face three challenges while managing their research projects. The first issue is related to the dissimilarity between English and Chinese languages. Many technical terms (for example, positivism or grounded-theory) found in traditional method books have no direct translation in the Chinese language. Most Chinese students found it difficult to comprehend these terms. I have to admit that the first time I saw the Chinese translation of the term "grounded-theory" (扎根理论) in a Chinese textbook, I failed to make the connection. Recent pedagogical research found that learning new contents through a foreign language can be ineffective, as the lack of language skills can interfere with content learning (Roussel, Joulia, Tricot, & Sweller, 2017). These authors suggest that learning with a translation into the native language is superior to learning entirely in a foreign language.

The second issue is associated with the unique social context of China. A large number of traditional textbooks of research methods are written by US and UK authors, for example Saunders, Lewis, and Thornhill (2015), and a few are written by scholars from other EU countries, for example Alvesson and Sköldberg (2018). Few, however, address issues faced by international students, with the noticeable exception of Marschan-Piekkari and Welch (2004). Yet, Chinese students frequently find it problematic to apply these methods to Chinese society without modifications. Third, the whole idea of developing new knowledge based on evidence-based research is alien to the majority of Chinese students. The essence of Western research is associated with reason, objectivity, truth and empiricism, as opposed to irrationalism, subjectivity, ignorance and faith (Bishop, 2006). Research is seen as a way of knowing, and the whole process is "a disciplined way of coming to know something about our world and ourselves" (Bouma, 2001, p. 5). Arguably, this subverts Chinese indigenous epistemology and methodology that emphasise experiential learning or knowing by doing (知行合一) and practical reasoning (实践出真理) (Chen, 2016). As a result, Chinese students often struggle to understand the nature of research and meet the requirements of overseas universities. As such, a significant reason for my translation activities is to facilitate learning. Whereas Xian and Meng-Lewis (2018) have addressed many issues related to points 2 and 3, the rest of the chapter will focus on point 1, as it is central to the discussion between language, translation and learning.

## Issues About Language, Translation and the Construction of Knowledge in Research

As stated earlier, there has been little discussion about how international researchers and students make sense of Western research methodology. There is evidence that this silence can be traced back to the lack of recognition about the roles of language and translation in cross-language business and management research (Chidlow et al., 2014; Piekkari & Tietze, 2011). Various scholars have used the metaphor of a "black box" to describe the hidden, yet important, decisions researchers make within a cross-language project (Chidlow et al., 2014; Xian, 2008). In this section, I will attempt to open this "black box" through considerations on language, translation and the ways they can impact on the construction of knowledge.

Language is an inseparable part of human life. In international research methodology, however, the notion of language is traditionally perceived to be unproblematic. This lack of debates on language and translation reflects a taken-for-granted assumption within the academic community that language is merely a tool for communication in scientific investigations and that translation is an objective and neutral process, in which meaning can be transferred between languages without changes or losses (Piekkari & Tietze, 2011; Wong & Poon, 2010). Translators are seen as "technicians" who can remain invisible in producing texts that carry forward all the original meaning from the source language to the target language without distortions. As pointed out by a number of international scholars, this thinking reflects an "equivalence paradigm", which dominates current literature on international and cross-language research methodology (Chidlow et al., 2014; Welch & Piekkari, 2006; Xian, 2008). In essence, this approach stipulates that there is "equivalence" between languages and translation is a quest for finding something identical or with "equal value" in another language. Peña (2007), for example, offers detailed explanations of four dimensions of equivalence in international research methodology. Linguistic equivalence is necessary to ensure that the words and linguistic meaning used in research instruments and instructions are the same for both languages. Functional equivalence addresses the incongruity in meanings and aims to make certain research instruments, questions and elicitation methods allow examination of the same construct or concept. Cultural equivalence focuses on the way members of different cultural and linguistic groups interpret the underlying meaning of an item or interview question, as culture may affect how people respond to research instruments. Metric equivalence refers to the level of difficulty in items of a questionnaire or interview questions, and is essential in ability tests, for example, English vocabulary assessments for children from different countries.

The equivalence approach appears to be grounded on a positivist standpoint that embraces both ontological and epistemological realism, and assumes an obtainable "reality" between languages through "accurate" translation. However, translators often run into trouble quickly, e.g. facing asymmetrical structures between languages or having to deal with concepts that are unique to a certain culture and language. To ensure the accurate transmission of meaning, a number of techniques have been recommended to overcome such problems. These techniques include back translation (Brislin, 1970) and team translation (Douglas & Craig, 2007), with an aim to produce a translated text that has the same response in a reader in the targeted language as the response of a reader in the original language.

In recent literature, however, many basic assumptions of the equivalence paradigm are questioned by authors who struggle with "the notion of what equivalence actually means and how it can be achieved" (Chidlow et al., 2014, pp. 564–565). There is a general recognition that language is ambiguous, unstable, context-dependent (Alvesson & Sköldberg, 2018; Björk Brämberg & Dahlberg, 2013) and even gendered (Abalkhail, 2018). Poststructuralist scholars further remind us that language is inseparable from culture, which incorporates systems of thinking, contextualised knowledge, values, beliefs, traditions, institutions or artefacts, shared by members of a society (Alvesson & Sköldberg, 2018). Language is not simply a tool for communication. Rather, it defines what is "normal" and carries logics about our sociocultural world (Foucault, 1972). Translation is therefore a process, which deliberately produces as well as conveys meaning across cultures (Björk Brämberg & Dahlberg, 2013). Wong and Poon (2010) argue that the understanding of culture, as systems of meanings, intertwined with language to (re)create sociocultural world, is critical to the debates about translation in cross-cultural research methodology. The assumption that a concept can be understood in the same way across cultures has been criticised for ignoring meaning embedded in culture (Venuti, 2008). In practice, many researchers are confronted with the asymmetrical features between languages and cultures. Sechrest, Fay, and Zaidi (1972) summarise a self-destructing logic of equivalence: the more equivalent the translation, the less likely that the research finds cultural differences. Another criticism to the equivalence approach is that what is "equivalent" is often a subjective matter (Gawlewicz, 2016). Take back-translation as an example. Whether the original and the back-translated versions are the "same" relies on subjective judgement of researchers. Inevitably, translators bring in their own understanding, experiences, preferred strategies and perceptions of the situations into the translation process (Björk Brämberg & Dahlberg,

2013; Venuti, 2008). Thus in international research methodology, translation is a form of knowledge co-production (Xian, 2008).

Following developments in the translation discipline, an alternative paradigm—the contextualised approach—has been proposed, which explicitly acknowledges the embeddedness between culture and language and the role of the translator as knowledge co-producer (Chidlow et al., 2014; Xian, 2008). Many scholars reject the positivist conception of language as a neutral medium which transmits information between languages. Instead, a range of philosophical positions has been used to underpin their practice of language and translation. These philosophies vary in their degree of acceptance of a subjective epistemology and a constructivist ontology, ranging from critical theory (Xian, 2008), feminist epistemology (Caretta, 2015), to poststructuralism (Wong & Poon, 2010). Proponents of the contextualised approach argue that it is impossible to produce a text in the target language, which contains all the features of the source culture and language (Gawlewicz, 2016; Xian, 2008). Translation is not seen as an exercise simply finding linguistic replacements in the target language. Rather, it is argued that translation is an interpretive and sense-making activity that starts from the translator's understanding of the source text then recontextualising it in another culture and language to a new audience (House, 2006). The act of recontexualisation is shaped by the translator's interpretation of the situation and requires his or her expert judgement of what works best in the target culture for a particular audience (Björk Brämberg & Dahlberg, 2013). As the response of the translated text is context dependent, there can be no "one best version" of translation. "Equivalence of response", if still relevant, is achieved at cultural level rather than at linguistic level.

## Translating Research Philosophy—(Re)contextualised Approach in Practice

As argued earlier, few articles have examined how international scholars and students make sense of Western methodologies. A noticeable difficulty faced by these scholars and students is that some key concepts may be absent in their own language and culture. Here in this section, I argue that this difficulty can be overcome through translation. In particular, I will put the contextualised approach into practice and further unpack the notion of recontextualisation. Examples of how I translated some philosophical concepts from Western research methodology and explained them in Chapter 3 of Xian and Meng-Lewis (2018) will be used as illustrations of contextualised translation. Like many of its English counterparts, such as Saunders et al. (2015) and Bryman and Bell (2011), this text is mainly for postgraduate taught students who pursue business or management-related master's degrees including MA, MSc and MBA in English-taught programmes, which often require the completion of an evidence-based research. Specifically, the primary target readers are those from the "Greater China" region, which, many believe, includes mainland China, Hong Kong, Taiwan, Macao and Singapore. A secondary target group is Chinese doctoral students and academics who wish to develop new research skills or explore new methods.

Translating between English and Chinese can be complicated and challenging. There are social concepts and expressions in English language that are difficult to say in Chinese, and vice versa. Becker (1991) argues that in every culture there is something unique and its uniqueness makes it unsayable in another language. Becker calls these unique concepts and expressions "silences", things in one language which have no counterpart in another. Xian (2008) identifies three difficulties when translating between English and Chinese. The first one is associated with the linguistic differences, as there is little similarity in terms of grammatical structure between the two languages. Tenses for instance are not used in Chinese. The second difficulty relates to the socio-cultural differences between Chinese and Western societies. There are concepts, idioms and proverbs, which came from historical events, stories or traditions that have no true equivalence in the other language. Third, in some cases, the "same" word can mean completely different things or concepts in the other language and culture. Therefore, a direct translation would be meaningless. Ree (2001) suggests two further complexities when translating philosophy. First, philosophical writing is mostly obscure and theoretical. Whereas philosophical terminologies are mostly concerned with concepts commonly related to truth, being, existence, nature, knowledge and authority, they are often remote from everyday vocabulary. Even native speakers can find these terminologies incomprehensible. This obscurity makes it impossible for translators to have one "true version" of understanding. At the end, translators have to make up their mind and stick to their own interpretations. A second complexity is that philosophical writing is dialogical (Ree, 2001). Philosophical writers tend to present their work in the form of a negotiation or debate with rival ideas. Readers can be left to exploit subjunctive, conditional and tenses in order to see a shifting multicity point of view. Translators are confronted with problems of "voice", obliquity and transparency. They have to choose between being "faithful" and "natural".

To deal with these complexities of translating Western research philosophy into Chinese text and facilitate learning, I have recontextualised philosophical concepts in a number of ways. First, I retained the dialogical feature of philosophical writing, as it helps to establish the unique arguments of each position by comparing them with those of other (especially similar) positions. Johnson and Duberley (2000) have observed that management research is characterised by the existence of an array of competing paradigms which disagree over basic epistemological and ontological assumptions. Engaging in such philosophical dialogues, in my view, helps to promote transparency and let readers make choices based on their interpretations rather than leaving them at the mercy of the translator. This, I argue, prevents a one-sided reductionism of philosophical translation.

Second, I have added a large amount of explanations to provide clarity. Nord (1997) warns that source text usually has presuppositions that are alien to the target audience. Nord suggests the translator has a crucial role, where "the cultural gap between the amount of information presupposed with respect to the source-text receivers and the actual cultural and world knowledge of the target-text addressees can sometimes be abridged by additional information or adaptations introduced by the translator" (Nord, 1997, p. 86). This is particularly useful for transferring concepts that do not exist in the Chinese language. From a learning point of view, additional explanations also help to overcome the increased difficulties of simultaneously learning contents and foreign language (Roussel et al., 2017). For example, one of the difficulties of translating "critical realism" is to explain what it means to "be critical", a concept which arguably does not exist in the Chinese language. The Chinese translation of the word "critical"—*pi pan shi* (批判式) comes from the word "to criticise"—*pi pan* (批判). This literal translation, however, can be misleading, as it does not capture the meaning in its English version, which is to evaluate different perspectives or to examine different evidence derived from different social positions of the same phenomenon. Moreover, "to criticise" can also run counter to social conventions, such as "respect" and "harmony" within the Chinese culture. Confucian teaching requires one to "treat others in a way one would expect to be treated". Actively criticising another person would seem harsh and jeopardise interpersonal relations. Thus, to translate "critical realism", I must distinguish between "being critical" and "to criticise" to my Chinese audience.

Therefore, when I translated, or more precisely explained, the concept of critical realism, I first compared it with "direct realism", then emphasised "being critical" is not the same as "to criticise". A "back translation" of the concept of critical realism (Xian & Meng-Lewis, 2018, p. 47, box "Key Concepts in Chinese: Realism") can be read as:

> Realism adopts an objective ontology. Thus, realists conduct research to seek an objective reality, independent of our cognition. However, realists do not all adopt the same epistemology. There are two main views: direct realism and critical realism. Direct realists believe in an objectivist epistemology. However, unlike positivism, realism focuses on whether the information collected by our senses (such as eyes, nose, ears, hand, and so on) can represent reality or truth. Direct realism proposes that what we see, listen and feel is what reality is. This is similar to the idea of "seeing is believing". On the other hand, critical realists tend to adopt a subjectivist perspective

of epistemology. "Being critical" here does not mean "to criticise". Being critical means when we analyse a situation, we must see beyond its superficial level.

Third, I used everyday examples to recontextualise these philosophical concepts, so that they can make sense in the Chinese culture. This approach is similar to what Caretta (2015) called "situated knowledge", in which translators use their local knowledge to redirect understanding so as to enhance trustworthiness of the text. In the same box, I went on to provide an example about how "reality" can be perceived differently thanks to people's different perspectives on organisational practice:

> For example, many organisations adopt flexible working hours. This means that employees, with their supervisors' agreement, can organise their own working hours. Those who benefit from the policy may think positively about this arrangement, because it helps them to achieve a better balance between work and life. Those who do not adopt this arrangement may find it disruptive. Critical realists believe although there is an objective reality (the consequences of flexible working hours), our knowledge of it can only be subjective (different people have different experience of it). . . . In social science, because many social concepts (such as organisational culture) have no physical shape, many researchers adopt a critical realist perspective to understand reality.

Fourth, as stated earlier, philosophical writing is often obscure and confusing. This obscurity can lead to negative receptiveness and create distance between texts and the audience. To reduce such distance between Western philosophy and my Chinese audience, I have "borrowed" relevant Chinese popular phrases that represent similar meaning. This can be illustrated by the example of "pragmatism" (Xian & Meng-Lewis, 2018, p. 49). In order to convey the central idea of pragmatism—truth of a belief lies in its consequences for experience and practice (James, 1975)—I "borrowed" a sentence from the late Chinese reformist Deng, Xiaoping who has been credited for engineering China's economic reform in the last four decades. In a public speech about how socialism can promote labour relations and increase productivity at the same time, Deng (1962) famously said, "It does not matter whether a cat is white or black. It is a good cat if it catches mice" to indicate that both planning and market forces are means of controlling economic activities and they should be used flexibly to encourage production and ultimately improve people's livelihood. After Deng, the same "cat metaphor" has been used widely in the Chinese language and writing to suggest that practical outcomes can sometimes legitimise the methods we use.

A back translation of the concepts of pragmatism (Xian & Meng-Lewis, 2018, pp. 49–50, Key Concepts in Chinese: Pragmatism, 2nd paragraph) can be read as:

> With regard to academic research, pragmatism emphasises two points. First, our research question or subject determines the method we adopt. If we study things that exist independently, we may use objective or neutral methods such as experiment or survey. But if we study things that exist subjectively, such as people's feelings or perceptions, we may use subjective methods, such as interview, to understand personal stories and feelings. Second, pragmatists believe that if truth exists, it must arise out of our practical experience. . . . To judge whether a theory is 'good' or not, we must see if it has practical consequences. A theory can be considered to be true if it has practical value, regardless the method from which it is developed. This is similar to a popular Chinese expression "it does not matter whether a cat is white or black. It is a good cat if it catches mice".

## Conclusion

The last few decades have witnessed a move towards a multilingual academic community both in research and education. However, the "black box" containing language and translation issues is rarely discussed in business and management research methodology, owing to an underlining assumption that non-native speakers can use English in the same way as native speakers do and meaning can be transferred smoothly between languages without any distortion (Tietze & Dick, 2013). Typically, the "equivalence paradigm" of translation sees language as purely a tool for communication and translation as technical problems to identify language functions in the same way (Chidlow et al., 2014). The dilemmas and difficult decisions translators have to make remain a negligible oversight. In this chapter, reflecting on my experience of translating Western research philosophical concepts into Chinese, I propose a contextualised approach, in which a translator interprets the source text using her "insider knowledge" of what works well in the target language and culture, and recontextualises that text to the target audience.

First, the approach will bridge cultural gaps between the source and target audiences (Nord, 1997). Translation is no longer a process aiming to maintain old-fashion "fidelity"—merely mirroring the content and style of the original text. The translated text in this case encompasses both foreign ideas that will enrich the target culture, as well as domestic elements that will help to make sense to the target audience. Indeed, this approach has long been argued in the sociological branch of translation studies. Venuti (1998) suggests that a translation always communicates an interpretation, a source text that is partial and altered, supplemented with features peculiar to the target language, no longer inscrutable foreign to the target readers but made comprehensible in a distinctively domestic style.

Second, specifically related to translating research methodologies, the contextualised approach is useful to facilitate learning by reducing the language and cultural deficits of the target audience. Roussel et al. (2017) show that students can benefit from bilingual learning materials when they have to learn new contents through a foreign language. Whereas this communication relies heavily on the translator's understanding and, as such, is inevitably partial, I argue that the approach can provide a translated text (e.g. philosophical concepts) that will function optimally in my target audience (e.g. Chinese students and researchers). But the translator has to be an expert both in intercultural communication and in Western research methodologies.

Furthermore, this chapter contributes to the practice of researcher and translator's reflexivity. It demonstrates that, rather than taking a neutral stance and a role of transmitting functional meaning between languages and cultures, a translator should critically engage with interpretation to enhance cross-cultural communication. Knowledge production is not a value-free process in translating research philosophy. The interference of the translator in providing additional contextual and sociocultural elements in the translated text is seen as an advantage. The contextualised method proposed here supports a reflexive analysis of one's approach and therefore may be valuable in researcher development. Whereas this chapter is based on my personal experience of translating Western research philosophy for Chinese students and academics, its applicability can be extended to translations within multilingual and cross-cultural research projects. Increasingly, researchers are expected to methodologically scrutinise their own work and advance reflectivity (Caretta, 2015; Reissner, 2018). Reflexivity allows me to challenge taken-for-granted assumptions and approaches in translation, disclose aspects of myself and propose an alternative approach.

## References

Abalkhail, J. M. (2018). Challenges of translating qualitative management data. *Gender in Management: An International Journal, 33*(1), 66–79.

Alvesson, M., & Sköldberg, K. (2018). *Reflexive methodology: New vistas for qualitative research*. London: Sage.

Becker, A. (1991). A short essay on language. In F. Steier (Ed.), *Research and reflexivity*. London: Sage.

Bishop, R. (2006). Research. *Theory, Culture and Society, 23*(2–3), 570–571.

Björk Brämberg, E., & Dahlberg, K. (2013). Interpreters in cross-cultural interviews. *Qualitative Health Research, 23*(2), 241–247.

Bouma, G. D. (2001). *The research process*. Melbourne: Oxford University Press.

Brislin, R. W. (1970). Back-translation for cross-cultural research. *Journal of Cross-Cultural Psychology, 1*(3), 185–216.

Bryman, A., & Bell, E. (2011). *Business research methods.* Oxford: Oxford University Press.

Caretta, M. A. (2015). Situated knowledge in cross-cultural, cross-language research: A collaborative reflexive analysis of researcher, assistant and participant subjectivities. *Qualitative Research, 15*(4), 489–505.

Cassell, C., Bishop, V., Symon, G., Johnson, P., & Buehring, A. (2009). Learning to be a qualitative management researcher. *Management Learning, 40*(5), 513–533.

Chartered Association of Business Schools. (2016). *UK business schools and international student recruitment: Trends, challenges and the case for change.* Chartered Association of Business Schools. Retrieved from https://chartered-abs.org/wp-content/uploads/2016/03/Chartered-ABS-International-Student-Recruitment-2016.pdf

Chen, X. (2016). Challenges and strategies of teaching qualitative research in China. *Qualitative Inquiry, 22*(2), 72–86.

Chidlow, A., Plakoyiannaki, E., & Welch, C. (2014). Translation in cross-language international business research: Beyond equivalence. *Journal of International Business Studies, 45*(5), 562–582.

Cooke, F. (2009). A decade of transformation of HRM in China: A review of literature and suggestions for future studies. *Asia Pacific Business Review, 47,* 6–42.

Deng, X. (1962). *How to restore agricultural production.* Communist Youth League Conference, Beijing.

Department of Education and Training. (2019). *International student enrolments in Australia 1994–2018.* Department of Education and Training, Australian Government. Retrieved from https://internationaleducation.gov.au/research/International-Student-Data/Pages/InternationalStudentData2018.aspx

Douglas, S. P., & Craig, C. S. (2007). Collaborative and iterative translation: An alternative approach to back translation. *Journal of International Marketing, 15*(1), 30–43.

Easterby-Smith, M., & Malina, D. (1999). Cross-cultural collaborative research: Toward reflexivity. *The Academy of Management Journal, 42*(1), 76–86.

Foucault, M. (1972). *The archaeology of knowledge and the discourse on language.* New York: Pantheon Books.

Gawlewicz, A. (2016). Language and translation strategies in researching migrant experience of difference from the position of migrant researcher. *Qualitative Research, 16*(1), 27–42.

HESA. (2019). *HE student data: Where do HE students come from?* Retrieved from www.hesa.ac.uk/data-and-analysis/students/where-from: Higher Education Statistics Agency

House, J. (2006). Text and context in translation. *Journal of Pragmatics: An Interdisciplinary Journal of Language Studies, 38*(3), 338–358.

Jack, G., & Westwood, R. (2006). Postcolonialism and the politics of qualitative research in international business. *Management International Review, 46*(4), 481–501.

James, W. (1975). *Pragmatism.* Cambridge, MA: Harvard University Press.

Johnson, P., & Duberley, J. (2000). *Understanding management research: An introduction to epistemology*. London: Sage.

Kornienko, A. A. (2015). Outline of synthesis of cognitive and socio-cultural foundations of scientific knowledge evolution in research programs of Western philosophy of science. *Procedia—Social and Behavioral Sciences, 166,* 387–392.

Lau, C.-M. (2002). Asian management research: Frontiers and challenges. *Asia Pacific Journal of Management, 19*(2), 171–178.

Marschan-Piekkari, R., & Welch, C. (2004). *Handbook of qualitative research methods for international business*. Cheltenham: Edward Elgar.

MOE. (2018). *Brief report on Chinese overseas students and international students in China 2017*. Beijing: Ministry of Education of the People's Republic of China.

Nord, C. (1997). *Translating as a purposeful activity: Functionalist approaches explained*. Manchester: St. Jerome.

Peña, E. D. (2007). Lost in translation: Methodological considerations in cross-cultural research. *Child Development, 78*(4), 1255–1264.

Piekkari, R., & Tietze, S. (2011). A world of languages: Implications for international management research and practice. *Journal of World Business, 46*(3), 267–269.

Quer, D., Claver, E., & Rienda, L. (2007). Business and management in China: A review of empirical research in leading international journals. *Asia Pacific Journal of Management, 24*(3), 359–384.

Ree, J. (2001). The translation of philosophy. *New Literary History, 32*(2), 223–257.

Reissner, S. C. (2018). Interactional challenges and researcher reflexivity: Mapping and analysing conversational space. *European Management Review, 15*(2), 205–219.

Roussel, S., Joulia, D., Tricot, A., & Sweller, J. (2017). Learning subject content through a foreign language should not ignore human cognitive architecture: A cognitive load theory approach. *Learning and Instruction, 52,* 69–79.

Saunders, M., Lewis, P., & Thornhill, A. (2015). *Research methods for business students*. New York: Pearson Education.

Sechrest, L., Fay, T. L., & Zaidi, S. M. H. (1972). Problems of translation in cross-cultural research. *Journal of Cross-Cultural Psychology, 3*(1), 41–56.

Stening, B., & Zhang, M. (2007). Methodological challenges confronted when conducting management research in China. *International Journal of Cross Cultural Management, 7*(1), 121–142.

Tietze, S., & Dick, P. (2013). The victorious English language: Hegemonic practices in the management academy. *Journal of Management Inquiry, 22*(1), 122–134.

Tsui, A. (2004). Contributing to global management knowledge: A case for high quality indigenous research. *Asia Pacific Journal of Management, 21*(4), 491–513.

Venuti, L. (1998). *The scandals of translation: Towards an ethics of difference*. London: Taylor & Francis.

Venuti, L. (2008). *The translator's invisibility: A history of translation*. London: Routledge.

Welch, C., & Piekkari, R. (2006). Crossing language boundaries: Qualitative interviewing in international business. *Management International Review*, 46(4), 417–437.

Wong, J. P.-H., & Poon, M. K.-L. (2010). Bringing translation out of the shadows: Translation as an issue of methodological significance in cross-cultural qualitative research. *Journal of Transcultural Nursing*, 21(2), 151–158.

Xian, H. (2008). Lost in translation? Language, culture and the roles of translator in cross-cultural management research. *Qualitative Research in Organizations and Management: An International Journal*, 3(3), 231–245.

Xian, H., & Meng-Lewis, Y. (2018). *Business research methods for Chinese students: A practical guide to your research project.* London: Sage.

# 4 Translatorial Linguistic Ethnography in Organizations

*Kaisa Koskinen*

Many if not most contemporary workplaces are multilingual and in numerous ways connected and networked across borders. The linguistic set-ups and communication needs take different shapes, but entirely monolingual work is a rarity in today's connected and globalized societies. Executives are recruited internationally or seconded to expatriate positions, and even if staying home they interact with their global peers and operate between company headquarters and local organizations. These higher echelons of work often operate with a controlled language regime and a combination of local languages and an international prestige language, in today's world often English. In comparison, the most multilingual workplaces may well be found in shop floors and low skills workplaces of Western countries, where people with immigrant backgrounds find employment. In these work communities the company language and the national language may be accompanied by a multitude of languages and locally relevant *lingua francas*.

All these multilingual workplaces are also *spaces of translation*, with their explicit or implicit language and translation policies (Meylaerts, 2011) and their organically grown and habitualized translation cultures (Prunč, 2008). Michael Cronin (2006) conceptualizes multilingual, multi-ethnic space as first and foremost a *translation space*, i.e. a space where translation needs to happen for mutual comprehensibility and where multilingual repertoires meet and mix. Translation, then, needs to be understood in a wide sense of transcultural and interlingual movement of verbalizations (Prunč, 2008, p. 19). Translation that takes place in organizational translation spaces is not only the kind executed by professional translators, for complete and final documents, labelled as translations and ordered from the in-house translation department or translation agencies. Translation is much more widespread in the everyday functioning of the organization, and much more fluid and porous. Recurrent orality, as opposed to written translation, adds to its ephemerality. This climate of constant movement between different languages can be called *tanslatoriality*, and once we start looking we realize that translatoriality is embedded in societal life in most corners of the contemporary, networked world.

These spaces can therefore also be conceptualized as *translatorial spaces*, a concept derived from Holz-Mänttäri's concept of *translatorial action* and signalling a space of translation activity emphasizing actors (Koskinen, 2017). Since the publication of Justa Holz-Mänttäri's now classic treatise in 1984, translatorial action has, in Translation Studies vocabulary, been used to denote a translator's activity that transgresses the boundaries of equivalence-based search for optimal correspondence between two texts. That is, the translation may radically deviate from word-to-word correspondence, and it may also be based on more than one source text. Holz-Mänttäri's research ethos was to empower and raise the status of professional translators. In recent research, her original focus on professional translators has been enlarged to all kinds of translation actors invested in the communication event in various ways, and the attribute 'translatorial' used to signal all kinds of parallel movement from one language to another, whether they are labelled as translation by the actors themselves or not (Koskela, Koskinen, & Pilke, 2017; Koskinen, 2017).

Organizations operating in more than one language need to develop practices of dealing with the movement from one language to another, i.e. for *managing translatoriality*. Even in situations where separate translation/interpreting units have been set up, the organizations are sometimes largely unaware of the effects of this movement in their daily activities, brand and image work, customer relations and, finally, economic success. An emerging research agenda in Organization Studies and International Business literature (Piekkari, Welch, Welch, Peltonen, & Vesa, 2013; Piekkari, Welch, & Welch, 2014; Chidlow, Plakoyiannaki, & Welch, 2014; Tietze, Tansley, & Helienek, 2017; Ciuk & James, 2015; Ciuk, James, & Sliwa, 2018) is beginning to address this under-researched area. For relevant methodology to study translatoriality in organizations, one logical avenue is to turn to Translation Studies, a wide-ranging and multidisciplinary field for researching translation and interpreting. From within the disciplinary perspective of Translation Studies, this chapter aims to support this emerging line of inquiry in two ways: 1) by providing conceptual tools for discussing and describing relevant related features, and 2) by indicating *translatorial linguistic ethnography* as one potential methodological avenue for future research. To illustrate the possibilities, two case examples of relevant studies within Translation Studies are discussed.

## Linguistic Ethnography and Translatoriality

### Linguistic Ethnography

During its forty odd years of existence, Translation Studies has provided a wealth of new knowledge on fields such as literary, business or audio-visual translation and the many modes of oral interpreting. Foci have varied from social and cultural contexts to agents and actors and to comparative analysis of source and target texts (for an overview see e.g. Munday, 2016). The sustained research focus closest to the current interest in workplace language practices is the branch of researching institutional translation (see Kang, 2009; Koskinen, 2011; Schäffner, 2018) where the workplace practices in various institutional settings have been studied with the help of ethnographic methods. In this chapter, particular emphasis will be given to linguistic ethnography as an avenue for understanding the roles of languages and their interplay in the functioning of organizations, and to translatorial linguistic ethnography (my neologism) in understanding translatoriality in multilingual organizations.

Linguistic ethnography is a largely UK-based line of research born organically around the turn of the millennium from a number of gatherings of like-minded scholars (Linguistic Ethnography Forum, 2004). It is reminiscent of linguistic Anthropology practices in the United States, and it builds on the foundational work of Frederick Erickson, John Gumperz, Dell Hymes and other classics of interaction research (Shaw, Copland, & Snell, 2015). Linguistic ethnography is not a set methodology nor a fixed research agenda, but Shaw et al. (2015) have identified a number of recurrent themes: 1) interdisciplinarity, 2) topic-oriented approach to ethnography (as opposed to anthropological full scale immersion), 3) use of multiple data sets, 4) an aspiration to improve social life and 5) combining linguistics with ethnography. The three first ones are rather self-evident in the sense that ethnography typically mobilizes different sources of data and ethnography employed outside Anthropology tends to be topic-oriented and interdisciplinary. The fourth one is more interesting as it signals an activist bend that is also visible in ethnography as it has been used in Translation Studies. Similar activist traits seem to be far less prominent in Organization Studies. This research position is not, however, in any way prescribed by the methodology and may be a consequence of other factors such as researcher personalities. What remains as the defining feature is the fifth and the most obvious one: the dominant role of linguistic data and its detailed analysis within an overall ethnographic framework, linking the micro elements of textual detail to the macro level of organizational practices.

Simply put, linguistic ethnography is a combination of ethnography and linguistic analysis (Shaw et al., 2015). Rampton (2007, p. 3) defines linguistic ethnography through these two foundational elements as follows:

1.   Its methodology is grounded in ethnography: "Meaning takes shape within specific social relations, interactional histories and institutional regimes, produced and construed by agents with expectations and repertoires that have to be grasped ethnographically."

2.  The role of language data is crucially important. Linguistic analysis is embedded in the research design, and verbalizations are researched in minute detail: "Meaning is far more than just the 'expression of ideas', and biography, identifications, stance and nuance are extensively signalled in the linguistic and textual fine-grain."

## Repertoires, Translatorial Encounters and Organizational Contexts

In practice, the combination of the over-arching cultural understanding and the microscopic study of textual data in linguistic ethnography allows for many kinds of research designs and a multitude of data sets and foci, ranging from members to situational encounters and institutional contexts.

First, Rampton's (2007, p. 3) long list of elements to observe and analyse in the members category includes

> their physical bodies, senses and perceptions; their cultural and semiotic repertoires, and the resources they have at their disposal; their capacities, habitual practices and dispositions; their likes and dislikes, desires, fears, commitments, and personalities; their social status and category memberships.

For the present purposes, I wish to particularly highlight repertoires and resources because of their importance to a translatorially focused linguistic ethnography. In sociolinguistics repertoire is traditionally defined as the variety of languages used by the members of a particular speech community, but in contemporary research and in this context it is also intended as a term for individual linguistic competence. What languages the members have at their disposal, to what level and in which variant or accent (i.e. their linguistic resources), and how skilfully they can employ various translatorial strategies (i.e. their translatorial repertoires) will crucially affect their position at the workplace and their possibilities for taking translatorial agency and using it for their purposes (see e.g. Chew, 2005). Habitual language and translation practices, and dispositions towards them, are also significant. Particularly in the absence of a robust translation policy, members of the organization will find workarounds and ways of organically sorting out their translatorial needs (Piekkari et al., 2013).

Second, Rampton's (2007, p. 3) listing of elements to observe in the situational encounters that members and texts—and, by extension, translatorial practices—are embedded in, is equally extensive:

> the events, genres and types of activity in which people, texts and objects interact together; actions, sequences of actions and the use

of semiotic materials (signs, language, texts, media); inferencing, interpretation and the efforts of participants to understand or influence each other; the physical arrangement of the participants and the material setting; origins, outcomes and wider links—how signs, actions and encounters fit with interactional and institutional processes over longer and broader stretches of time and space.

In this kind of ethnography the "use of semiotic materials" is the centre of attention. In ethnography, a repeated guideline for fieldwork is "follow the actors". In linguistic ethnography it is equally important to *follow the texts* as the participants take efforts to model and mould them, also through translation processes, for the various organizational purposes, and texts travel in various forms of distribution from one member, department, organization and sometimes country to another. It is therefore important to ask what are the texts used for, how and by whom: who writes or speaks, for which purposes and to influence who and how; who distributes and through which channels and media; who is targeted and expected to read and who is excluded (because of limited access or lacking language resources); who will take the role of explaining to others and how and why; who translates, how and for whom; who revises and reinterprets and for which purposes; who stores and archives and is this organizational memory referred to. And so on.

The third layer of contextualization consists of more or less durable institutions, groups and communities of practice, and research is expected to look into how "institutions shape, sustain and get reproduced through texts, objects, media, genres and practices" as well as how they produce, control and manage "persons, resources, discourses, representations, ideologies, spaces" and so forth (Rampton, 2007, p. 3). Many modern organizations and institutions are entirely text-based in that their output is entirely written or spoken material. They are talked into being (Heritage, 1984, p. 290), written into being, and in a multilingual and translatorial world they are also translated into being (Koskinen, 2008, p. 3). The texts that workers produce at work *create* the work.

The three layers are interlinked: "With varying degrees of friction and slippage, repertoires get used and developed in encounters, encounters enact institutions, and institutions produce and regulate persons and their repertoires through the regimentation of encounters" (Rampton, 2007, p. 3). Rampton (ibid.) labels the three levels as 'persons', 'encounters' and 'institutions'. This is not too far removed from what was developed within Translation Studies for the purposes of an ethnography of translation work at the European Commission (Koskinen, 2008) around the same time. With no explicit reference to linguistic ethnography, the study employs a similar architecture, with three levels, but whereas the linguistic ethnography of Rampton tacitly prioritizes spoken encounters, Koskinen (2008) operates on written texts, and the most micro-level inspection is that of a gradual drafting of a Commission document in English and the gradual gestation of its translation into Finnish through the various intermittent text versions and revisions. The "meso-level" is that of persons—the professional translators and the community of practice they have in the Finnish translation unit (I will return to this case later in "Case 1. Translating the European Union").

## Agents of Translation

In a manner typical for most Translation Studies research, Koskinen's research (2008) focuses on professional translators, and also the analysis of the translations is employed to support the aim of understanding their workplace culture. Ethnography is about people in their social and cultural environment, and also linguistic ethnography focuses on people, even if also through the lens of the texts they produce. The power positions of the various actors and their aims and motivations (their *skopoi*) play a significant role in defining how the translation events will unfold. Holz-Mänttäri (1984; see also Koskinen, 2017) identifies six key roles of a translatorial event as follows:

a.   the initiator, who needs a translation for a purpose
b.   the client, who commissions translatorial action
c.   the source-text producer
d.   the translator
e.   the user of translation (i.e. the one who needs the translation to accomplish a task)
f.   the addressee (i.e. the end-user of the translation)

In organizations these roles can be played by many actors, and people may alternate in different roles, resulting in different set-ups and hierarchies depending on language, text type and other situational factors. These roles may be quite distinct in cases when full translation of an existing text is requested from a professional translator, but in the case of more fluid translatoriality, things can be much more fuzzy. As Koskela et al.'s (2017) data indicate, role-taking may be quite subtle and even subconscious, but it is also dependent on the institutional status and position of different actors (see "Case 2. Translation Practices in a Bilingual Formal Meeting" later). Not everybody can push themselves forward as translators, and not everybody is in the position of demanding translatoriality even when in need. Arguably, this latter form of translatoriality, the one without professional translators and interpreters, is the more common one, in the world at large and in organizations. In workplaces, various translatorial activities are constantly carried out by translators who are doing it alongside their other occupational tasks, not necessarily labelling them translating or even recognizing their translatorial nature (which can be a challenge for interview studies as the full extent of translatoriality may be difficult to capture through members' self-reports). These actors are professionals and translators but not professional translators. In Translation Studies this group has recently been labelled as *paraprofessional* translators (Koskela et al., 2017), to differentiate them from both professional translators and non-professional translation that takes place entirely outside the occupational and salaried realm.

This group—the consultants, the CEOs and other paraprofessional translators in organizations—are an interesting sub-group of boundary spanners (see e.g. Williams, 2002) spanning interlingual boundaries as they reverbalize and set in motion meanings that circulate across languages. They are also a theoretically interesting group from the perspective of Translation Studies because their translation practice is unconstrained by the professional norms nor controlled by codes of conduct, professional ideologies of good translation or inbuilt understandings of translator habitus. Some evidence indicates that they might be willing and able to exert more agency and resort to bolder translation strategies than professional translators (Buzelin, 2014), thus pushing the boundaries of translational behaviour. This is why understanding them, and their translatorial behaviour, is highly relevant also for Translation Studies.

## From Linguistic Ethnography to Translatorial Linguistic Ethnography

It needs to be noted that *linguistic* ethnography is not a label often used within Translation Studies whereas ethnography in itself has become a trendy method. Linguistic ethnography was first introduced into Translation Studies by Peter Flynn (2006) in his PhD on literary translation and Moira Inghilleri (2006) in the context of her ethnographic research of asylum interpreting, and more recently by Wine Tesseur (2014) in her PhD research on translation practices and policies in Amnesty International. This is not a strong lineage of previous research yet, but many more works that combine ethnography with translation and interpreting topics could easily be placed under this umbrella term, although it has not been in active use (Tesseur, 2017). For example Koskinen (2008, p. 36), one of the first to introduce ethnography into the study of translation practices, only mentions it in passing. One reason may be that it is not yet, and even less so a decade ago, an established research tradition in sociolinguistics where it originates from, but rather still an emerging field (Rampton, 2007; Shaw et al., 2015). It also needs to be noted that in linguistic ethnographies conducted outside Translation Studies, translation issues are rarely topicalized. Still, what has been done in this area seems particularly well adapted to complement the research thus far conducted on organizations and their translatoriality. The methodology of *linguistic* ethnography promises to fill a gap in existing research because of its consistent foregrounding and close attention to languages as they manifest in the micro features of language use in the everyday life.

The crucial question is what adding the linguistic, and more specifically translatorial, layer to the research design can add. Is the added value worth the effort for those interested in organizational life and not in the subtleties of linguistic structures? In my opinion, yes. In the case of written translatoriality, where the "same" text exists in more than one language, the resulting paper trail of transformations available for a comparative analysis allows for pinpointing interpretive challenges and ideological touchstones. The translatorial practices themselves are revealing in terms of interactional and institutional hierarchies and power structures: Which languages are selected, which are not? Are the versions produced simultaneously or is there a temporal difference that signals prioritization? Are all versions equally official or are some groups only served by accidental or voluntary linguistic support from their co-workers similar to what Svetlana Probirskaja (2017) has labelled linguistic first aid? Are there institutionalized translation processes, regulatory guidelines and nominated translators, or is the practice irregular, non-resourced and uncontrolled? Oral translatoriality leaves less traces unless multilingual oral interactions are recorded for research purposes, but if those data are available (and often in contemporary ethnographies it may be the case), the minutiae of multilingual interaction will likely reveal a rich pool of evidence for example on the usability of personal linguistic repertoires in controlling interpretations and on inclusion and exclusion via translation strategies (e.g. by providing swift summary translation to keep all participants up to speed about an ongoing discussion, see Koskela et al., 2017).

Importantly, the micro data of everyday action allow for a triangulation of data: interview study, the currently dominant method for understanding translation work in organizations in International Business, offers possibilities for understanding the ideologies, values, aims and targets of optimal performance; documented translatorial behaviour explains what goes on in practice. In any human action, words and deeds form a complex dialectical relationship. The ensuing triangulation of different data sets is unlikely to result in simply validating one another in any straightforward manner. Rather, it will make findings more complex.

In this case [translating in the European Commission], the question of triangulation is confused: on the one hand—the different sets of data and different methods tell the same story; on the other hand, the story they all repeat is a story of incongruence, of a continuous battle between the readers and the institution.

The benefit of mixing different kinds of data and viewpoints is in understanding their tensions and interrelatedness. The translators' own views of their roles are seasoned by a look at the official documents which *both* ignore them completely *and* offer them a potentially significant role. Similarly, translators' laments of not being able to take the readers into account are balanced by an analysis of the case translation where the translator obviously does a lot precisely to enhance readability.

(Koskinen, 2008, p. 150, emphasis in original)

Language, and by extension translation, is a complex tool for human interaction, but its social nature is not necessarily fully obvious to scholars in other fields. It may therefore seem unnecessary to pay attention to language issues in one's object of study, or in one's research design for that matter (multilingual workplaces will often place demands on language skills of the research teams, and interpreters and fixers are often used to facilitate fieldwork without too much reflexion on how this may affect the results; see Tietze & Dick, 2013). Incorporating textual data into the research design may therefore appear a pointless exercise of nitty-gritty grammatical analysis. Research into translation in institutions within an explicit or implicit linguistic ethnography framework consistently agrees in seeing linguistic data as an element of micro analysis, but it equally consistently argues that observations on linguistic features and source-target comparisons are not only interesting for those who are into linguistic structures. On the contrary, "Language and the social world are mutually shaping," and analyzing situated language use can provide "both fundamental and distinctive insights into the mechanisms and dynamics of social and cultural production in everyday activity" (Linguistic Ethnography Forum, 2004, p. 2). Linguistic ethnography is not concerned with the micro-level linguistic features of themselves, but with how the language use in interaction is socially and institutionally framed (Inghilleri, 2006). Furthermore, the entire disciplinary understanding of translatorial action is socio-culturally-oriented. As opposed to lay expectations of mechanical sameness between source and target texts, *shifts* (of meaning, expression, connotation and so forth) are in Translation Studies considered a universal feature of translation (Toury, 2012). These shifts provide openings into the social and institutional framing of translatoriality (see Koskinen, 2008, Ch. 6). A close comparative analysis of the shifts of meaning in situated language use, as documented in the different language versions, functions as the looking glass of microspection that allows us to have whole worlds reflected in it (Cronin, 2012).

## Researching Translatoriality in Organizations

In the study of multinationals and global businesses, social and cultural differences have been identified as a significant boundary to be crossed, and organizational boundary spanners and "translators" who adapt and localize incoming practices have been a target of extensive research. It is much rarer to find studies that would take the linguistic understanding of translation seriously and engage directly with textual translatorial data, either written translations or oral interpretations. This situation is now changing, as many fields of inquiry are witnessing a "translation turn" (Evans, 2018), beginning to pay attention to and problematize the translatorial practices encountered in the contexts studied, and turning to Translation Studies for support (Piekkari et al., 2019).

A growing body of research into organizational life contains interlingual translations as a core element of analysis. In this current organization studies literature on translation in multilingual organizations, the levels of people and institutional context are typically covered. Researchers looking into translation engage in fieldwork observations and conduct extensive interviews on actors identified as central for translation work, be they outside consultants (Tietze et al., 2017), the local CEO (Logeman & Piekkari, 2015) or local branch middle management (Ciuk & James, 2015; Ciuk et al., 2018). Shop floor translatoriality is less prominent in International Business research, but it might indeed prove interesting to follow the translations down all organizational layers and to also include the reception end in the analysis. A recent study of the language policy of the global manufacturer Wärtsilä located in Finland indicates that some hiccups in the transfer of practices may well be caused by insufficient translatoriality between ladders of the organizational hierarchy. Here's a quote from a factory worker (Malkamäki & Herberts, 2014, p. 53; my translation):

> Well I did not understand all of it myself, let alone those whose language proficiency is even lower, and they were quite confused. Well, afterwards maybe something was sent in writing about what had been discussed for those who do not understand at all, something has to come, like, someone then translated the main points.

The case studies mentioned previously are, for the time being, exceptional in their disciplinary context in their direct engagement with the linguistic level of analysis of translatoriality. Still, from the perspective of a Translation Studies scholar it seems that to fully benefit from the explanatory potential of translatorial data they could still be pushed further in the direction of translatorial linguistic ethnography. I suggest three areas of development:

1. Deeper engagement with translation data: A comparative analysis of source and target texts from the viewpoint of shifts and translation strategies would provide tangible evidence of power relations, politeness issues, taboos, cultural differences and so on.
2. Integrating analysis: An integrated analysis of the three levels discussed in the previous section, comparing and contrasting textual data with translatorial discourses and statements (typically obtained

by interviews) and with the institutional aims and constraints. The way in which Ciuk et al. (2018) use *skopos* (a term in Translation Studies for the purposes of the translation) as one such connector between textual evidence and higher level aims is a good indicator of the potential for bringing Translation Studies concepts and theories in contact with the disciplinary aims of Organization Studies.

3.  Following the translation: Current research provides snapshots of translation but does not necessarily retract back to the origin of the translation trail nor follow it through during its full organizational extent, differentiating between a *translation act* (the process of producing the translation) and the *translation event* (Toury, 2012) from its gestation in the form of a perceived need by someone up to its reception and its social afterlife. The diagram by Piekkari et al. (2014) provides a good model for an organizational analysis of a translation event.

Integrative research designs combining Translation Studies and Organization Studies viewpoints would naturally also be enriching for Translation Studies. Although the explanatory power of context has long been recognized as crucially important in Translation Studies, the disciplinary tradition tilts towards textual analysis, and translation scholars would benefit greatly from a more fine-tuned organizational understanding. Although fieldwork methods are gaining popularity in Translation Studies, research skills in this area are not widely taught, making fieldwork a learning experience for most researchers. Even more importantly, the theoretical conceptualizations of organizational issues are not as robust as they might be if an interdisciplinary team were working together (for an example of an extensive textual analysis of translation in a MNC with a clear opening for input form the OS side see Brunelière, 2017).

A closer look at language issues and translatorial movements between languages provides documented evidence of the political processes at play. Looking into challenges of translatability of the concept of social inclusion into Hungarian within the context of policy transfer from the European Union to Hungary within a framework that closely resembles translatorial linguistic ethnography, Noémi Lendvai (2015, p. 142) underlines the importance of acknowledging the "spaces beneath the surfaces of the 'common' the 'shared', the 'same' language and the breakdown of the supposed linear assembly-line process of policy transfer and policy learning". She defines interlingual translation not only as a matter of language but as "a broader process of policy production and assemblage". The struggles for meaning during "awkward encounters" of languages, language re-engineering by strategic back-translation and the productive lacunae in languages allow her to identify translation as an immensely important process: "Translating across languages not only transmits, transfers and transplants but also makes, crafts and alters, policies" (p. 154). Similar emphasis of translation as a tool for micro-political soft power can be found in Logemann and Piekkari (2015), Tietze et al. (2017), Ciuk et al. (2018), in Organization Studies/International Business literature, and also in Inghilleri (2006), Koskinen (2008), and Tesseur (2017) in Translation Studies. Translation is seen as "a site of struggle occupied by many actors with different power positions bound to different institutional ideologies" (Tesseur, 2017, p. 18). In research, it is overlooked and taken for granted at the researcher's risk and peril.

## Two Examples of Researching Translatoriality in Organizations

The previous sections have argued for a more intense engagement with translatorial data in studying multilingualism at work from a meta-level perspective. In this section I aim to show what kinds of findings one can gain from paying attention to the linguistic detail and the shifts therein in the movement from one language to another. I have selected two cases at two extremes of the scale between global and local perspectives. First, I return to the case of the European Union that has already come up a number of times in the discussion earlier. Drawing on a number of different studies, both my own and by others, I aim to highlight some general translatorial factors that often come to play when policies and practices are moved across borders, and therefore also across linguistic and cultural boundaries. The second case is much narrower in scope. It is based on the research I conducted with two colleagues (Koskela et al., 2017), and it provides a snapshot of organizational everyday bilingual practices, and the translatorial strategies used in oral discourse. The purpose of the latter case is to give ideas of how the more fuzzy areas of paraprofessional translatoriality can be addressed in research. The context of case 2 is one typical of most organizations: a meeting.

### Case 1. Translating the European Union

Among supranational institutions the European Union is unique in both its relentless multilingualism and its penetration into the national spheres of its member states. The policies and practices aim at harmonizing the European regulatory and ideological framework in many domains of life. Hence also the need for many languages: To succeed in getting the ideologies and pragmatic applications accepted and adopted in the various local contexts, the European Union needs to make itself understood and accepted, and speaking the local language is a crucial element in this project (Koskinen, 2008, Ch. 4). In practice, this is accomplished by running the biggest translation and interpreting services in the world. The European Union therefore functions well to highlight a number of relevant issues in organizational translatoriality in multinational organizations.

*Acceptability* (Toury, 2012) is one of the key concepts in Translation Studies, reflecting a strong target-orientedness at the heart of the discipline. In the EU context, at stake is not only the acceptability of the translation but also the acceptability of the entire institutional system *through* translations. Translation strategies have not always been successful, as testified by a long trail of complaints about unclear, foggy and alienating reading experiences both in the press and in research literature. It is not entirely by coincidence that Lendvai (2015, p. 154) states a personal sense of alienation as the origin of her research interest into how European texts travel in translation, referring back to a similar origin of Koskinen's research.

The constant battle between readability (the target) and institutional constraints (the source) is a consistent finding in Koskinen (2008), through all data sets from the institution's own communication strategies to translator's talk and to the actual translation strategies, and the translations are indeed one site of that struggle. The necessity to strike a balance between staying close to the source text form, content and style and matching the new text to the target context is a foundational, and unresolvable, problem of translation and therefore also one that will unavoidably be at play in organizational contexts. The line between localizing and telling local lies (Logemann & Piekkari, 2015) is blurry, and successful translatoriality often requires a degree of free reinterpretation (see e.g. Ciuk & James, 2015). Very literal rerendering of the original wording is often clumsy at best and incomprehensible at worst (Koskinen, 2008, p. 133). To add complexity, also extremely localizing translation strategies can cause alienation in the readers. This is what also happened in the early Finnish EU translations that suffered from an "overdomestication" tendency through an excessive avoidance of loan words, for example by translating the word 'report' as 'kertomus' ("story") rather than using the more common localized loan word 'raportti', or having 'yhteensovittaa' ("to fit together") instead of 'koordinoida' to translate 'to coordinate' (Koskinen, 2012; cf. Koskinen, 2008, p. 134).

A recurrent translatorial challenge is caused by *realia*, i.e. linguistic expressions for elements in the social and cultural life that are specific to one context and hence not verbalized in the other. Much of EU terminology has been resistant to translation because the target culture lacks a similar concept. Lendvai (2015) reports the difficulties of translating social inclusion into Hungarian. The situation is quite similar to the "discursive void" encountered in translating Western business terms into the post-socialist Slovak reality (Tietze et al., 2017). Because the European Union is a political institution, its discourse is also often intentionally fuzzy (and therefore difficult to translate)—Lendvai (2015, p. 145) calls it "fiction-writing"—and its terminology is sometimes unstable because of the rapidly evolving political scene around the terms (see Marani, 2018, for an analysis of the migration of the term 'migration' in EU discourse).

Identifying these contested terms and words that resist easy translation can be used to highlight ideological, social and cultural boundaries, and analyzing their successful and failed translations can be revealing in terms of pinpointing the nature of that boundary.

Source and target-oriented translation strategies and solutions for realia translation are elements translators can consciously work on, and professional translators are trained to find workable tactics for getting around them. These have been called *optional shifts* in translation theory (Vinay & Darbelnet, 1958). Translation also entails *obligatory shifts* that result from the differences between language systems and reflect on what a particular language either can or has to make explicit. For example, in English you are expected to signal the gender of the person in the third person pronoun; in my native language Finnish we only have pronoun ('hän'). These shifts, too, can affect the target text reception, sometimes significantly. For example, the different systems of modal verbs in English and Finnish, and the standardized practice of translating them, were found to lead to softening of the degree of directiveness in EU communication (Koskinen, 2008, pp. 142–144), and the variation of idiomaticity in metaphors leads to a loss of a connotation to 'heart', and hence reduced affectivity, in language versions other than English (ibid., p. 137).

## Case 2. Translation Practices in a Bilingual Formal Meeting

EU translation is a massive undertaking, employing thousands of in-house and freelance translators and interpreters. But organizational life also contains an equally massive amount of everyday translatoriality that often goes unnoticed, by management, researchers and participants alike. In the article by Koskela et al. (2017), the researchers zoom into the micro level of oral translatoriality within a bilingual formal meeting where no professional translating or interpreting was provided. The fine-grained analysis of the turns, and a consensus-based matching of content to define the degree and kind of translatoriality, reveals a number of elements. For example, it shows how extensively translatoriality is being used to forward the aims of the meeting and how flexibly different translation strategies are brought to play. Summary translation, i.e. condensing the gist of the turn in another language, in particular, appears an efficient and time-saving method of involving all participants. Next, the expert's presentation of an issue in Swedish activates the chair to engage in summarizing to make sure also the Finnish-speaking participants are up to speed, thus safeguarding inclusion of all members. However, he only provides the essentials, cutting the length of the turn to less than one half:

EXPERT: Jo, ordförande, det här är ett projekt som det här baserar sig på att vi ska få en matbutik, en market där och läget är ju på det viset nuförtiden att det här våra investeringspengar har strukits ner till noll, så vi har inte möjlighet att börja med sådana här projekt alls mera utan den här finansieringen måste sökas på andra håll. Prisma öppnar en ny stor market, men som alstrar mycket trafik, så det måste göras en rondell vid bland annat för att få det här att löpa, trafiken, och de här planerna är klara och kostnadskalkylen är (168000 euro). Finansieringen är sådan att kommunen betalar hälften och ELY pengarna då andra hälften.

CHAIR: Elikkä tää on kaupan liikekeskuksen liikennejärjestelyjen turvaamiseksi ja Luodon keskuksen kehittämisen turvaamiseksi, niin nämä liikennejärjestelyt, ja rahojen vähyys niin johtaa siihen, että tällaista aluekehittämisrahaakin on käytettävä tällaisiin kohteisiin.

[EXPERT: Yes, chair, this is a project that concerns a grocery shop, a super market we will get, and the situation today is that since the money for investments has been cut down to zero, so we cannot invest in projects like this without getting financing somewhere else. Prisma will open a large supermarket that will bring about a lot of traffic which is why we need a roundabout in order to get the traffic going, and these plans are ready and the cost estimate is 168000 euro. The financing is such that the municipality will pay half and ELY money the other half.

CHAIR: So this concerns securing the traffic arrangements of a commercial centre and development of the centre of Luoto, these traffic arrangements, and the lack of money leads to the need of using regional development money for this type of purposes.]

It also becomes evident in the article that formal contexts endow some participants with more translatorial agency than others. In the context of a formal meeting, the chair plays a key role, and having a chair person willing and able to perform translatorially can significantly enhance democratic language use and inclusion of all. The data were collected from a habitually bilingual meeting, and it shows how the chair's performance dominates on that of other participants, showing the chair to be a crucially important role for supporting equal participation and community-building through translation.

Methodologically, the article by Koskela et al. describes how naturally occurring speech data can be mapped and classified according to translatorially relevant categories that can be used to create a typology of translation practices and a classification of actor roles. In the absence of professional translators, questions such as who is in a position to demand translation and for whom, and who takes on the role of the translator, are not clear-cut and can be used to identify organizational key actors who engage in translatorial boundary spanning.

## Conclusions

Even among those interested in languages and multilingualism, interlingual translation may sometimes be overlooked as a technicality, not interesting as such. My aim in this chapter has been to show that this is not the case. On the contrary! Translation—in particular the challenges of correspondence and the resulting discursive voids—makes visible and highlights the crossing of cultural boundaries, and the organization of translation practices offers a window to the language ideologies, power structures, hierarchies and cultural affiliations in and between organizations and stakeholder groups.

This chapter has forwarded a particular research agenda that combines ethnographic fieldwork and interview data with a close analysis of linguistic data from a translatorial perspective, i.e. *translatorial linguistic ethnography*. It was argued that multilingual workplaces are full of translatoriality, not only in the form of professional translation and interpreting, but also—and more often—in more ephemeral and ever-present forms of everyday movement between languages both in the form of self-translation and in jumping in to take the role of the translator as the need arises, in addition to one's other workplace roles and occupational tasks. This legion of paraprofessional translators in organizations engages in translatorial boundary spanning. Their activities leave a paper trail of values, attitudes and ideologies of cultural mediation, documented in their translations and available for researchers through a comparative analysis of source and target texts. Following these translations, and recordings of oral translation practices, provides avenues for researchers interested in studying multilingual workplaces.

## References

Brunelière, J. F. (2017). Business and translation as power games: The automotive industry in Brazil. *Cadernos de traduçao, 37*(3), 185–213.

Buzelin, H. (2014). How devoted can translators be? Revisiting the subservience hypothesis. *Target, 26,* 63–97.

Chew, K.-S. (2005). An investigation of the English language skills used by new entrants in banks in Hong Kong. *English for Special Purposes, 24,* 423–443.

Chidlow, A., Plakoyiannaki, E., & Welch, C. (2014). Translation in cross-language international business research: Beyond equivalence. *Journal of International Business Studies, 45*(5), 562–582.

Ciuk, S., & James, P. (2015). Interlingual translation and transfer of value-infused practices: An in-depth qualitative exploration. *Management Learning, 46,* 565–581.

Ciuk, S., James, P., & Sliwa, M. (2018). Micropolitical dynamics of interlingual translation processes in an MNC subsidiary. *British Journal of Management.* doi:10.1111/1467-8551.12323

Cronin, M. (2006). *Translation and identity.* London and New York: Routledge.

Cronin, M. (2012). *The expanding world: Towards a politics of microspection.* Winchester, UK: Zero Books.

Evans, L. (2018). Language, translation and accounting: Towards a critical research agenda. *Accounting, Auditing & Accountability Journal, 31*(7), 1844–1873. doi:10.1108/AAAJ-08-2017-3055

Flynn, P. (2006). *A linguistic ethnography of literary translation: Irish poems and Dutch-speaking translators* (Unpublished PhD thesis). Ghent University, Ghent.

Heritage, J. (1984). *Garfinkel and ethnomethodology.* Cambridge: John Wiley & Sons.

Holz-Mänttäri, J. (1984). *Translatorisches Handeln. Theorie und Methode.* Annales Academia Scientiarum Fennicae B 226. Helsinki: Helsingin tiedeakatemia.

Inghilleri, M. (2006). Macro social theory, linguistic ethnography and interpreting research. *Lingustica Antwerpiensia. Themes in Translation Studies, 5,* 57–68.

Kang, J.-H. (2009). Institutional translation. In M. Baker & G. Saldanha (Eds.), *The Routledge encyclopedia of translation studies* (pp. 41–145). Abingdon and New York: Routledge.

Koskela, M., Koskinen, K., & Pilke, N. (2017). Bilingual formal meeting as a context of translatoriality. *Target, 29*(3), 464–485.

Koskinen, K. (2008). *Translating institutions: An ethnographic study of EU translation.* Manchester, UK: St. Jerome.

Koskinen, K. (2011). Institutional translation. In Y. Gambier & L. van Doorslaer (Eds.), *Handbook of translation studies* (Vol. 2, pp. 54–60). Amsterdam and Philadelphia: John Benjamins Publishing Company.

Koskinen, K. (2012). Domestication, foreignization and the modulation of affect. In H. M. Kemppanen, M. Jänis, & A. Belikova (Eds.), *Domestication and foreignization in translation studies* (pp. 13–32). Berlin: Frank & Timme.

Koskinen, K. (2017). Translatorial Action in non-professional translation communities: The Tampere city council in 1875. In K. Taivalkoski-Shilov, L. Tiittula, & M. Koponen (Eds.), *Communities of translation and interpreting* (Vita Traductiva) (pp. 37–61). Montreal: Éditions québécoises de l'oeuvre.

Lendvai, N. (2015). Soft governance, policy fictions and translation zones: European policy spaces and their making. In J. Clarke, D. Bainton, N. Lendvai, & P. Stubbs (Eds.), *Making policy move: Towards a politics of translation and assemblage* (pp. 131–156). Bristol and Chicago: Polity Press.

Linguistic Ethnography Forum. (2004, December). *UK linguistic ethnography: A discussion paper.* UK Linguistic Ethnography Forum 1. Coordinating Committee. Retrieved from www.lancaster.ac.uk/fss/organisations/lingethn/documents/discussion_paper_jan_05.pdf

Logemann, M., & Piekkari, R. (2015). Localise or local lies? The power of language and translation in the multinational corporation. *Critical Perspectives on International Business, 11,* 30–53.

Malkamäki, A., & Herberts, K. (2014). *Case Wärtsilä: Flerspråkighet i arbetssituationer/Monikielisyys työtilanteissa/Multilingualism in work situations.* Vaasan yliopiston julkaisuja, selvityksiä ja raportteja 194. Vaasa: Vaasan yliopisto.

Marani, J. (2018). *Migration in translation: The role of terminology and transediting in shaping the crisis in EU Institutions* (PhD thesis). University of Verona, Verona.

Meylaerts, R. (2011). Translation policy. In Y. Gambier & L. van Doorslaer (Eds.), *Handbook of translation studies* (Vol. 2, pp. 163–168). Amsterdam and Philadelphia, PA: John Benjamins.

Munday, J. (2016). *Introducing translation studies* (4th ed.). London and New York: Routledge.

Piekkari, R., Tietze, S., & Koskinen, K. (2019). Metaphorical and interlingual translation in moving organizational practices across languages. *Organization Studies.* https://doi.org/10.1177/0170840619885415

Piekkari, R., Welch, D. E., & Welch, L. S. (2014). *Language in international business: The multilingual reality of global business expansion.* Cheltenham and Northampton: Edward Elgar.

Piekkari, R., Welch, D. E., Welch, L. S., Peltonen, J.-P., & Vesa, T. (2013). Translation behaviour: An exploratory study within a service multinational. *International Business Review, 22*(5), 771–783.

Probirskaja, S. (2017). Does anybody here speak Finnish? Linguistic first aid and emerging translational spaces on the Finnish-Russian Allegro train. *Translation Studies, 10*(3), 231–246.

Prunč, E. (2008). Zur Konstruktion von Translationskulturen. In L. Schippel (Ed.), *Translationskultur—ein innovatives und produktives Konzept* (pp. 19–42). Berlin: Frank & Timme.

Rampton, B. (2007). *Linguistic ethnography and the study of identities* (Working Papers in Urban Language & Literacies 43). London: King's College London.

Tesseur, W. (2014). *Transformation through translation: Translation policies at amnesty international* (PhD thesis). Aston University, Birmingham.

Tesseur, W. (2017). Incorporating translation into sociolinguistic research: Translation policy in an international non-governmental organisation. *Journal of Sociolinguistics, 21*(5), 629–649.

Tietze, S., & Dick, P. (2013). The victorious English language: Hegemonic practices in the management academy. *Journal of Management Inquiry, 22*(1), 122–134.

Tietze, S., Tansley, C., & Helienek, E. (2017). The translator as agent in talent management knowledge transfer. *International Journal of Cross Cultural Management, 17*, 151–169.

Toury, G. (2012). *Descriptive translation studies—And beyond: Revised edition.* Benjamins Translation Library, 100. Amsterdam: John Benjamins Publishing Company.

Vinay, J.-P., & Darbelnet, J. (1958). *Stylistique comparée du français et de l'anglais. Méthode de traduction.* Paris and Montreal: Didier, Beauchemin.

Williams, P. (2002). The competent boundary spanner. *Public Administration, 80*, 103–124.

Schäffner, C. (2018). Translation and institutions. In J. Evans & F. Fernandez (Eds.), *Routledge handbook of translation and politics.* London and New York: Routledge.

Shaw, S. E., Copland, F., & Snell, J. (2015). An introduction to linguistic ethnography: Interdisciplinary explorations. In J. Snell, S. E. Shaw, & F. Copland (Eds.), *Linguistic ethnography: Interdisciplinary explorations* (pp. 1–13). Basingstoke: Palgrave Macmillan.

# Section 2

# Empirical Research on Language at Work

*Editor: Philippe Lecomte*

# Innovation in Empirical Studies
## The Individuals' Reflexivity

*Philippe Lecomte*

More than 30 years ago, language issues emerged in IB research (Marschan, Welch, & Welch, 1997; Luo & Shenkar, 2006). In the following decades the number of articles dedicated to the role of language in firms' international business operations constantly grew (Brannen, Piekkari, & Tietze, 2014). During this period this research stream evolved from language as an instrument in the 1970s–1990s to language as "a central construct in IB" (2012–2016) (Brannen & Mughan, 2016, p. 8). Interconnected with parallel developments in other disciplines such as the social sciences, these changing attitudes about the role of languages in IB are reflected in different epistemological and methodological choices. Epistemologically, language is no longer viewed as mirroring, but as constructing the social reality (Angouri & Piekkari, 2018; Alvesson & Kärreman, 2000). This has important methodological implications such as understanding language and organisations as fluid and constantly evolving entities (Angouri & Piekkari, 2018), as well as adopting a qualitative approach and advocating an emic stance (see the following).

## Language as a Social Practice

According to Tenzer, Terjesen, and Harzing (2017) the share of qualitative studies regularly rose and reached up to 47,9% between 1987 and 2016 against 42,6% for quantitative studies, 4,2% using both methodologies. How can we explain the relative predominance of qualitative studies when quantitative ones are rather the mainstream in IB research (Marschan-Piekkari & Welch, 2004)? The main reason is that quantitative studies don't allow scholars to observe and understand as closely as possible what happens in the black box of social and linguistic interactions. Moreover, one of the major developments of the last decade in the vein of globalisation is the rapid rise of multicultural teams which profoundly transformed the traditional workplace in a global workplace. Thus there is a need to capture the reality of language interactions in time, space and history and at the micro-level of the team and/or of the individual, in order to understand "how individuals draw on multiple linguistic repertoires to construct, transmit and apply knowledge" (Tenzer et al., 2017, p. 838). Thus, it is not surprising that language-sensitive research made a shift from a functional approach to a conceptualisation of language as a social practice (Karhunen, Kankaanranta, Louhiala-Salminen, & Piekkari, 2018) and as an operative capacity to face multilingual situations (Welch & Welch, 2015). However, Tenzer et al. (2017) note that only 19 articles from a total of 92 articles studied are based on this social constructionist approach. They argue that the perspective taken on language remains influenced by the functional theories of language acquisition and those of linguistic pragmatics (ibid., p. 994). This means that the social practice view of language represents a huge avenue for further language-sensitive research.

In organisational studies, the "Communicative Constitution of Organization" (CCO) stream brought forward the view of organisations as a social construct constituted by ongoing and interconnected communicative acts (Cooren, Kuhn, Cornelissen, & Clark, 2011; Cooren, Vaara, Langley, & Tsoukas, 2014). Accordingly, the firm is viewed as "a social constellation which emerges in everyday interactions" (Karhunen et al., 2018, p. 1002). In the language-sensitive research stream scholars have heeded a call for conceptualising the firm as something dynamic and for capturing language fluidity (Angouri & Piekkari, 2018; Karhunen et al., 2018). The authors of the chapters displayed in this section share this view of language as a social construct and practice. Consequently, they put a strong focus on language interactions at the micro-level of the individual as part of the global conceptualisation of language as constitutive of and creative of social reality.

## An Emic Stance and the Importance of Contextualisation

Another aspect of the qualitative approach lies in its emic dimensions of knowledge production (i.e. in-depth contextual approach without generalising aims) which the etic nature of quantitative studies (measuring and quantifying approach with generalisation effects) does not allow. As a result, context plays a considerable role in the study of language interactions. The importance of contextualisation has been highlighted in a case study on the mistakes made by the Walt Disney company during their internationalisation process in France (Brannen, 2004). The study explains the famous firm's flop caused by the ignorance of specific features of the foreign culture and the blind application of successful methods in the country of origin.

## Language and Culture

Historically, the concept of language has for a long time been subsumed under the concept of culture. Nevertheless, Brannen et al. note that one of the three salient turns in the development of the language stream in IB has been "the decoupling of language from culture" (Brannen et al., 2014, p. 499). Tenzer et al. argue that "it was [the] emerging differentiated concept of culture that prepared the ground for a new research stream in international business, one that only gradually took off in the first decade of the new millennium: studies on language differences" (Pudelko et al., 2015, p. 87). On the other hand, as Karhunen et al. (2018) note, the two concepts of language and culture are strongly intertwined in studies in which language is conceptualised as an individual characteristic of MNC employees. However, the emphasis is often on the negative implications of language leading to ingroup/outgroup divisions and therefore to exclusion (Karhunen et al., 2018).

This section aims at examining the role played by empirical studies in advancing our knowledge of how language operates in concrete multilingual/multinational settings. It explores the agentic role of individuals in negotiating language strategies across boundaries. Two chapters (one by Barner-Rasmussen and Langinier, the other by Wilczewski, Søderberg and Gut) refer to the strong link between language and culture. One of them shows how local language use is influenced by global historical and cultural factors. The other focuses on the failure of Polish expatriates in China to understand the Chinese cultural background.

## Overview of the Chapters

The first chapter by Tenzer and Pudelko examines the state of the art of language-sensitive research on language diversity in multinational teamwork. Far from being an exhaustive review of the literature of the field which would go beyond the scope of this book, the authors focus on five thematic clusters: power issues, identity, emotions, trust building and knowledge sharing. Recent studies addressing these major issues are analysed, unravelling the more significant knowledge advances and ingeniously coupling research outcomes with practical implications and advice to multinational team leaders. In a second part, the authors suggest new avenues for further research and point to understudied topics such as transition processes, defined as whenever team members reflect on previous performances and plan for future work. Tenzer and Pudelko share the view of language as a social practice rather than as a formal system, and they call for new orientations of language effects studies focusing on more innovative dimensions such as innovation, customer relations, project quality or decision making and creativity rather than on communication barriers. Other still understudied areas are mentioned such as virtual teams, which tend to be more and more the norm in IB, or the impact of communication technology. To sum up, this chapter provides a rich description of the recent literature on language diversity and insightful suggestions for developing the field.

Translanguaging by Barner-Rasmussen and Langinier (i.e. the use and combination of multiple language repertories in order to create shared meaning) is one of these innovative topics which represent genuine discourse strategies employed by multilingual team members in the workplace. In line with the global orientation of the section dedicated to micro-level research the authors deliver an intriguing qualitative study which captures fine-grained creative processes for language interactions in multinational teams. The study describes highly context-embedded language practices, while exploring translanguaging patterns in two highly different IB contexts according to their conceptual and methodological framework. They draw on the concept of language ecology, which allows them to mix a local and a global approach of the field studied and on the interpretive approach, borrowed from cross-cultural management studies (see Romani, Barmeyer, Primecz, & Pilhofer, 2018) in order to highlight language practices embedded in their specific environment (contextualisation) and to understand the historic (cultural) dimension of language use, which "refers to cultural memories enacted in words".

The originality of this chapter also lies in its comparative aspect. The two authors, addressing the call for "cross-national research collaborations" (Tenzer et al., 2017, p. 815; see also Brannen et al., 2014, on the increasing collaboration of researchers from various geographical locations), are both IB scholars coming from two highly different geographic areas (the French-German border and Finland with its Swedish component). Being embedded in their own culture but aware of the culture of their counterpart and studying the same topic (translanguaging practices i.e. co-creating of meaning in two highly different geographic areas), the authors are able to understand and interpret similarities of translanguaging patterns, which would have been mistakenly interpreted as a local phenomenon in a single case study. The authors claim: "Such confrontation of perspectives, ideas and insights between colleagues each immersed in their own field but both familiar with the core theoretical concepts of joint interest provides alternative understandings of how things might be connected". Finally, the chapter offers an example of coupling the two dimensions of language and culture in the same study, linking the local with the global. Language use is studied in its very "real" nature, whereas culture contributes to highlight the historical dimensions of linguistic occurrences.

The third chapter by Detzen and Löhlein also examines highly contextual language practices at the micro-level, but from another perspective. The focus here is on individuals' responses to language asymmetry. Multilingual team interactions have already been studied, but this piece is original in two ways. First it concentrates on individuals and second the linguistic context is permanently changing, compelling the team members to continually adapt their strategies of communication. The study is conducted in the Luxembourg branches of the Big Four accounting firms, a domain which is scarcely explored in language-sensitive IB research. The Luxembourgish environment of the accounting firms is particularly interesting due to its extreme diverse linguistic nature (three official languages; English corporate language; other expatriates' languages). The multilingual teams are invited to speak in the client's language. This is a huge linguistic challenge. The individuals' responses to linguistic barriers are examined through the theoretical lens of language skills (proficiency) and reflexivity, echoing Tenzer and Pudelko's call for a reflexive approach of transition processes (see page 96). The authors find four strategies depending on the variables proficiency and reflexivity: avoidance, confrontation, adaptation and activation. What is interesting in this study is apart from the already mentioned extreme variety of work situations, the choice of the concept of linguistic reflexivity to examine how multinational team members confronted with the linguistic barrier can avoid miscommunication and qualitatively improve their response to such a situation. Indeed, the highlighted categories are not static, the boundaries are malleable and the authors give examples of speakers who succeed in moving from one category to another one (e.g. from avoidance to confrontation or from adaptation to activation). The authors also explain how team members can improve their linguistic skills while choosing the appropriate strategy in a given context—a reflexive skill that develops over time.

This section's last chapter, by Wilczewski, Søderberg and Gut, deals with the difficulties encountered by Polish expatriates in China. This qualitative study examines the cultural learning of Polish expatriate managers and experts in a Chinese subsidiary of a Western European MNC. The experts were delegated between 2011 and 2015 to China to train and coach the local personnel and, in general, support building the subsidiary. The method is based on critical incidents. Through narrative inquiry (a qualitative method of analysis based on storytelling in order to understand how people create meaning through their life experiences), the chapter explores how the expatriates learnt about such processes as communication and collaboration, management, decision making, working styles and organisational culture in a Chinese business setting. In addition to the narrative approach, which enhances a reflexive understanding of experiences from an expatriate's perspective, the authors propose an application of a four-fold taxonomy of intercultural learning processes, which encompasses two explicit and two implicit forms of learning processes in order to explore expatriates' qualitatively different learning processes and how they develop the capacity to function in multicultural situations despite linguistic and cultural barriers. The four categories (explicit learning, attributional reasoning, implicit social learning and conditioning) are illustrated in three case studies. The originality of this chapter is that, in line with the global orientation of this book, it tackles the issue of cross-cultural collaborators from an individual perspective rather than from the organisational level and also that it responds to the call for contextualised research, be it in the linguistic or in the cross-cultural field. It is a context-sensitive approach. This study has in common with Chapter 3 that it uses the concept of reflexivity, but from a cultural perspective rather than from a linguistic one. The chapter examines how the expatriates retrospectively interpret their experience through the lens of critical incidents, how they apply acquired knowledge and how they position themselves in relation to the local staff. One of the practical implications for cross-cultural education is that "not all cultural knowledge expands the individual capacity to navigate multicultural and multilingual contexts, especially when it is stereotypical or based on generalisations". This statement will add grist to the mill of cross-cultural scholars who call for contextualised qualitative rather than worldwide macro-level quantitative studies.

In sum, this section contributes to enhance our knowledge of what is really at stake when language is defined as a social practice and consequently when language use is scrutinised in its very nature. To achieve this goal, the authors of the section adopt a qualitative approach for studying *language in context* at the level of the individuals. We argue that the most innovative aspect of this empirical section lies in the use of the concept of *reflexivity* that helps scholars and managers better understand the famous black box.

## References

Alvesson, M., & Kärreman, D. (2000). Taking the linguistic turn in organizational research: Challenges, responses, consequences. *The Journal of Applied Behavioral Science, 36*, 136–158.

Angouri, J., & Piekkari, R. (2018). Organising multilingually: Setting an agenda for studying language at work. *European Journal of International Management, 12*(1–2), 8–27.

Brannen, M. Y. (2004). When Mickey loses face: Recontextualisation, semantic fit, and the semiotics of foreignness. *Academy of Management Review, 29*(4), 593–616.

Brannen, M. Y., & Mughan, T. (2016). Introduction. In M. Y. Brannen & T. Mughan (Eds.), *Language in international business: Developing a field* (pp. 1–19). Cham, Switzerland: Springer International Publishing AG.

Brannen, M. Y., Piekkari, R., & Tietze, S. (2014). The multifaceted role of language in international business: Unpacking the forms, functions and features of a critical challenge to MNC theory and performance. *Journal of International Business Studies, 45*, 495–507.

Cooren, F., Kuhn, T., Cornelissen, J. P., & Clark, T. (2011). Communication, organizing and organization: An overview and introduction to the special issue. *Organization Studies, 32*(9), 1149–1170.

Cooren, F., Vaara, E., Langley, A., & Tsoukas, H. (2014). *Language and communication at work: Discourse, narrativity, and organizing*. Oxford: Oxford University Press.

Karhunen, P., Kankaanranta, A., Louhiala-Salminen, L., & Piekkari, R. (2018). Let's talk about language: A review of language-sensitive research in international management. *Journal of Management Studies*, 55(6), 980–1013.

Luo, Y., & Shenkar, O. (2006). The multinational corporation as a multilingual community: Language and organization in a global context. *Journal of International Business Studies*, 37(3), 321–339.

Marschan, R., Welch, D., & Welch, L. (1997). Language: The forgotten Factor in multinational management. *European Management Journal*, 15(5), 591–598.

Piekkari, R., & Welch, C. (2004). Qualitative research methods in international business: The state of the art. In R. Piekkari, C. Welch, & L. Welch (Eds.), *Handbook of qualitative research methods for international business* (pp. 5–24). Cheltenham and Northhampton, MA: Edward Elgar.

Pudelko, M., Tenzer, H., & Harzing, A.-W. (2015). Cross-cultural management and language studies within international business research: Past and present paradigms and suggestions for future research. In N. Holden, S. Michailova, & S. Tietze (Eds.), *The Routledge companion to cross-cultural management* (pp. 85–94). London and New York: Routledge/Taylor and Francis Group.

Romani, L., Barmeyer, C., Primecz, H., & Pilhofer, K. (2018). Cross-cultural management studies: State of the field in the four Research paradigms. *International Studies of Management & Organization*, 48, 247–263.

Tenzer, H., & Pudelko, M. (2017). The influence of language differences on power dynamics in multinational teams. *Journal of World Business*, 52, 45–61.

Tenzer, H., Terjesen, S., & Harzing, A.-W. (2017). Language in international business: A review and agenda for future research. *Management International Review*, 57, 815–854.

Welch, D., & Welch, L. (2015). Developing multilingual capacity: A challenge for the multinational enterprise. *Journal of Management*, 44(3), 854–869.

# 5 The Impact of Language Diversity on Multinational Teamwork

## Helene Tenzer and Markus Pudelko

Given the increasing complexity of global business, multinational teams comprising members from two or more countries (Earley & Gibson, 2002) constitute "a key feature of today's business environment" (Kassis-Henderson, 2005, p. 66). Global corporations need these teams to perform at their best (Butler, 2011) by reaping the benefits of diversity while avoiding its pitfalls (Stahl, Maznevski, Voigt, & Jonsen, 2010). Whereas multinational teams research has a long-standing tradition of studying the impact of cultural diversity on teamwork (Cohen & Kassis-Henderson, 2012; Vigier & Spencer-Oatey, 2017), the fact that multinational teams are also composed of members with different linguistic backgrounds (Fleischmann, Folter, & Aritz, 2017) has been neglected for surprisingly long and was described as "largely ignored" just a few years ago (Butler, 2011, p. 225). More recent work, however, has recognized the "primordial role" (Cohen & Kassis-Henderson, 2012, p. 187) of verbal communication in intercultural interactions and has focused on language diversity as a "distinguishing feature" (Chen, Geluykens, & Choi, 2006, p. 670) of global teams.

Whenever a team consists of employees speaking different mother tongues, its members need to select a common working language. In most cases, English is chosen for this purpose, as it has reached the status of "lingua franca in business communication" (Nickerson, 2015, p. 390). If English proficiency levels are unequally distributed among team members, however, the need to speak this foreign language in team meetings creates communication barriers (Butler, 2011); gives rise to misunderstandings, lack of trust, and team conflicts (Paunova, 2017); and constitutes obstacles for effective teambuilding and cooperation (Cohen & Kassis-Henderson, 2012). Recent years have seen a surge in studies aiming to understand the complex influence of language on multinational teams (Tenzer, Terjesen, & Harzing, 2017; Cohen & Kassis-Henderson, 2017). This chapter will review the main trends in this nascent research area and point out directions for further investigation.

## Current Status of the Research Field

Research on language diversity, foreign language use, and language barriers in multinational teams has grown exponentially over the last few years, but largely still concentrates on a limited set of team processes that are subject to linguistic influences. In the following, we will summarize the current status of the field according to the following thematic clusters which we consider to be of particular importance: language-induced power distortions, issues regarding social identity formation, emotional conflict, obstacles to trust building, and hurdles to knowledge sharing.

### The Impact of Language Diversity on Power Relations in Multinational Teams

Power relations are crucial to teamwork, as power differentials influence the extent to which team members contribute to the team's tasks (Janssens & Brett, 2006). Language is highly influential in this respect, because power is exerted through communication which necessitates the use of language.

Various studies have conceptualized an individual's linguistic background as a source of power, which determines the degree of deference received from colleagues (Paunova, 2017). Most of this research has established that power relations in multinational teams are strongly impacted by the choice of the team's working language and the proficiency in that language across team members. Whenever an official working language is designated, native speakers enjoy a privileged position and higher influence within the team (Méndez García & Pérez Cañado, 2005). Individuals with sub-par proficiency in that tongue are limited in their conversation abilities, may be excluded from critical exchanges of information (Fredriksson, Barner-Rasmussen, & Piekkari, 2006), are less involved in decision making (Louhiala-Salminen, Charles, & Kankaanranta, 2005), and thus experience a loss of power (Luo & Shenkar, 2006). As refined speech is typically associated with higher status, intelligence, competence, and dependability, those linguistically privileged employees signal leadership potential (Paunova, 2017) while simultaneously hindering contributions from colleagues who struggle to express their opinions in the working language (Janssens & Brett, 2006). Critical management scholars have therefore portrayed the choice of an official team language as "a particular application of power" (Wilmot, 2017, p. 85) or an "act of coercion" (Wilmot, 2017, p. 89), which "will enfranchise some team members and disenfranchise others" (Janssens & Brett, 2006, p. 133; Janssens, Lambert, & Steyaert, 2004). Because the majority of multinational teams select English as their working language, native or highly fluent English speakers are likely to dominate discussions (Butler, 2011) and exert a higher influence within the team (Méndez García & Pérez Cañado, 2005).

Besides being a strong source of power in itself, language was also found to moderate other power sources such as position power based on formally assigned leadership positions or expert power. As Tenzer and Pudelko (2017) demonstrated, team leaders' position power is reinforced if it coincides with superior proficiency in the team's working language. In contrast, leaders find it hard to enact their formally assigned power if they are linguistically disadvantaged compared to their subordinates. Similarly, technical experts, who should enjoy particular influence on strategic decisions due to their superior task competence (Finkelstein, 1992), may be unable to adequately leverage their expertise due to linguistic disadvantages. The extent of these language-induced power distortions in multinational teams depends on the disparity between team leader's and members' proficiency levels in the chosen working language. Whenever a multinational team unites low-fluency speakers with colleagues of (near) native proficiency, the latter can play out their language-based power. Only if everyone speaks the working language as a foreign tongue on similar proficiency levels, colleagues meet on equal footing (Tenzer & Pudelko, 2017). As a result, language-induced power distortions lead to process losses in information extraction and decision making, as they may silence the voices of low-proficiency team members despite the potential importance of their contributions (Janssens & Brett, 2006).

Regarding practical implications, multinational team leaders should mitigate any undeserved advantages or disadvantages language might convey to individual team members. Furthermore, they should be very perceptive towards any potential dissatisfaction among team members and assist the unrestricted communication between language groups, giving particular attention to team members with lower proficiency in the team language (Tenzer & Pudelko, 2016).

### The Impact of Language Diversity on Social Identity Formation in Multinational Teams

The previously described power contests in multilingual teams are also frequently accompanied by the formation of linguistic subgroups (Hinds, Neeley, & Cramton, 2014). In more general terms, multinational teams are characterized by salient and potentially divisive differences between their members. Building a common identity therefore constitutes a particularly complex challenge for multinational teams (Cohen & Kassis-Henderson, 2012). According to Tajfel and Turner's (1986) seminal social identity theory, individuals define their identities by classifying their social environment into in-groups they seek to belong to and out-groups they wish to distinguish themselves from.

Out-groups are constantly compared to in-groups with particular focus on their differences. Given people's tendency towards in-group favoritism and out-group discrimination (Lauring, 2008), these distinctions can activate problematic fault-lines within multinational teams (Vigier & Spencer-Oatey, 2018).

Because social identities are formed and reinforced through interaction (Hinds et al., 2014), which takes place through language (Lauring & Selmer, 2010), language is consistently portrayed as a crucial marker of an individual's identity (Harzing & Feely, 2008; Woo & Giles, 2017). Some even consider it a more important aspect of people's self-concept than demographic attributes such as age, gender, or race because of the solid functional and psychological barriers it creates for communication (Giles & Johnson, 1981; Cohen & Kassis-Henderson, 2017). Woo and Giles (2017) argue that social categorization based on spoken language is particularly salient as long as team members have not yet developed personal relationships, which might indicate that language-based identification and subgroup formation affects particularly the early phases of newly established teams. However, Hinds et al. (2014) claim that proficiency disparities in a team's working language and subgroup identification fuel each other on a constant basis, as differences between highly fluent and less fluent speakers are reinforced in daily communication, and therefore keep subgroup identifications alive also later in a multinational team's life.

Because individuals tend to show negative behaviors to out-group members (Riek, Mania, & Gaertner, 2006), research based on social identity theory established that language diversity can be highly problematic, for example with regard to knowledge transfer (Reiche, Harzing, & Pudelko, 2015) and linguistic identity and subgroup formation (Bordia & Bordia, 2015). Language-based subgroup formation within multinational teams is particularly problematic, as it exacerbates the communication barriers already imposed by language diversity. In-group solidarity among highly proficient speakers and separate solidarity among less proficient teammates goes along with limited interaction between these linguistic subgroups. This in turn restricts opportunities for informal exchange, perpetuates mutual stereotypes (Woo & Giles, 2017), and ultimately hampers the communication needed to accomplish the team's tasks (Cohen & Kassis-Henderson, 2017). These effects are compounded by the fact that language asymmetries and the related social identification represent deeply emotional issues for multinational team members.

With regard to practical implications, leaders of multinational teams should take care for all team members to be accepted as in-group members, in particular when language is an important factor of social categorization within the team. Stressing the common values and objectives within the team can help to establish a common team identity across linguistic boundaries.

## The Impact of Language Diversity on Emotional Conflict in Multinational Teams

Severe social categorization and resulting subgrouping, as we outlined previously, are often linked to negative emotional states (Hinds et al., 2014) and frustrations, mistrust, and tensions (Vigier & Spencer-Oatey, 2018). In fact, the investigation of employees' emotions has emerged since the late 1990s as a major topic in organizational behavior (Gooty, Gavin, & Ashkanasy, 2009). In the wake of this research, team scholars came to agree that emotions play a powerful role also in teams and that emotional conflicts with teams exert a strong negative influence on team performance (von Glinow, Shapiro, & Brett, 2004).

Language diversity in multinational teams presents particular emotional challenges, because non-native speakers of the designated working language tend to feel apprehensive, uncomfortable, and tongue-tied (Neeley, Hinds, & Cramton, 2012); fear status loss (Neeley, 2013); face negative evaluations (Tenzer & Pudelko, 2015); and experience high levels of stress, helplessness, or even physical exhaustion (Aichhorn & Puck, 2017). Researchers have captured these feelings in the concept of "foreign language anxiety", conceptualized as "a situational anxiety reaction specifically related to communication in a non-native tongue" (Aichhorn & Puck, 2017, p. 750).

Language-induced anxiety among multinational team members has been portrayed as "a fundamental threat for effective communication in the workplace" (Aichhorn & Puck, 2017, p. 755), as team members who lack linguistic confidence often remain silent during meetings (Hinds et al., 2014; Tenzer & Pudelko, 2015). If anxiety becomes too acute, they may even avoid anxiety-inducing situations by eschewing meetings in which they anticipate having to speak in the foreign language (Neeley et al., 2012; Hinds et al., 2014).

Many low-fluency team members also strive to alleviate their anxiety through switching into their mother tongue during meetings. While such deviations from the agreed-upon working language are therefore often caused by negative emotions by some team members, they can also result in additional negative emotions by other team members who cannot follow these side conversations. Often considered as "annoying, rude and disrespectful" (Vigier & Spencer-Oatey, 2017, p. 24), code-switching can produce anger, frustration, offense, and discouragement (Hinds et al., 2014; Tenzer & Pudelko, 2015; Aichhorn & Puck, 2017) among those who feel excluded from conversations they cannot understand. These individuals experience linguistic ostracism (Dotan-Eliaz, Sommer, & Rubin, 2009) with concomitant feelings of being devalued, disrespected, neglected, and lonely (Neeley et al., 2012, p. 239). As a consequence, they might demand language discipline or even leave meetings in protest, leaving everyone more sensitive to language failures than before (Neeley et al., 2012, p. 238). In the worst case, a negative cycle of emotional dynamics ensues. Neeley et al. (2012, p. 238) speak in this context of a "hot potato" cycle, as team members pass their language discomfort on to each other as quickly as the proverbial hot potato. This vicious cycle starts with low-fluency team members' anxiety and their subsequent avoidance behaviors, continues with high-fluency speakers' anger or frustration about the language lapses, and is perpetuated by everyone's strategies to deal with those negative feelings. Consequently, code-switching reduces trust between employees from different language groups (Lauring & Selmer, 2010) and therefore has the potential of becoming highly disruptive to a multinational team's emotional climate.

Multinational team leaders should consider in terms of practical implications the following: First, they should be aware of the emotional impact of language barriers and recognize in particular how the less proficient team members are affected. In addition, they should manage language-induced negative emotions to reduce the impact of language barriers, for example by moderating code-switching, allocating speaking time, and communicating redundantly (Tenzer & Pudelko, 2015).

## The Impact of Language Diversity on Trust Relationships in Multinational Teams

The previously described disturbed emotional climate due to language diversity between team members can also seriously impede their propensity to trust each other (Noteboom & Six, 2003). With trust being acknowledged as "the glue that holds most cooperative relationships together" (Lewicki & Bunker, 1996, p. 129), scholars have recently recognized the importance of looking at trust formation also in multilingual business settings. Research on inter-unit relationships in multinational corporations indicated, for example, that language diversity influences trust relations between subsidiaries in different countries (Barner-Rasmussen & Björkman, 2007). If linguistic impediments to trust formation already become salient in communications between different business units, they are likely to be even more acute for highly interdependent multinational teams.

Trust is commonly defined as "the willingness of a party to be vulnerable to the actions of another party" (Mayer, Davis, & Schoorman, 1995, p. 712), which depends on the perceived trustworthiness of the other party, i.e. the "characteristics that inspire positive expectations" among trustors (Colquitt, Scott, & LePine, 2007, p. 909). Trustworthiness is cognitively assessed according to trustees' perceived professional ability, their integrity, and benevolence towards the trustor (Mayer et al., 1995). In line with Kassis-Henderson's (2005, p. 71) finding that team members infringing the rules of speech behavior will be considered "unprofessional", "ignorant", or "unprepared", Tenzer, Pudelko, and Harzing

(2014) discovered that low-fluency speakers of a multinational team's working language are typically rated low on ability-based trustworthiness. They also found that linguistic misunderstandings often make colleagues appear less dependable and consequently reduce their perceived integrity-based trustworthiness. The previously described frustration about code-switching additionally portrays teammates speaking different mother tongues in a negative light and hampers benevolence-based trust formation (also see Neeley et al., 2012).

Next to those cognitive evaluations of trustworthiness, trust also emerges from emotional bonds between coworkers and mutual feelings of emotional security (McAllister, 1995; Noteboom & Six, 2003). The foreign language anxiety described earlier reduces multinational team members' willingness to trust colleagues with relatively higher proficiency in the team's working language for fear of being exploited (Tenzer et al., 2014). Antagonism between language-based in-groups and out-groups as shown previously can further undermine the trust needed for effective teamwork (Neeley et al., 2012).

The previously reviewed work portrays the negative relationship between language diversity and trust formation in a way that language barriers hamper team communication, which in turn influences the level of trust in a multinational team, i.e. trust is a consequence rather than a determinant of communication. Other studies have focused on the reverse relationship, i.e. they identified trust as enhancing communication quality (Gibson & Manuel, 2003). This implies that a "feedback loop" (Tenzer et al., 2014, p. 530) in the form of a vicious cycle can occur in multinational teams: first, restricted communication due to language barriers impedes trust formation; subsequently, the resulting lack of trust relationships further aggravates communication barriers between team members.

Regarding practical implications, team leaders should proactively promote trust within the team. To foster ability-based trust, team leaders might highlight task-related achievements of each team member, in particular of those with weaker proficiency in the team language; to promote integrity-based trust, team leaders should reduce misunderstandings and subsequent attributions of low dependability, for example by regularly summarizing and paraphrasing discussion outcomes during team meetings; and finally, to augment benevolence-based trust, team leaders should not allow code-switching to become too frequent in team meetings and guide code-switchers quickly back to the team's shared language (Tenzer et al., 2014).

### The Impact of Language Diversity on Knowledge Sharing in Multinational Teams

The previously described skillful management of communication to foster trust formation in multinational teams is crucial, also for facilitating knowledge sharing (Cohen & Kassis-Henderson, 2012; Aichhorn & Puck, 2017). In fact, effective knowledge sharing is a key prerequisite for competitive advantage in our globalized knowledge economy (Acs, de Groot, & Nijkamp, 2013). Multinational teams play an important role in this respect, as they can develop common global business solutions in the multinational corporation by combining local knowledge from different world regions (Lagerström & Andersson, 2003). It is only the sharing of a common language which allows for this crucial knowledge to be exchanged (Barner-Rasmussen & Björkman, 2005; Welch & Welch, 2008). This implies that individuals without the appropriate language skills are excluded from key information processes (Feely & Harzing, 2003; Lauring & Selmer, 2010).

On the most basic level, knowledge exchange is slowed down if team members share only a limited vocabulary, cannot produce correctly structured sentences in the working language, or strongly mispronounce expressions (Tenzer & Pudelko, 2012). Differences in the way speakers from different cultures use language to create meaning also give rise to frequent misunderstandings among multinational team members (Kassis-Henderson, 2005; Tenzer & Pudelko, 2012). In addition, language diversity influences knowledge sharing through team members' previously described behaviors in response to negative language-induced emotions. If those with low proficiency in the working language skip meetings due to foreign language anxiety, they lose out on important information while withholding their contributions from those who do attend. If they switch to their mother tongue mid-meeting and later boil those discussions down to short summaries in the working language, they further reduce knowledge sharing with high-fluency speakers (Neeley et al., 2012).

These issues are compounded by the fact that managers often maintain a façade of understanding and refrain from asking for clarification to avoid embarrassment and save face (Harzing & Feely, 2008; Aichhorn & Puck, 2017). Piekkari, Oxelheim, and Randøy (2015) found such effects even in multinational teams at the highest corporate level. Their study yielded evidence of impoverished and silenced discussions in linguistically diverse management boards, some members of which struggled to contribute to board meetings and to voice disagreement. The most pernicious effects of language diversity were found to arise, however, if team members falsely believe they have a shared knowledge base and act upon this imagined consensus, although in reality they are talking at cross-purposes (Tenzer & Pudelko, 2012).

In terms of practical suggestions, research proposed frequent face-to-face interactions, for example in the form of regular meetings. This will not only facilitate knowledge exchange but help individuals to feel more at ease in cross-language knowledge exchange and ultimately should even increase their proficiency in the working language (Reiche et al., 2015). Furthermore, multilingual teams are often geographically dispersed, so that communication has to take place virtually. Language diversity necessitates in this case specific considerations, for example the provision of a suitable media infrastructure, the adoption of new media, and the use of redundant media (Tenzer & Pudelko, 2016).

## Opportunities for Future Research

Based on our review of the current state of knowledge, we now indicate several promising avenues for further research on language diversity in multinational teams.

### Consider Additional Team Processes and Emergent States

Whereas power, social identity, emotions, trust, and knowledge sharing have by now been extensively studied under a linguistic lens, the influence of language on other team processes and emergent states has yet to be investigated in depth. *Team processes* are defined as "members' interdependent acts that convert inputs to outcomes through cognitive, verbal, and behavioral activities directed toward organizing task work to achieve collective goals" (Marks, Mathieu, & Zaccaro, 2001, p. 357; Mathieu, Hollenbeck, van Knippenberg, & Ilgen, 2017, p. 458), whereas *emergent states* constitute "properties of the team that are typically dynamic in nature and vary as a function of team context, inputs, processes, and outcomes" (ibid.).

The former can be classified into three categories: *Transition processes* happen whenever team members reflect on previous performances and plan for future work. They set the stage for *action processes*, which start as soon as team members focus on accomplishing their tasks, coordinate, and monitor progress. *Interpersonal processes* of conflict and affect management or motivation building accompany all other process phases (Marks et al., 2001; Mathieu et al., 2017).

*Transition processes* have received only limited attention in general team research and have, to the best of our knowledge, not yet been taken up by language researchers. This gap could be fruitfully addressed by investigating how language diversity influences the planning and organizing capabilities of multinational teams. As transition team processes based on planning and organizing capabilities depend on extensive communication and require sophisticated mutual understanding among multinational team members, language effects which are similar to those already identified for knowledge sharing are likely to apply. In terms of *action processes*, future research could study the impact of language diversity on team coordination. Here, the focus should be on the orchestration and timing of team members' interdependent actions or decision making, i.e. the process of "gathering, processing, integrating, and communicating information in support of arriving at a task-relevant decision" (Cannon-Bowers, Salas, & Converse, 1993, p. 222). Team monitoring and backup behavior, during which team members provide each other with verbal feedback or coaching (Marks et al., 2001), may also be prone to language-induced process losses. In the area of *interpersonal processes*, future studies could expand on von Glinow et al.'s (2004) and Lauring and Selmer's (2010) work on language-related conflict between multinational team members. Both preemptive conflict management, during which teams establish conditions to prevent, control, or guide team conflict, and reactive conflict management, which requires them to work through interpersonal disagreements (Marks et al., 2001), are verbally based and therefore highly prone to language effects.

In the realm of emergent states, existing work on the emotional impact of language diversity on team members could inform more specific research into linguistic influences on team affective states such as affective tone, i.e. the "consistent or homogenous affective reactions within a group" (George & King, 2007, p. 98), psychological safety, i.e. the "shared belief held by team members that the team is safe for interpersonal risk taking" (Bradley, Postlethwaite, Klotz, Hamdani, & Brown, 2012, p. 152), or cohesiveness, i.e. the "extent to which group members are attracted to each other, feel satisfied with each other and socialize with each other" (Lauring & Selmer, 2010, p. 271). Given that team learning depends on collective team identification (van der Vegt & Bunderson, 2005) and on teammates' feeling of safety to make mistakes for the purpose of learning (Neeley et al., 2012), both language-induced subgroup formation and foreign language anxiety may affect this crucial process in multinational team settings. Furthermore, extant studies on language-based avoidance and withdrawal behaviors suggest that individual team members' motivation for teamwork can suffer in the face of linguistic challenges. Future studies might fruitfully take this motivational research to the group level by studying the collective motivation of multinational teams through several related constructs. Team efficacy and team potency both address team members' collectively perceived capability of working together to achieve tasks (Collins & Parker, 2010). The former is geared towards joint beliefs of successfully performing a specific task (Gully, Incalcaterra, Joshi, & Beaubien, 2002), whereas the latter comprises a more general, collective evaluation of team capability (Collins & Parker, 2010). Team confidence similarly addresses the extent to which team members "place confidence in their group's ability to perform well" (De Dreu & Beersma, 2010, pp. 1111–1112). A fine-grained understanding of how language diversity affects these emergent states could substantially enhance our understanding of multinational team functioning.

### Investigate the Linguistic Challenges of Virtual Teams

Globalization has dramatically increased multinational corporations' use of virtual teams, i.e. teams that are geographically dispersed and rely on communication technology for their interaction (Gilson, Maynard, Jones Young, Vartiainen, & Hakonen, 2015). Functioning as channels for organizational knowledge sharing (Klitmøller & Lauring, 2013), these teams have become crucial for connecting the linguistically diverse units of today's multinational enterprises (Klitmøller, Schneider, & Jonsen, 2015). Despite the pervasive use of virtual teams in corporate practice, only a few pioneering studies have investigated the challenges of selecting appropriate communication media and using them skillfully to bridge language barriers in globally dispersed team communication. Klitmøller et al. (2015) found that language-based social categorization is more likely to occur if multilingual virtual teams use verbal as opposed to written communication media, whereas Klitmøller and Lauring (2013) suggested modifications to the predictions of media richness theory in multilingual team settings. Similarly, Tenzer and Pudelko (2016) revisited media synchronicity theory in multilingual virtual teams.

Future studies could build on this work and probe other theories such as media naturalness theory (DeRosa, Hantula, Kock, & D'Arcy, 2004) under conditions of language diversity. Whereas most virtual teams research to date has focused on time-tested communication media such as e-mail, chat, and discussion boards (Gilson et al., 2015), language scholars could also expand their investigation to new and emerging collaboration tools such as document sharing and co-creation technologies, meeting tools, project management tools, or social networking platforms (for an overview see Gilson et al., 2015) as enablers of multilingual virtual team communication. For example, Gao's (2017) recent finding that virtual team members' propensity to use machine translation as a support tool depends on various contextual factors could stimulate further research into the success factors of geographically dispersed and linguistically diverse teams. Her idea that private communication channels with selected team members on computer-based communication platforms may allow for code-switching without creating feelings of exclusion indicates the need to test extant knowledge on language effects in co-located teams for its applicability to virtual settings. We agree with Klitmøller et al. (2015, p. 270) that a better understanding of language dynamics in virtual teams "would lay the foundation for effective virtual management in multinational corporations".

### Study the Performance Outcomes of Language Diversity in Teams

In terms of the traditional input-process-outcome logic of team research (McGrath, 1964), existing studies have overwhelmingly focused on language diversity as an input factor influencing team processes. The subsequent relationship between altered team processes and team outcomes has received much less scholarly attention. Several studies hint at the negative performance effects of communication barriers in general (Lauring & Selmer, 2012) and language barriers in particular (Neeley et al., 2012), but these mechanisms are rarely in the focus of investigation. Future studies could emphasize the importance of language effects in teamwork by studying their impact on different dimensions of team effectiveness such as innovativeness (Liu & Philips, 2011), customer satisfaction (Gibson, Zellmer-Bruhn, & Schwab, 2003), project quality (Altschuller & Benbunan-Fich, 2010), quality of decisions made (Pridmore & Phillips-Wren, 2011), or the time and resources it takes to arrive at these decisions (Gibson et al., 2003). Hitlan et al.'s (2006) experimental study on the consequences of perceived linguistic ostracism indicates that affective outcomes such as multinational team members' commitment to their organization and their organizational citizenship behaviors may also be studied as a function of language diversity in field settings. Team members' job satisfaction (Kirkman & Shapiro, 2001) in multilingual team environments could be additionally scrutinized.

Expanding on Dotan-Eliaz et al.'s (2009) experimental investigation of the connection between linguistic ostracism and creative performance, the relationship between language diversity and creativity should be further explored in the field. This line of work would be highly relevant given the importance of creativity in today's complex, fast-paced, and competitive work environment (Gilson et al., 2015). Even more interestingly, it might also complement the research field with an innovative angle. Whereas extant studies were almost exclusively concerned with the negative effects of language diversity, the idea that this type of diversity might also affect multinational teamwork positively has been hardly pursued. Because diversity and divergent thinking are known as important drivers of team creativity (Gilson et al., 2015), Cohen and Kassis-Henderson (2017) recently suggested that linguistic diversity may help multinational team members understand and accept different discursive practices. If managed well, they postulate, language may over time turn from a divisive to a cohesive and creativity-enhancing factor. Future research into this direction could fruitfully diversify our understanding of language effects in multinational teamwork.

Having summarized the burgeoning research on linguistic diversity in multinational teams, this review has highlighted the complex and multifaceted role of language in teamwork. Despite the sharp rise in research output over the past years, opportunities for further theorizing and practically oriented studied still abound in the field. We hope that we could provide some inspiration for the further development of this vibrant research area.

# References

Acs, Z. J., de Groot, H. L., & Nijkamp, P. (Eds.). (2013). *The emergence of the knowledge economy: A regional perspective.* Berlin: Springer Science & Business Media.

Aichhorn, N., & Puck, J. (2017). I just don't feel comfortable speaking English: Foreign language anxiety as a catalyst for spoken-language barriers in MNCs. *International Business Review, 26*(4), 749–763.

Altschuller, S., & Benbunan-Fich, R. (2010). Trust, performance, and the communication process in ad hoc decision-making virtual teams. *Journal of Computer-Mediated Communication, 16*, 27–47.

Barner-Rasmussen, W., & Björkman, I. (2005). Surmounting interunit barriers factors associated with interunit communication intensity in the multinational corporation. *International Studies of Management & Organization, 35*(1), 28–46.

Barner-Rasmussen, W., & Björkman, I. (2007). Language fluency, socialization and inter-unit relationships in Chinese and Finnish subsidiaries. *Management and Organization Review, 3*(1), 105–128.

Bordia, S., & Bordia, P. (2015). Employees' willingness to adopt a foreign functional language in multilingual organizations: The role of linguistic identity. *Journal of International Business Studies, 46*(4), 415–428.

Bradley, B. H., Postlethwaite, B. E., Klotz, A. C., Hamdani, M. R., & Brown, K. G. (2012). Reaping the benefits of task conflict in teams: The critical role of team psychological safety climate. *Journal of Applied Psychology, 97*(1), 151–158.

Butler, C. L. (2011). I know how! You know how! We know how! The multinational matter of language use in task teams. *International Journal of Human Resources Development and Management, 11*(2–4), 221–234.

Cannon-Bowers, J. A., Salas, E., & Converse, S. (1993). Shared mental models in expert team decision making. In N. J. Castellan (Ed.), *Individual and group decision making: Current issues* (pp. 221–245). Hillsdale, NJ: Lawrence Erlbaum Associates.

Chen, S., Geluykens, R., & Choi, C. (2006). The importance of language in global teams: A linguistic perspective. *Management International Review, 46*(6), 679–695.

Cohen, L., & Kassis-Henderson, J. (2012). Language use in establishing rapport and building relations: Implications for international teams and management education. *Management & Avenir, 55*(5), 185–207.

Cohen, L., & Kassis-Henderson, J. (2017). Revisiting culture and language in global management teams: Toward a multilingual turn. *International Journal of Cross Cultural Management, 17*(1), 7–22.

Collins, C. G., & Parker, S. K. (2010). Team capability beliefs over time: Distinguishing between team potency, team outcome efficacy, and team process efficacy. *Journal of Occupational and Organizational Psychology, 83*(4), 1003–1023.

Colquitt, J. A., Scott, B., & LePine, J. (2007). Trust, trustworthiness and trust propensity: A meta-analytic test of their unique relationships with risk taking and job performance. *Journal of Applied Psychology, 92*(4), 909–927.

De Dreu, C. K., & Beersma, B. (2010). Team confidence, motivated information processing, and dynamic group decision making. *European Journal of Social Psychology, 40*(7), 1110–1119.

DeRosa, D. M., Hantula, D. A., Kock, N., & D'Arcy, J. (2004). Trust and leadership in virtual teamwork: A media naturalness perspective. *Human Resource Management, 43*(2–3), 219–232.

Dotan-Eliaz, O., Sommer, K., & Rubin, Y. (2009). Multilingual groups: Effects of linguistic ostracism on felt rejection and anger, coworker attraction, perceived team potency, and creative performance. *Basic and Applied Social Psychology, 31*, 363–375.

Earley, P. C., & Gibson, C. B. (2002). *Multinational work teams: A new perspective.* Mahwah, NJ: Lawrence Erlbaum Associates.

Feely, A. J., & Harzing, A. W. (2003). Language management in multinational companies. *Cross Cultural Management: An International Journal, 10*(2), 37–52.

Finkelstein, S. (1992). Power in top management teams: Dimensions, measurement, and validation. *Academy of Management Journal, 35*(3), 505–538.

Fleischmann, C., Folter, L. C., & Aritz, J. (2017). The impact of perceived foreign language proficiency on hybrid team culture. *International Journal of Business Communication.* doi:10.1177/2329488417710440

Fredriksson, R., Barner-Rasmussen, W., & Piekkari, R. (2006). The multinational corporation as a multilingual organization: The notion of a common corporate language. *Corporate Communications: An International Journal, 11*(4), 406–423.

Gao, G. (2017). *A Kaleidoscope of languages: Understanding the dynamics of language use and its effects on daily communication in multilingual teams* (Doctoral dissertation, Cornell University). Retrieved from https://ecommons. cornell.edu/handle/1813/56789

George, J. M., & King, E. B. (2007). Potential pitfalls of affect convergence in teams: Functions and dysfunctions of group affective tone. In E. A. Mannix, M. A. Neale, & C. P. Anderson (Eds.), *Affect and groups* (pp. 97–123). Bingley: Emerald Group Publishing Limited.

Gibson, C. B., & Manuel, J. A. (2003). Building trust: Effective multicultural communication processes in virtual teams. In C. Gibson & S. G. Cohen (Eds.), *Virtual teams that work: Creating conditions for virtual team effectiveness* (pp. 59–86). San Francisco, CA: Jossey-Bass.

Gibson, C. B., Zellmer-Bruhn, M. E., & Schwab, D. P. (2003). Team effectiveness in multinational organizations: Evaluation across contexts. *Group & Organization Management, 28*(4), 444–474.

Giles, H., & Johnson, P. (1981). The role of language in ethnic group relations. In J. C. Turner, & H. Giles (Eds.), *Intergroup behavior* (pp. 199–243). Oxford: Blackwell.

Gilson, L. L., Maynard, M. T., Jones Young, N. C., Vartiainen, M., & Hakonen, M. (2015). Virtual teams research: 10 years, 10 themes, and 10 opportunities. *Journal of Management, 41*(5), 1313–1337.

Gooty, J., Gavin, M., & Ashkanasy, N. M. (2009). Emotions research in OB: The challenges that lie ahead. *Journal of Organizational Behavior, 30*, 833–838.

Gully, S. M., Incalcaterra, K. A., Joshi, A., & Beaubien, J. M. (2002). A meta-analysis of team-efficacy, potency, and performance: Interdependence and level of analysis as moderators of observed relationships. *Journal of Applied Psychology, 87*(5), 819.

Harzing, A. W., & Feely, A. J. (2008). The language barrier and its implications for HQ-subsidiary relationships. *Cross Cultural Management: An International Journal, 15*(1), 49–61.

Hinds, P. J., Neeley, T. B., & Cramton, C. D. (2014). Language as a lightning rod: Power contests, emotion regulation, and subgroup dynamics in global teams. *Journal of International Business Studies, 45*(5), 536–561.

Hitlan, R. T., Kelly, K. M., Schepman, S., Schneider, K. T., & Zarate, M. A. (2006). Language exclusion and the consequences of perceived ostracism in the workplace. *Group Dynamics: Theory, Research, and Practice, 10,* 56–70.

Janssens, M., & Brett, J. M. (2006). Cultural intelligence in global teams: A fusion model of collaboration. *Group & Organization Management, 31*(1), 124–153.

Janssens, M., Lambert, J., & Steyaert, C. (2004). Developing language strategies for international companies: The contribution of translation studies. *Journal of World Business, 39*(4), 414–430.

Kassis-Henderson, J. (2005). Language diversity in international management teams. *International Studies of Management & Organization, 35*(1), 66–82.

Kirkman, B. L., & Shapiro, D. L. (2001). The impact of cultural values on job satisfaction and organizational commitment in self-managing work teams: The mediating role of employee resistance. *Academy of Management Journal, 44*(3), 557–569.

Klitmøller, A., & Lauring, J. (2013). When global virtual teams share knowledge: Media richness, cultural difference and language commonality. *Journal of World Business, 48*(3), 398–406.

Klitmøller, A., Schneider, S. C., & Jonsen, K. (2015). Speaking of global virtual teams: Language differences, social categorization and media choice. *Personnel Review, 44*(2), 270–285.

Lagerström, K., & Andersson, M. (2003). Creating and sharing knowledge within a transnational team—The development of a global business system. *Journal of World Business, 38*(2), 84–95.

Lauring, J. (2008). Rethinking social identity theory in international encounters: Language use as a negotiated object for identity making. *International Journal of Cross Cultural Management, 8*(3), 343–361.

Lauring, J., & Selmer, J. (2010). Multicultural organizations: Common language and group cohesiveness. *International Journal of Cross Cultural Management, 10*(3), 267–284.

Lauring, J., & Selmer, J. (2012). Knowledge sharing in diverse organisations. *Human Resource Management Journal, 22*(1), 89–105.

Lewicki, R. J., & Bunker, B. B. (1996). Developing and maintaining trust in work relationships. In R. M. Kramer & T. R. Tyler (Eds.), *Trust in organizations: Frontiers of theory and research* (pp. 114–139). Thousand Oaks, CA: Sage.

Liu, Y., & Phillips, J. S. (2011). Examining the antecedents of knowledge sharing in facilitating team innovativeness from a multilevel perspective. *International Journal of Information Management, 31*(1), 44–52.

Louhiala-Salminen, L., Charles, M., & Kankaanranta, A. (2005). English as a lingua franca in Nordic corporate mergers: Two case companies. *English for Specific Purposes, 24*(4), 401–421.

Luo, Y., & Shenkar, O. (2006). The multinational corporation as a multilingual community: Language and organization in a global context. *Journal of International Business Studies, 37*(3), 321–339.

Marks, M. A., Mathieu, J. E., & Zaccaro, S. J. (2001). A temporally based framework and taxonomy of team processes. *Academy of Management Review, 26,* 356–376.

Mathieu, J. E., Hollenbeck, J. R., van Knippenberg, D., & Ilgen, D. R. (2017). A century of work teams in the Journal of Applied Psychology. *Journal of Applied Psychology, 102*(3), 452.

Mayer, R. C., Davis, J. H., & Schoorman, F. D. (1995). An integrative model of organizational trust. *Academy of Management Review, 20*(3), 709–734.

McAllister, D. J. (1995). Affect- and cognition-based trust as foundations for interpersonal cooperation in organizations. *Academy of Management Journal, 38*(1), 24–59.

McGrath, J. E. (1964). *Social psychology: A brief introduction.* New York: Holt, Rinehart & Winston.

Méndez García, M., & Pérez Cañado, M. L. (2005). Language and power: Raising awareness of the role of language in multicultural teams. *Language and Intercultural Communication, 5*(1), 86–104.

Neeley, T. B. (2013). Language matters: Status loss and achieved status distinctions in global organizations. *Organization Science, 24*(2), 476–497.

Neeley, T. B., Hinds, P. J., & Cramton, C. D. (2012). The (un)hidden turmoil of language in global collaboration. *Organizational Dynamics, 41*(3), 236–244.

Nickerson, C. (2015). The death of the non-native speaker? English as a lingua franca in business communication: A research agenda. *Language Teaching, 48*(3), 390–404.

Noteboom, B., & Six, F. (2003). Introduction. In B. Noteboom & F. Six (Eds.), *The trust process in organizations: Empirical studies of the determinants and the process of trust development* (pp. 1–15). Cheltenham: Edward Elgar.

Paunova, M. (2017). Who gets to lead the multinational team? An updated status characteristics perspective. *Human Relations, 70*(7), 883–907.

Piekkari, R., Oxelheim, L., & Randøy, T. (2015). The silent board: How language diversity may influence the work processes of corporate boards. *Corporate Governance: An International Review, 23*(1), 25–41.

Pridmore, J., & Phillips-Wren, G. (2011). Assessing decision making quality in face-to-face teams versus virtual teams in a virtual world. *Journal of Decision Systems, 20,* 283–308.

Reiche, B. S., Harzing, A.-W., & Pudelko, M. (2015). Why and how does shared language affect subsidiary knowledge inflows? A social identity perspective. *Journal of International Business Studies, 46*(5), 528–551.

Riek, B. M., Mania, E. W., & Gaertner, S. L. (2006). Intergroup threat and outgroup attitudes: A meta-analytic review. *Personality and Social Psychology Review, 10*(4), 336–353.

Stahl, G. K., Maznevski, M. L., Voigt, A., & Jonsen, K. (2010). Unraveling the effects of cultural diversity in teams: A meta-analysis of research on multicultural work groups. *Journal of International Business Studies, 41*(4), 690–709.

Tajfel, H., & Turner, J. C. (1986). The social identity theory of intergroup behavior. In S. Worchel & W. G. Austin (Eds.), *Psychology of intergroup relations* (2nd ed., pp. 1–24). Chicago, IL: Nelson-Hall.

Tenzer, H., & Pudelko, M. (2012). The impact of language barriers on shared mental models in multinational teams. *Academy of Management Proceedings, 2012*(1), 1. Academy of Management.

Tenzer, H., & Pudelko, M. (2015). Leading across language barriers: Managing language-induced emotions in multinational teams. *The Leadership Quarterly, 26*(4), 606–625.

Tenzer, H., & Pudelko, M. (2016). Media choice in multilingual virtual teams. *Journal of International Business Studies, 47*(4), 427–452.

Tenzer, H., & Pudelko, M. (2017). The influence of language differences on power dynamics in multinational teams. *Journal of World Business, 52*(1), 45–61.

Tenzer, H., Pudelko, M., & Harzing, A.-W. (2014). The impact of language barriers on trust formation in multinational teams. *Journal of International Business Studies, 45*(5), 508–535.

Tenzer, H., Terjesen, S., & Harzing, A.-W. (2017). Language in international business: A review and agenda for future research. *Management International Review, 57*(6), 815–854.

Van Der Vegt, G. S., & Bunderson, J. S. (2005). Learning and performance in multidisciplinary teams: The importance of collective team identification. *Academy of Management Journal, 48*(3), 532–547.

Vigier, M., & Spencer-Oatey, H. (2017). Code-switching in newly formed multinational project teams: Challenges, strategies and effects. *International Journal of Cross Cultural Management, 17*(1), 23–37.

Vigier, M., & Spencer-Oatey, H. (2018). The interplay of rules, asymmetries in language fluency, and team dynamics in culturally diverse teams: Case study insights. *Cross Cultural & Strategic Management, 25*(1), 157–182.

Von Glinow, M. A., Shapiro, D. L., & Brett, J. M. (2004). Can we talk, and should we? Managing emotional conflict in multicultural teams. *Academy of Management Review, 29*(4), 578–592.

Welch, D. E., & Welch, L. S. (2008). The importance of language in international knowledge transfer. *Management International Review, 48*, 339–360.

Wilmot, N. V. (2017). Language and the faces of power: A theoretical approach. *International Journal of Cross Cultural Management, 17*(1), 85–100.

Woo, D., & Giles, H. (2017). Language attitudes and intergroup dynamics in multilingual organizations. *International Journal of Cross Cultural Management, 17*(1), 39–52.

# 6 Exploring Translanguaging in International Business. Towards a Comparison of Highly Context-Embedded Practices

## Evidence From France and Finland

*Wilhelm Barner-Rasmussen and Hélène Langinier*

When translanguaging, interlocutors mobilize and combine multiple languages repertoires, creating new words and expressions to improve comprehension (García, 2009). This and similar practices such as code-switching, long recognized by linguists and sociolinguists, have only recently received significant interest among language-sensitive international business (IB) scholars, and the understanding of their dynamics in the context of cross-border business and management relationships remains limited. This chapter thus documents an inroad into relatively uncharted territory, with all that this entails of unexpected challenges and answers generating new questions at each turn.

Our overarching ambition is to explore translanguaging patterns in two different IB contexts, and discuss in what sense and under what epistemological assumptions such patterns might meaningfully be compared across these contexts. Based on interviews in the subsidiary of a German multinational corporation (MNC) located in France at the French-German border, and in Finnish businesses with large exposure to Sweden, we shed new light on translanguaging practices in MNCs by describing and analyzing patterns of language use. We want to understand how individuals relate to their translanguaging at work, and the role(s) it may grant them in the organization.

Translanguaging practices are deeply embedded in, and derive much of their legitimacy from, the socio-historical environment of the geographical areas where they occur. Hence, a traditional positivist comparison of such practices makes little sense. What is possible is to analyze and contrast how these practices relate to their separate contexts and thereby attempt to decode the "areas of meaning" (Romani, Barmeyer, Primecz, & Pilhofer, 2018) that make individuals in the respective contexts resort to translanguaging. Such comparison can stimulate our understanding of translanguaging in cross-boundary business contexts as a practice embedded not only in an organizational, but also a social and societal context (Heller, 1988), with various degrees of interplay between these. This helps answer recent calls for IB research on translanguaging and on language(s) in international business and management overall (Brannen, Piekkari, & Tietze, 2014).

Distinguished anthropologist and historian Alan Macfarlane (2004) has argued that comparison in the social sciences plays an important role in distancing the over-familiar, familiarizing the distant, making absences visible and testing answers (ibid., p. 95–98). Research on adult education has found that comparison of cases promotes learning processes by encouraging appropriate analysis, inspiring curiosity and generating abstracting principles (Loewenstein, Thompson, & Gentner, 2003, p. 125). We believe that the approach outlined later does generate at least some of these valuable benefits.

To this topic, we apply the theoretical lens of language ecology (Haugen, 1972; Fill & Mühlhäusler, 2006, Van Lier, 2006). Language ecology engages with the relation between languages and their environment in specific areas, with a focus on interpersonal co-creation of meaning. It offers several possible approaches to understanding situated language practices. We follow Kramsch and Whiteside (2008) in drawing upon language ecology to explain hybrid language use in multilingual settings by referring to three main dimensions: history, time and space.

Methodologically, we are inspired by current approaches in cross-cultural management (CCM) as outlined by Romani et al. (2018). We leverage international collaboration between researchers to explore interview data on embedded practices from two contexts that the researchers individually know very well. Previous research from a language ecology perspective has insisted on highly immersive methodologies such as ethnomethodology; compared to this, our empirical approach trades depth for breadth, and detailed context-specific insight for insight generated by distancing from the familiar through contrast and dialogue. Compared to traditional positivist research on cross-cultural management, again, which has tended to focus on "quantifiable relationships between national culture (. . .) and management and organizational practices" (Romani et al., 2018, p. 249), our approach is highly context-sensitive and immersive. This aligns us with the *interpretive* view on cross-cultural management (Romani et al., 2018).

## Literature Review

### *Language(s) in IB*

Increased heterogeneity of local environments (Jaussaud & Mayrhofer, 2014) forces global businesses to take into account local specificities and calls for a new understanding of relationships between global and local

(Mayrhofer & Very, 2013). This entanglement of universality and par-
ticularity (Janssens & Steyaert, 2014) implies understanding MNCs as
sites where local practices reflect global embeddedness, where global and
local co-construct reality. This simultaneous interest in the global and the
local has also guided language-sensitive IB research from a focus on discrete national languages and barriers between these (see e.g. Marschan-
Piekkari, Welch, & Welch, 1999) to a more refined understanding of
processes associated with linguistic diversity in MNC contexts.

Janssens and Steyaert's (2014) concept of *multilingual franca* highlights a negotiated, situated approach to English[1] as a lingua franca in
continuation with other languages where speakers use multiple linguistic resources in complex ways to express voice. Ricento (2015) and colleagues also stress the situated importance of the environment for choices
made by language managers in international contexts. This interest in the
multilingual potential of collaborators in cross-boundary business contexts forms an important avenue of future inquiry in language-sensitive
IB research (Brannen et al., 2014).

## Translanguaging

The notion of languages that are distinct and almost impermeable to each
other is linked to the rise of the nation-state in Europe. In many other
historical periods and other geographical and anthropological contexts,
the emphasis is on the links between communicative systems of different human groups. For example, Romaine (1994, p. 12), describing the
complex language situation in Papua New Guinea, has argued that "Any
attempt to count distinct languages will be an artefact of classificatory
procedures rather than a reflection of communicative practices".

Present-day contact linguistics does not insist on the number of languages used or their denomination, but rather on speakers' capacity to
draw on a range of linguistic elements in interactions with specific partners in specific contexts (Fill & Mühlhäusler, 2006; Canagarajah, 2016).
By contrast, IB research still tends to focus on different autonomous languages and the organizational and/or individual consequences of knowing or not knowing these. With the exception of some research on issues
such as code-switching (e.g. Harzing, Köster, & Magner, 2011; Boussebaa,
Sinha, & Gabriel, 2014; Gaibrois, 2018), few have heeded Janssens and
Steyaert's (2014) call for a more "cosmopolitan" approach, even if exploring the context-specific mixing of linguistic resources offers a fruitful way
towards understanding "real" language use in the business world.

Next, to capture these mixing practices, we use the notion of *translanguaging*. It was introduced by the linguist García (2009, p. 40), who
defined it as

> the act performed by bilinguals of accessing different linguistic
> features or various modes of what are described as autonomous

languages, in order to maximize communicative potential. It is an approach to bilingualism that is centred, not on languages as has often been the case, but on the practices of bilinguals that are readily observable in order to make sense of their multilingual worlds.

When translanguaging, interlocutors mobilize different languages simultaneously (e.g. French, German and English), sometimes in the same sentence, and even create new words in order to improve comprehension. This shifts our focus to language-in-use, opening up significant potential to understand complex interplays of languages within MNCs. This can help bridge divides between proponents of common corporate languages (e.g. Luo & Shenkar, 2006; Harzing et al., 2011) and critics of the imperialistic and hegemonic effects of such linguae francae (especially English) on actors in local subsidiaries (e.g. Piekkari, Vaara, Tienari, & Säntti, 2005; Tietze, 2008).

A focus on translanguaging may also help MNCs benefit more from employees' existing linguistic skills. When translanguaging, interlocutors break free from grammatical rules, draw on all their language repertories and combined different national languages and dialects to make themselves understood in a specific context (García, 2009). In this perspective, MNC employees who lack officially recognized language qualifications and are reluctant to learn languages in traditional classrooms may find creative ways to communicate efficiently with foreign colleagues in the context of their subsidiary. This ability constitutes a Language Operative Capacity for the company (Welch & Welch, 2018). Language is approached as a social practice where language is negotiated in situation (Karhunen, Kankaaranta, Louhiala-Salminen, & Piekkari, 2018).

## Language Ecology

To help understand how translanguaging practices are embedded in wider cultural and historical processes (Heller, 1988), we locate our exploration within the framework of language ecology (Haugen, 1972; Fill & Mühlhäusler, 2006; Van Lier, 2006). Language ecology explains the relation between languages and their environment in a specific area with a focus on the interpersonal co-creation of meaning.

In IB, multilingual practices have often been attributed to the individual behaviors and capabilities of a small elite labelled e.g. "language nodes" (Marschan-Piekkari et al., 1999). An ecolinguistic framework points beyond individuals to account also for the contexts in which speakers communicate and highlights that each member of a community has the potential to cross linguistic and cultural boundaries; the main limitation to this is not of linguistic nature, but due to unequal distribution of power. Following Kramsch and Whiteside (2008), *history*, *time* and *space* form the main dimensions of our inquiry into translanguaging practices. "Time" refers to when interlocutors resort to translanguaging, on what occasion and with whom. "Space" refers to the geographical location(s) of actors in relation to the use of specific languages. "History" refers to cultural memories enacted in words and how history is recreated in today's multilingual interaction.

Analyzing our data within a language ecology framework helps illuminate what specific linguistic practices owe to their context and helps account for their links to different spatial and temporal timescales. This enables us to answer calls for more research on the links between language and culture (Brannen, 2004; Barner-Rasmussen, Ehrnrooth, Koveshnikov, & Mäkelä, 2014), especially on the influence of linguistic specificities of regional culture (Hofstede, Hofstede, & Minkov, 2005; Davoine, Schroeter, & Stern, 2014).

*Empirical Approaches to Translanguaging and*
*Cross-Cultural Management*

As mentioned earlier, previous research from a language ecology perspective has insisted on highly specific data and a deep understanding of each empirical field to explore the meaning potential of interactions in a specific context. For example, ethnomethodology has been used to help understand how history (e.g. colonial domination or former territorial affiliation) is recreated in today's multilingual interactions, how the location in a specific territory impacts the co-creation of meaning or how these macro dimensions interplay with corporate culture. Ecolinguists analyze situated language interactions based on transcripts but linked with other data such as field maps or geographic or historical accounts of the analyzed context. In Kramsch and Whiteside (2008), actors with roots in Yucatan in a mainly Mexican area of San Francisco used Maya as a form of public resistance to Spanish colonial discourses which hold Maya in low esteem among Mexicans. Mühlhäusler (2003) used a language ecology approach to natives' pidgins and creoles to show how the introduction of colonial English in Australia was interwoven with an increasingly detrimental relation to the environment and the abuse of natural resources. Such deeply embedded approaches differ from traditional methods in the fields of cross-cultural management and IB, where quantitative comparative studies at high levels of analysis (e.g. units, MNCs, countries) form an important fundament of empirical activity.

As a middle road between these extremes, we follow what Romani and colleagues (2018) have termed an *interpretive* approach in the context of CCM. This implies an interest in "the systems of meaning and national institutions [and] underlying historical rooted assumptions that reveal national management practices" (ibid., p. 250), and a view of "interpersonal interactions . . . as a system of social interactions with negotiated contextual meanings" (p. 251). The advantage of this approach is illustrated by our initial empirical insight that some translanguaging patterns in our data were very similar even if they occurred in quite different contexts. An approach strongly focused on a single context might misinterpret such a pattern as specific to a particular locale, thereby ignoring dynamics generating similar patterns also in other conditions. An approach focused on the general might ignore important context-specific factors. In short, the value of the kind of comparison we advocate here is to enable the training of empirical interpretations against a varied base of practices at both organizational and social/societal levels, while remaining sensitive to the forms and consequences of translanguaging practices in different contexts.

Such an approach requires accord between researchers who know their "own" context and data very well, including in-depth historical, cultural and linguistic knowledge that is hard to convey to outsiders. The challenge is to expose the insights generated by such in-depth understanding for collegial examination and critique while remaining receptive to the alternative insights generated by that dialogue. This requires biases and pet interpretations to be openly recognized as part of the research process.

Such confrontation of perspectives, ideas and insights between colleagues each immersed in their own field but both familiar with the core theoretical concepts of joint interest provides alternative understandings of how things might be connected. For instance, the finding that Swedish-speaking Finns from the Helsinki region label their translanguaging practices as "sloppy language" raised the awareness of the French researcher of the pride that the French interviewees at the French-German border attached to their translanguaging. In Paris, such practices might have been despised as well; dialogue around these dynamics helped us to characterize employees' special relation to translanguaging in cross-border settings.

## Method

### Data Collection

To understand language diversity through a translanguaging perspective we need to focus on how and why individuals draw on all their language repertoires. For this paper we approach such language practices primarily through interview data, supplanted by on-site observations as well as internal and external secondary data (see e.g. Jarzabkowski, 2008; Lincoln & Guba, 1985). These data were collected in one company in France at the German border and in seven Finnish companies with strong links to Sweden in the Helsinki region. Our empirical examples are thus of translanguaging between organizational units straddling neighbor countries with intensive business and cultural links (implying extensive interaction in both scale and scope, as well as rich opportunities for inter-action) but mutually non-intelligible languages (implying specific exper-tise in both languages is needed to cross between them).

The data collections were independent and the decision to compare translanguaging practices across the contexts was made *post hoc*, but followed similar procedures in both contexts. In France, we looked for occurrences referring to border-crossing situations with a focus on lan-guage, local specificities of the organization, the way global and local were intertwined in relation to language and what such practices could bring to the organization. At the end of the interview, interviewees were asked to complete a language biography, to indicate what language(s) they use or used at a certain period of their lives and also at what level of competency and under what circumstances. In Finland, the focus of the interviews was more varied, but individuals' own language competences, their practices of language use—especially in relation to the local-global tension—and organizational specifics that influenced language use were topics of interest at all stages of the data collection.

In both locations we interviewed employees from different backgrounds, with different language skills, working for different departments, of dif-ferent hierarchical status, age, gender and professional experience. Thus our conceptual argumentation is informed by a varied range of empirical material. We conducted all our interviews in the language preferred by our respondents (Welch & Piekkari, 2006). Each interview in France was conducted by two researchers, one native German and one native French. In Finland, all interviews were carried out by either one of two research-ers who were bilingual in Finnish and Swedish.

## Data Analysis

The recorded and transcribed interviews were open-coded (see e.g. Strauss & Corbin, 1998) for evidence of communicative activities by the respondents or their colleagues that could be described as translanguag-ing (García, 2009). For the Finnish data, this step was conducted by a bilingual Finnish management scholar. For the French data, the analysis was conducted by a German linguist bilingual in French and German and a French researcher from the management science field with some knowledge in German. Next, we carried out an in-depth cross-contextual analysis together based on the ecolinguistic approach, focusing on the impact of context on translanguaging practices. Time, space and history form the main dimensions of our inquiry as environmentally conditioned factors that may affect the willingness to enact translanguaging practices (Kramsch & Whiteside, 2008).

The combination of two contexts and three dimensions, illustrated in Figure 6.1, constitutes the structural backbone of the results presentation which follows after short descriptions of the studied contexts. Findings

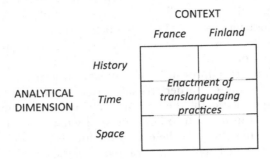

*Figure 6.1* Analytical framework

from each analytical dimension and context are discussed separately before an analysis across both contexts and dimensions.

## Context Descriptions

### The French Case

We investigated language practices in the car plant *smart* (subsidiary of the German group Daimler AG) mainly because linguistic borders in the organization were a matter of concern for the leadership and because of its cross-border location in France at Hambach near the French/German border. The territory where *smart* is located has belonged alternatively to France and Germany throughout history. Here locals are often bilingual; most of the time they have family links to Germany, they go out or go shopping in Germany, and they tend to develop a bicultural and bilingual identity (Hemker, 2014). The use of the Franconian dialect drawing on French and German can act as a communicative bridge between both sides of the border. The development of these skills has been supported locally by the educational system in the eastern part of Lorraine. However, a growing number of students choose to learn English.

This fact played an important role in the choice of Hambach for Daimler, along with economic factors like the lower labor cost in France compared to Germany. There were also strategic factors like market development, as *smart* considered France to be the most important market for this new car model (Dörrenbächer & Schulz, 2008). *smart* counts 800 employees, the majority of which is French-speaking; only 5% of the employees are German, working mostly in administrative support functions. However, the firm is headed by a German. Although no formal and explicit linguistic policy is communicated at *smart*, French and German linguistic skills appear as recruitment criteria at least for support and management functions.

We interviewed the CEO, the director of human resources and the communication director. We also met 15 employees and discussed with them based on a semi-directed dialogue guideline, and the interviewees were asked to complete a language biography and to draw their space of living at the end of their interview. Finally, we compiled internal documentation like statistics on employees and internal corporate documentation. We triangulated interviews with the employees with the ones conducted with the management team.

## The Finnish Case

Eighteen interviews were carried out with top and middle management members and regular staff in two Finnish MNCs with large subsidiaries in Sweden, and five Finnish subsidiaries of Swedish-owned firms, all located in the Helsinki region. The MNCs included a state-owned utility and a family-owned alimentation company. The subsidiaries belonged to firms active in both the service and manufacturing sectors. This forms a representative selection of Finnish businesses with a significant interface to Sweden. This choice is relevant for our study because both Finnish and Swedish are official languages of Finland. Until 1809, when it became a Russian grand duchy, Finland was part of Sweden for some 500 years. The national economies of Sweden and Finland are among the most integrated in the world, and cross-border ownership and pan-national organizations are common. However, Finnish and Swedish belong to different language families and are mutually unintelligible, whereas Swedish is closely related to Danish and Norwegian.

Since Finnish independence from Russia in 1917, the status of Swedish as a second national language is constitutionally enshrined but not unequivocally accepted. It has been interpreted by some even in postcolonial terms (see e.g. Vaara, Tienari, Piekkari, & Säntti, 2005) and has not fitted easily with efforts to craft a Finnish national identity. Still, perhaps due to the widely recognized importance of positioning Finland as part of the Nordics and not of the East, Swedish remains a mandatory school language alongside Finnish and English, and basic knowledge of Swedish is required for civil service positions. These rules have majority public support despite frequent criticism that they are inefficient and counterproductive; the mandatory school Swedish is colloquially known as "forced Swedish".

Of Finns, 5.2% are formally Swedish-speaking (Statistics Finland, 2019), but in the Greater Helsinki region most are bilingual, work in Finnish and speak Swedish mainly in private. The Swedish slang of the region has absorbed many Finnish words and more recently also structures. The spoken Swedish of schoolchildren and youngsters today is only partly comprehensible for Swedish-speakers who do not know Finnish.

# Findings

## *Time*

In our framework, this analytical dimension is related to when interlocutors resort to translanguaging, under what occasion and with whom. In France translanguaging occurs spontaneously between locals at the Hambach site; the main objective is to be understood by one's interlocutors, regardless of grammatical rules or vocabulary accuracy. A German project manager explains:

> With one colleague, I speak German, with others French, with others a mix of everything.

Our respondents mobilize accurate technical vocabulary to develop cars or get information from suppliers or maintenance firms; some words are simply not translated in French. In parallel, mobilizing French words or dialect elements around technical German words helps convey the right message to colleagues with a lesser command of German, thus fostering knowledge sharing between *smart* and the Daimler head office. This is important because all reporting activities at *smart* are in German, as are 90% of suppliers. Thanks to their translanguaging practices mixing French and German, local employees act as boundary spanners between the German HQ and the Hambach plant. Even employees at lower hierarchical levels, who are often excluded from this kind of dialogue (Barner-Rasmussen & Aarnio, 2011), can join it.

Similar translanguaging patterns emerge in Finland. Swedish-speaking Finns will speak Swedish to each other and to Swedes, but the bulk of their work in Finland is carried out in Finnish, and many also use English on a daily basis. This creates office microenvironments where respondents typically say, "We speak a mix of everything, everyone speaks whatever comes first to mind", and interlocutors produce translations as well as mixed-language expressions and constructions. However, native Swedish-speakers are aware that when interacting with Swedes, they have to control their accent and vocabulary to produce Swedish that is "Swedish" enough. One respondent noted that her children would always know when she was on the phone to Sweden due to the linguistic adaptations she would make. Still, Finns who know Swedish and interface with Swedes in their job tend to benefit from their language skills, which enable them to play bridging or boundary spanning roles in many daily interactions. At higher hierarchical levels, they are able to talk directly to Swedish top managers and boards, and also at lower levels they often gain career advantages related to visibility, participation and effectiveness.

In both research contexts we find that employees are willing to adapt to their interlocutors, highlighting the pragmatic use of translanguaging to improve comprehension among colleagues. In both cases we also find respondents—including at lower hierarchical levels—whose language skills enable them to act as boundary spanners.

### Space

Space relates to the relevance of specific language skills in relation to the geographical location(s) of the firm. Most of the French employees are locals from the cross-border region where *smart* is located. They are bicultural and bilingual, or master at least the common dialect used on both sides of the borders; they live, go out or go shopping in France as in Germany; some of them are married with people from the other side of the border. They strongly identify with this cross-border region as a third space where the border between France and Germany is blurred. We observed their pride at belonging to this region and at performing translanguaging, when we referred to the introduction of English at *smart* because of a new project with a French car producer from Paris. A local project manager shared his experience: "On the project team you had the French from Paris and the Germans from Stuttgart". For him the cross-border region appears as a third space where he is proud to resort to translanguaging practices to help French and German colleagues avoid misunderstandings when they struggle in English.

In Finland, the picture is more complex. Geographically, translanguaging between Swedish and Finnish is mainly done in Finland, because few Swedes know Finnish: Compared to the French case, there is no "cross-border region" where mixing languages is mutually accepted as a social practice. Those who do engage in it often feel they occupy a position as intermediaries or middlemen, and are able to broker or translate between Swedes and Finns. However, for native Swedish-speakers in the Helsinki region, this position also makes them outsiders to some extent. Speaking "proper Swedish" takes a significant effort, whereas the colloquial accented Swedish with many Finnish words is illegitimate in both Sweden and Finland as "sloppy language" or "not proper Swedish". A native Finnish speaker highly fluent in Swedish commented on the mixed-language practices of Swedish-speaking Finns:

> If a third of the words are Finnish, some contorted Finnish, well I think that's totally awful. My daughter-in-law is a Swedish-speaking Finn and I listen to her and look at her facebook postings,[2] well, dear God what language.
> Yeah, maybe that's a bit true.

It really is, it's not just a bit, especially here in Southern Finland, you hear like, "det var huisin kiva där på Särkänniemi" [structure Swedish, several words Finnish], and I think [. . .] soon I will go and tell these people off because all their talk is like this.

These different perceptions of translanguaging highlight the difference between the geographical areas where these practices occur: a regional cross-border area versus a capital more distant from the country of the language used for translanguaging. They also made us aware of the French employees' strong identification with the territory where *smart* is located.

### History

History is recreated in today's multilingual interactions: In Lorraine, the region at the French German border, a strong common history between territories on both sides of the border explains a strong identification of the employees to the region along with a bicultural-bilingual identity (Hemker, 2014). This territory has alternatively been French and German, most locals have family links with Germany, and both border regions suffered from the demise of a formerly flourishing mining industry that structured the whole life of locals. This explains the common identification of both French and Germans to this region and the pride at resorting to translanguaging practices related to the region.

If French and German can be said to be kept together by history in Lorraine, Finnish and Swedish are perhaps slowly being torn apart by history in the Helsinki region. In Finland, the Swedish language has longstanding historical associations to privilege and, despite its evident usefulness for business and cultural contacts to Sweden, has been an uneasy fit with efforts to develop a Finnish national identity and raise the status of Finnish. This somewhat conflicted historical background may help explain why efforts to engage in translanguaging practices mixing Finnish and Swedish can raise emotional reactions among Finnish-speakers, even if done to smoothen the comprehension between MNC units. Native Swedish-speakers in Finland risk alienating both Swedes and native speakers of Finnish with "sloppy" Swedish-Finnish translanguaging.

Analyzing our data from the perspective of history thus alerts us to the salience of identification with a cross-border entity as opposed to either of two separate country contexts in explaining how translanguaging efforts are received.

### Discussion

We find that in both contexts, employees combine languages to improve comprehension between interlocutors, and individuals' willingness to engage in specific translanguaging practices is influenced by their identification with a region, group or common history. This aspect may be conceived in terms of how socially acceptable it is to cross certain language boundaries.

Some respondents—while immersed in broader national-cultural contexts that emphasize French and Finnish—construct their own identity partly or even extensively around German and Swedish, and belong to cultural subgroups that have historically bridged these cultures and languages. In the context of such spatial and historic dynamics, some individuals perceive translanguaging as a natural and accepted part of their identity.

In France, we observe a pragmatic approach towards language more than the desire to cross borders; employees are not aware of crossing a boundary while mixing French and German. As mentioned earlier, local employees at *smart* in the French-German cross-border area are often bilinguals and biculturals; they live in France or Germany, have Germans in their family, and the notion of boundary in itself does not make sense to them.

In Finland, there is greater awareness on behalf of bilinguals— especially native Swedish-speakers—that they act as cultural boundary spanners. The geographical distance to Sweden makes the boundary more perceptible, although this is mitigated by frequent trips to Sweden, family members and work experience there, Swedish media etc. They do mostly not think of themselves as bicultural, but rather as "between cultures", although sufficiently familiar with both cultures to be able to broker between them. As suggested by Wismann (2012), who highlights a weaving between thinking and cultures enacted in language use, these individuals think between cultures. As for language use, they do think of themselves as bilingual but also are aware that their variety of Swedish is not identical to the one spoken in Sweden.

We observe in both areas the development of some jargons specific to the firm or work situation, for instance mixing German words in French sentences or Finnish words in Swedish sentences, or vice versa. However, these practices are perceived differently. In France, they mix words very naturally, a practice supported by the use of the Franconian dialect from both side of the borders mixing French and German with some liberty towards to the grammatical rules of these languages, even if the use of this dialect is declining. In Finland, the mobilization of both Swedish and Finnish also occurs smoothly in the context of "Greater Helsinki slang", but results in a conflict for Swedish-speaking Finns torn between the goals to be speaking "proper Swedish" and remaining in the comfort zone of their Finnish context. These respondents are very aware that their translanguaging breaks the boundary of correct, "acceptable" language.

In organizational terms, our bilingual respondents in both Finland and France play a role of boundary spanners in the sense of Barner-Rasmussen et al. (2014). In both cases, bilingual individuals span the linguistic boundary between organizational entities in their working environment, aiming for better comprehension through a pragmatic approach to language. The main difference lies in the way they experience their translanguaging practices.

The ecolinguistic approach helps understand these differences in light of the histories of our research contexts. The specific location of the company studied in France at the cross-border area with Germany is extremely important. Germans and French in this region on both sides of the border have a common history, local employees from Germany and French have strong ties outside the professional context, and they naturally mobilize all their language repertoires to understand each other without any constraint to do so. It is important to specify that this occurs even if in this working environment, languages are not free from power influence, and mastering German is a prerequisite to progress in the hierarchy.

In Finland, the somewhat conflicted position of Swedish-speaking Finns is explained by the history and present status of Swedish in Finland. Historical tensions between the language groups in combination with the emphasis on being able to produce "normal" Swedish and not a local dialect influenced by Finnish fosters a less serene approach to language than in France among both Swedish- and Finnish-speakers.

## Conclusion

Exploring contextually embedded translanguaging practices in Finland and France with a focus on comparing "areas of meanings" in the sense of Romani et al. (2018) proves fruitful. A language ecology oriented data analysis highlights how translanguaging practices relate to the history, time and space in the territory where they occur. These categories offer us "tertia comparationis" and give the opportunity to distinguish different phenomena peculiar to each context, enabling both of us to distance us from our respective fields (Macfarlane, 2004).

Drawing on ecolinguistics helps understand the significant influence of context on translanguaging practices. Highlighting the role of actors anchored in different local specific contexts through their translanguaging practices illustrates Janssens and Steyaert's (2014) view on cosmopolitanism, pointing out how local practices reflect global embeddedness. Our cross-country study helps clarify the concept of translanguaging in MNCs and the circumstances in which it may support communication between different organizational entities. These insights facilitate future IB research on translanguaging and related issues and advance the overall understanding of language(s) in international business and management, for example by highlighting how history as recreated through multilingual interactions interplays with corporate culture—an important contribution overlooked in current research. While doing so we illustrate a way to approach language as a social practice, thus answering the call of Karhunen et al. (2018).

Against the background of recent calls for research problematizing the nature of intercultural communication processes in international business (e.g. Szkudlarek, Nardon, & Osland, 2017), we note that there is much that firms can do to encourage employees to draw upon translanguaging as a positive resource for themselves as well as the organization. The workplace has two important advantages over educational settings: People spend a lot of time there, and they really have to communicate in authentic situations. Especially in manual activities like on the production line of a car factory, the context gives an important frame for the exchange, providing an excellent means of fostering linguistic exchange and mutual comprehension or even the acquisition of another language.

Translanguaging can take different shapes (García & Wei, 2014). It can consist in translation and interpretation with intercultural sensitivity and linguistic awareness, or be driven by a desire to promote improvement in a second language (García, 2009). Originally translanguaging referred to a pedagogy that encouraged the use of two languages (Welsh and English) so as to promote the acquisition of Welsh (Lewis, Jones, & Baker, 2012). Another aspect of the productive use of translanguaging is the development of receptive bilingualism, where each person speaks his or her language. Such practices may enable employees with limited educational background at lower hierarchical levels to be included in exchanges with HQ.

## Notes

1. The fundamental dynamics of this process extend beyond the use of any specific language; the key point is the use of multiple linguistic resources
2. Respondent uses Anglicism "postaus" in Finnish.

## References

Barner-Rasmussen, W., & Aarnio, C. (2011). Shifting the faultlines of language: A quantitative functional-level exploration of language use in MNC subsidiaries. *Journal of World Business*, 46(3), 288–295.

Barner-Rasmussen, W., Ehrnrooth, M., Koveshnikov, A., & Mäkelä, K. (2014). Cultural and language skills as resources for boundary spanning within the MNC. *Journal of International Business Studies*, 45(7), 886–905.

Boussebaa, M., Sinha, S., & Gabriel, Y. (2014). Englishization in offshore call centers: A postcolonial perspective. *Journal of International Business Studies*, 45(9), 1152–1169.

Brannen, M. Y. (2004). When Mickey loses face: Recontextualization, semantic fit, and the semiotics of foreignness. *Academy of Management Review*, 29(4), 593–616.

Brannen, M.-Y., Piekkari, R., & Tietze, S. (2014). The multifaceted role of language in international business: Unpacking the forms, functions and features of a critical challenge to MNC theory and performance. *Journal of International Business Studies, 45*(5), 495–507.

Canagarajah, S. (2016). Shuttling between scales in the workplace: Reexamining policies and pedagogies for migrant professionals. *Linguistics and Education, 34,* 47–57.

Davoine, E., Schroeter, O. C., & Stern, J. (2014). Cultures régionales des filiales dans l'entreprise multinationale et capacités d'influence liées à la langue: Une étude de cas. *Management International, 18,* 165–177.

Dörrenbächer, P., & Schulz, C. (2008). The organization of the production process: The case of Smartville. In P. Pellenbarg & E. Wever (Eds.), *International business geography: Case studies of corporate firms* (pp. 83–96). London: Routledge.

Fill, A., & Mühlhäusler, P. (Eds.). (2006). *Ecolinguistics reader: Language, ecology and environment.* London: Continuum.

Gaibrois, C. (2018). "It crosses all the boundaries": Hybrid language use as empowering resource. *European Journal of International Management, 12*(1–2), 82–110.

García, O. (2009). *Bilingual education in the 21st Century: A global perspective.* Oxford: Wiley-Blackwell.

García, O., & Wei, L. (2014). *Translanguaging: Language, bilingualism and education.* Basingstoke: Palgrave Macmillan.

Harzing, A.-W., Köster, K., & Magner, U. (2011). Babel in business: The language barrier and its solutions in the HQ-subsidiary relationship. *Journal of World Business, 46*(3), 279–287.

Haugen, E. (1972). *The ecology of language.* Stanford: Stanford University Press.

Heller, M. (1988). *Codeswitching: Anthropological and sociolinguistic perspectives.* Berlin: Mouton de Gruyter.

Hemker, G. (2014). Sprachbewusstsein und regionale Identität in Ost-Lothringen. In S. Ehrhart (Ed.), *Europäische Mehrsprachigkeit in Bewegung: Treffpunkt Luxembourg, Des plurilinguismes en dialogue: Rencontres luxembourgeoises* (pp.35–55). Bern: Peter Lang.

Hofstede, G., Hofstede, G. J., & Minkov, M. (2005). *Cultures and organizations: Software of the mind.* New York: McGraw-Hill.

Janssens, M., & Steyaert, C. (2014). Re-considering language within a cosmopolitan understanding: Toward a multilingual franca approach in International Business Studies. *Journal of International Business Studies, 45*(5), 623–639.

Jarzabkowski, P. (2008). Shaping strategy as a structuration process. *Academy of Management Journal, 51*(4), 621–650.

Jaussaud, J., & Mayrhofer, U. (2014). Les tensions global-local: l'organisation et la coordination des activités internationales. *Management International, 18*(1), 18–25.

Karhunen, P., Kankaaranta, K., Louhiala-Salminen, L., & Piekkari, R. (2018). Let's talk about language: A review of language sensitive research in international management. *Journal of Management Studies, 55*(6), 980–1013.

Kramsch, C., & Whiteside, A. (2008). Language ecology in multilingual settings: Towards a theory of symbolic competence. *Applied Linguistics, 29*(4), 645–671.

Lewis, G., Jones, B., & Baker, C. (2012). Translanguaging: Origins and development from school to street and beyond. *Educational Research and Evaluation, 29*(7), 641–654.

Lincoln, Y. S., & Guba, E. G. (1985). *Naturalistic inquiry*. London: Sage.

Loewenstein, J., Thompson, L., & Gentner, D. (2003). An examination of analogical learning in negotiation teams. *Academy of Management Learning and Education*, 2(2), 119–127.

Luo, Y., & Shenkar, O. (2006). The multinational corporation as a multilingual community: Language and organization in a global context. *Journal of International Business Studies*, 37(3), 321–339.

Macfarlane, A. (2004). To contrast and compare. In V. K. Srivastava (Ed.), *Methodology and fieldwork* (pp. 94–111). New Delhi: Oxford University Press.

Marschan-Piekkari, R., Welch, D. E., & Welch, L. S. (1999). In the shadow: The impact of language on structure, power and communication in the multinational. *International Business Review*, 8(4), 421–440.

Mayrhofer, U., & Very, P. (Eds.). (2013). *Le Management International à l'écoute du local*. Paris: Editions Gualino.

Mühlhäusler, P. (2003). *Language of environment—Environment of language: A course in ecolinguistics*. London: Battlebridge.

Piekkari, R., Vaara, E., Tienari, J., & Säntti, R. (2005). Integration or disintegration? Human resource implications of a common corporate language decision in a cross-border merger. *International Journal of Human Resource Management*, 16(3), 330–344.

Ricento, T. (Ed.). (2015). *Language policy and political economy: English in a global context*. Oxford: Oxford University Press.

Romaine, S. (1994). *Language in society: An introduction to sociolinguistics*. Oxford and New York: Oxford University Press.

Romani, L., Barmeyer, C., Primecz, H., & Pilhofer, K. (2018). Cross-cultural management studies: State of the field in the four research paradigms. *International Studies of Management and Organization*, 48(3), 247–263.

Statistics Finland. (2019). *Finnish population statistics as of Dec 31, 2018: Population according to language 1980–2018*. Retrieved December 2, 2019, from www.stat.fi/til/vaerak/2018/vaerak_2018_2019-03-29_tau_001_en.html

Strauss, A., & Corbin, J. (1998). *Basics of qualitative research: Techniques and procedures for developing grounded theory*. Thousand Oaks, CA: Sage.

Szkudlarek, B., Nardon, L., & Osland, J. (2017). Intercultural communication in international business research. *Journal of World Business*, special issue call for papers. Retrieved from July 11, 2017, from www.journals.elsevier.com/journal-of-world-business/call-for-papers

Tietze, S. (2008). *International management and language*. London: Routledge.

Vaara, E., Tienari, J., Piekkari, R., & Säntti, R. (2005). Language and the circuits of power in a merging multinational corporation. *Journal of Management Studies*, 42(3), 595–623.

Van Lier, L. (2006). *The ecology and semiotics of language learning: A sociocultural perspective* (Vol. 3). Amsterdam: Springer Science & Business Media.

Welch, C., & Piekkari, R. (2006). Crossing language boundaries: Qualitative interviewing in international business. *Management International Review*, 46(4), 417–437.

Welch, D., & Welch, L. (2018). Multilingual capacity: A challenge for the multinational enterprise. *Journal of Management*, 44(3), 1568–1593.

Wismann, H. (2012). *Penser entre les langues*. Paris: Albin Michel.

# 7 Towards a Framework of Individuals' Responses to Language Asymmetry

*Dominic Detzen and Lukas Löhlein*

Understanding the consequences of multilingualism is a fundamental issue in international business research. Prior literature extensively studied the implications of language on intra-organisational dynamics, such as power (Aichhorn & Puck, 2017; Gaibrois & Steyaert, 2017), knowledge transfer (Klitmøller & Lauring, 2013; Welch & Welch, 2008), performance (Hinds, Neeley, & Cramton, 2014), and exclusion (Klitmøller, Schneider, & Jonsen, 2015; Kulkarni, 2015). However, few studies have assessed how individuals actively *respond* to and navigate through multilingual contexts (e.g., Angouri & Piekkari, 2018; Hinds et al., 2014; Lønsmann, 2017; Neeley, 2013; Steyaert, Ostendorp, & Gaibrois, 2011). This chapter adds to this literature in two ways. First, we investigate the responses of individuals who are confronted with a continually *changing* linguistic context and thus need to *constantly* renegotiate their responses to the language asymmetry experienced. In this way, we respond to recent calls to view "languages in flux, [. . .] which prioritises fluid and hybrid language practices (language-in-use) rather than national languages or varieties" (Angouri & Piekkari, 2018, p. 18). Second, our analysis suggests that individuals' responses to language asymmetries are not only determined by their language skills, but also by what we call language *reflexivity*. That is, whereas prior literature has argued that language asymmetries result in status loss (Neeley, 2013) or serve as a lightning rod in teams (Hinds et al., 2014), we demonstrate that *reflexive* individuals are aware of their situatedness in a particular language context and are able to (at least partially) overcome constraints resulting from language asymmetries.

Based on interviews in multinational accounting firms, we find that these two dimensions—skill and reflexivity—result in four distinct strategic responses to language asymmetries: Avoidance, Confrontation, Aspiration, and Activation. We argue that the strategies produce a sense of comfort or stress in the individuals, which is exacerbated by the temporary character of their work assignments and the resulting constant (re)adjustment of their discursive strategy. Whereas our identified responses likely represent antecedents for individual and collective counter-reactions, we focus on individuals' responses to language asymmetry in isolation from team members' reactions. In this way, we hope that our model sets the ground for further investigations into the circuit of actions and reactions in multilingual settings.

## Literature Review: Agency in Multilingual Settings

The lack of a shared native language and limited language proficiency trigger potent intra-organisational asymmetries. Where multiple languages co-exist, language not only has the capacity to create a linguistic "shadow structure" (Marschan-Piekkari, Welch, & Welch, 1999), which affects communication, trust, and performance (Kassis-Henderson, 2005; Lauring & Klitmøller, 2015; Neeley, 2013; Tenzer, Pudelko, & Harzing, 2014), it also becomes an instrument of power and status (Aichhorn & Puck, 2017; Gaibrois & Steyaert, 2017; Lønsmann, 2014; Hinds et al., 2014), as well as of resistance (Gaibrois, 2015; Logemann & Piekkari, 2015) and identity (Detzen & Loehlein, 2018; Harzing & Feely, 2008; Hinds et al., 2014). Whereas prior research has largely focused on the implications of language asymmetries, insights about individual's responses to language asymmetry remain scarce (e.g., Angouri & Piekkari, 2018; Hinds et al., 2014; Lønsmann, 2017; Neeley, 2013; Steyaert et al., 2011).

A substantial part of this exploration of actors' responses to language asymmetries is connected to the rise and spread of English as a corporate lingua franca. Dor (2004), for instance, postulated the possibility for individuals to actively resist processes of "Englishization" by using and maintaining local languages. Steyaert et al. (2011, p. 277) confirmed that "language users are not necessarily pawns directed by a blunt kind of linguistic dominance", but that communication involves dynamic negotiations between employees. Language choice is thus a social and context-dependent phenomenon (Fredriksson, Barner-Rasmussen, & Piekkari, 2006), which is "hard to control or regulate by central language policies and management approaches" (Bellak, 2014, p. 302). Individuals may thus actively resist the use of corporate English, such as by insisting on the use of another language or by critically remarking on others' use of English (Gaibrois, 2015).

By following prior research that has started to explore the motives and ways organisational actors react to linguistic diversity (e.g., Angouri & Piekkari, 2018; Bordia & Bordia, 2014; Hinds et al., 2014; Kassis-Henderson, 2005; Lønsmann, 2017; Neeley, 2013), we argue that two key factors determine individuals' responses to language asymmetries in multinational teams: language skills and language reflexivity.

*Language skill* refers to an individual's proficiency with language. Individuals with high language skills are proficient in "the rules of phonology, syntax, and semantics, and are capable of clear expression"

(Kassis-Henderson, 2005, p. 69), whereas low such skills trigger misunderstandings due to "'the unfamiliar vocabulary', 'the speed of speech', 'the strong accent', or 'too many mistakes'" (Kassis-Henderson, 2005, p. 70). Yet, as language is primarily targeted at enabling communication, language skill also and foremost relates to an individual's ability to communicate in another language. Bordia and Bordia (2014), for instance, argue that individuals with foreign language competencies are more willing to accept a common corporate language.

*Language reflexivity* entails individuals' awareness of their position in multilingual contexts, and to what extent they take for granted existing social arrangements (Ripamonti, Galuppo, Gorli, Scaratti, & Cunliffe, 2016; Suddaby, Viale, & Gendron, 2016). Reflexive individuals thus acknowledge that their actions and behaviour have an impact on social and organisational settings, and they may actively try to shape interactions to overcome potential constraints. Indeed, research suggests that actors who possess *language reflexivity* respond actively to linguistic structures in corporate contexts. Principally, employees tend to operate across language barriers by using customised communication norms or ad hoc strategies, thereby deviating from formal company policies (Kassis-Henderson, 2005; Fredriksson et al., 2006). Lønsmann (2017) suggests that employees particularly resist language policies when these are perceived as not helpful to their work, but are rather interpreted as instruments for long-term strategies. In turn, team members' responses to language asymmetries in polarised teams may reinforce exclusion and the potential negativity of subgrouping, but also entail strategies that keep power dynamics alive (Hinds et al., 2014). Importantly, it seems to be the self-assessed and perceived, rather than objective, level of fluency that has a strong impact on the status of employees after the adoption of English (Neeley, 2013). These findings imply that responding to language asymmetries requires a contextual and dynamic competence for individuals to become "boundary crossers" (Kassis-Henderson, Cohen, & McCulloch, 2018). Hence, language reflexivity corresponds to individuals' capacity to respond actively to linguistic situations, and we argue that it is the interplay of both language skill and language reflexivity that results in four distinct discursive strategies.

## Methods

Our study draws on the same empirical material as Detzen and Loehlein (2018) and is informed by semi-structured interviews with 25 professionals, all of them having relevant work experience at the Luxembourg branches of the Big Four accounting firms (Deloitte, EY, KPMG, PwC; see Appendix). The Grand Duchy of Luxembourg is a small European country, where the country's three official languages—Luxembourgish,

French, and German—mix with other expatriate languages and the corporate language of English. Across all of the firms we studied, about a third of the staff are French, the Germans and Belgians constitute a fifth each, and almost a tenth are Luxembourgers. The remainder come from other countries, primarily in Europe.

As is the nature of auditing, individuals work in temporary teams of varying sizes, with the objective of auditing a client's financial statements. In prior work, we have established that in Luxembourg the Big Four firms segment their branch offices into language teams based on the client's language (Detzen & Loehlein, 2018). These teams primarily consist of individuals who are fluent in the client's language but also include members from other language groups, thereby introducing asymmetries, which constantly change as teams are staffed only for a particular audit engagement. As such, individuals need to renegotiate their responses due to the temporary nature of audit teams, and they need to respond to different languages, as they may be assigned consecutively to a French-speaking team and then to a German-speaking team. We understand language asymmetries as constituted in situations where an individual works in a team that uses a language other than the individual's primary language. At the extreme, this may be a language that the individual does not speak at all, but it may also be one that is not the individual's most comfortable language. These individuals need to respond to this situation so as to contribute to the team effort, but also to avoid becoming an outsider. Importantly, our interviewees are required to actively collaborate with one another in the respective audit team, which differs from prior research (e.g., Neeley, 2013), where interactions are often limited to meetings or electronic or informal communications.

To account for the multilingual nature of the firms, interviewees were included from 12 different countries. Interviews, lasting on average 40 minutes, were carried out in 2016 and 2017. One of the co-authors conducted all the interviews, either in German or English. During the interviews, attempts were made to shed light on how individuals experience their multilingual environments, and how they respond to their firm's formal language policies and informal language practices. Interview excerpts in German were translated into English and are marked in the following with "TR". Both authors listened to the audio files separately and read the transcripts individually, before discussing them jointly. Insights from the interviews were reflected on and discussed throughout the data-gathering process, both to enrich further interviews and to develop theoretical viewpoints. Once the four strategies of how individuals deal with language asymmetries emerged, we went through all transcripts again to produce the theoretical and empirical exposition in the following.

## Findings: Individuals' Responses to Language Asymmetries

Our analysis revealed four distinct strategies of how individuals respond to language asymmetries in multilingual teams: Avoidance, Confrontation, Adaptation, and Activation. These are determined by an individual's language skill and reflexivity (see Figure 7.1). The four strategies produce a sense of comfort or stress in the professionals (Tenzer & Pudelko, 2015), which is exacerbated by the temporary character of audit assignments and the resulting constant renegotiation of their discursive strategy.

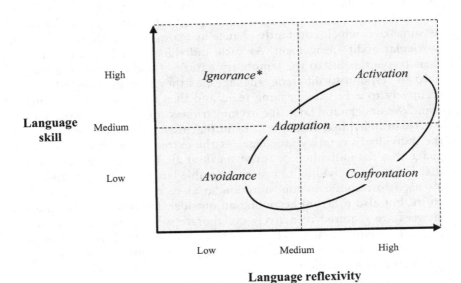

*Figure 7.1* Discursive strategies to respond to language asymmetries

Note: * Individuals with high language skills and low language reflexivity are not exposed to a language asymmetry that they need to react to. As these individuals seemingly *ignore* the effects of language, we exclude this "strategy" in our analysis.

### Avoidance

Individuals that follow an *avoidance strategy* have low language skills and low language reflexivity. Low levels in both dimensions are crucial factors, particularly when professionals are assigned to audit teams randomly. Such allocation to what is perceived as a "wrong" team (e.g., an auditor being assigned to a French team without speaking French) can produce anxiety:

> That is hard. I felt a lot of pressure at the time. But the people in the team were nice as well. They also explained things to me in English.

But, still, for example, when the senior manager came, we all had a question about the testing. Actually, I was doing the testing, [and] I raised the question to the senior and he didn't know how to do it as well. So, when the senior manager passed by, he asked the question. The senior manager answered the question very well, but in French. And I didn't understand all of that, so only after the senior manager left, the senior explained it to me [. . .] in English.

(I#11, Intern, Chinese)

The intern was thus excluded from a conversation due to language asymmetry. Accepting this differential as a barrier meant that she "withdrew" from the discourse (Neeley, 2013) and received an explanation only after the senior manager left, through a "language mediator" (Marschan-Piekkari et al., 1999). It thus implies a sense of passivity, as the interviewee avoids taking any measures to bridge the language gap, which is perceived as a constraint rather than something that can be overcome. The interviewee argued that she had previously been in a team where she "managed totally fine with English", so she now "wasn't really used to this" situation, which may in part explain her passive response.

Interviewees widely considered it "normal" or "more efficient" that team members were at liberty to converse in their "comfortable language", thus accepting to be excluded from the team:

They tend to [have] some conversations by themselves, using French. So, they are not aware that somebody else is also curious about what they are laughing at, talking about [. . .] It's not quite easy, I mean, they would keep talking until, I don't know, at one point, they explain and then they switch back to French.

(I#18, Junior, Chinese)

Because if they want to talk to me about work, about the task I was performing they would talk to me in English. But otherwise, if they talk about something else, a lot of times, not very specifically linked to my job, they would speak in French. And for me, I wouldn't realise that it may be helpful for my job, and that's the problem.

(I#19, Junior, Chinese)

Interviewees were well aware of the constraints that their team's language structure imposed on them. Yet, rather than responding actively to this asymmetry, they placed the onus on others to mitigate the language gap, and thus their negative emotions (Tenzer & Pudelko, 2015).

To sum up, individuals with low language skills and reflexivity find themselves unable to fully access the organisational experience and, as a result, run the risk of remaining within their linguistic boundaries. Neeley (2013, p. 486) suggested that "low-fluency speakers also had low anxiety" about their language use, likely because they were still able to do their work. In our case though, interviewees display a strong sense of discomfort, as they strongly rely on team interactions for their work. This implies that they are effectively excluded from the team, as they wait for language mediators or empathetic colleagues to bridge the gap. The exclusion resulting from the *avoidance strategy* may have implications for individuals' status (Neeley, 2013), but also others' assessment of their competence (Śliwa & Johansson, 2014). It not only means that these auditors are unable to fully access the corporate experience, it also prevents them from participating in interactions that are vital to advance in organisational contexts.

## Confrontation

Individuals who follow a *confrontation strategy* have low language skills but exhibit a medium level of language reflexivity. They confront fellow team members about feeling excluded due to the language asymmetry and their inability to follow conversations and access information. Such confrontation may be subtle and polite, but also direct, especially when individuals experience frustration as a result of being excluded:

> There are cases, where, let's say, I am the only non-French speaker and the teacher [in a seminar] is also French. There is the tendency within groups, but this is natural that, you know, people ask questions in French and maybe the answer is also in French. But, I mean, then you just need to point out: "Listen, here, please, this is an English class!"
>
> (I#2c, Junior, Italian)

> And I believe that's how it is, when there are many French speakers together. They switch automatically back into their language. I mean, I am hardly ever at a loss for words. I am someone who says: "Hey, guys, can we get back to English again?" [. . .] But sometimes it *is* somewhat difficult. It is [difficult].
>
> (I#8, Senior, German, TR)

Recognising the impact and consequences of language asymmetry, but also acting upon them, requires some level of language reflexivity. The preceding interviewee argued that her lack of French-language skills affected her post-engagement evaluation, which she openly discussed:

> For example, I worked as a junior in a team [in which] they always spoke French. And I said: "I don't understand that." And when they talked to me, of course, they switched to English or German, but there are so many [situations], when you sit together in a room at

the client's and you're not able to follow each and every aspect, that still [would be relevant], and afterwards, I didn't get good feedback on [the engagement], because they said: "Hey, you were not motivated." [And I said:] "Well, I sat there the whole day and didn't understand a thing."

(I#8, Senior, German, TR)

In the *confrontation strategy*, individuals are thus partly able to bridge the language asymmetry, but they need to repeatedly remind fellow team members to remain inclusive. The effectiveness of this strategy may also be questioned, as the individual quoted previously was still aware of her outsider role, which required efforts from others to alleviate, yet still negatively affected her performance evaluation.

That one meets sympathetic others may be an optimal outcome of the *confrontation strategy*, but may be unattainable because mitigating a language asymmetry requires effort, as interviewees suggest. This aspect may play a particular role in audit teams, who often work under time pressure. Such time constraints may make team members reluctant to help others out or make them pursue the most efficient way of communication, which often is in their native language. Interviewees thus become painfully aware of the excluding role of language:

I just always asked: "Hold on, I don't understand. Could you repeat this?" Sometimes even emails came in French. And I just wrote: "Could you please write in English? I don't understand this." I think that slows down everything a bit. You could work quicker and more efficiently if the communication was a bit quicker.

(I#9, Intern, German, TR)

Interviewees argued that such situations led to "frustration" (I#16) or "a mess" and "a big problem" (I#19). *Confrontation* may thus not fully alleviate an individual's sense of discomfort, in that teamwork may still be experienced as distressing. Notably, in all excerpts, interviewees referred to what they "always" do in "such cases", suggesting that individuals may develop over time the reflexivity required for *confrontation*. That is, in the *avoidance* case, interviewees admitted to experiencing a new situation, whereas individuals here refer to some kind of routine response that they draw on. Importantly, this response also needs to be invoked repeatedly, both to remind team members to remain inclusive and due to changing team memberships. Individuals thus need to start all over again in a new team, which may be the main source of our interviewees' frustration.

We note that the strategy is somewhat related to Neeley's (2013, p. 489) "tempering", where individuals interrupt interactions to diminish the "rhetorical domination" of their colleagues. However, our interviewees were not in the position to interrupt their team members, but rather strove to re-gain access to conversations, so as to contribute to the team effort. The *confrontation strategy* may thus enable individuals to re-access organisational knowledge flows, because they can make themselves heard and actively reach out for help. This may go some way in terms of participating in the team but will still produce discomfort in the individuals.

### Adaptation

Individuals who follow an *adaptation strategy* have medium language skills and medium language reflexivity. Under this strategy, auditors exert efforts to understand communications, either by not immediately admitting that they are not fully versed in the team language or by actively trying to overcome this issue by other means:

> Even someone like me, who never had French [in school], will at one point get the basics, so that you say: "OK, if an email comes in, I understand in principle what they want from me."
>
> (I#8, Senior, German, TR)

Individuals applying this strategy have some level of foreign-language skill that lets them work around certain situations or that allows them some form of communication. They use their possibly limited language skills to adapt to their surrounding language structures. They may, for example, try their "best to use as much French as they can", when assigned to a French team (I#11, Intern, Chinese), leading to a moment of successful *adaptation*:

> I am learning French now. [Laughs] At the beginning, I told my colleagues: "OK, I don't speak French." And they thought I would not understand. But when they are talking about something, sometimes I do understand and once it was funny, so I laughed [and they responded]: "Oh, no, you understand." So, they were, like, quite surprised. So, I kept on trying to understand as much as I can.
>
> (I#11, Intern, Chinese)

Besides the ability to comprehend conversations, the excerpt further suggests that individuals become aware of the benefits of accessing the social reality of their teams. As a result, individuals strive to bridge language gaps, such as by making sense of information in its context, which might be enabled by the specificity of audit-related terminology. A Chinese junior explains how she worked on an audit engagement that was conducted in a language that she does not speak fluently:

> Even though I don't speak much German, I still manage to audit a portfolio in German, I don't know why. Because in audit we only

usually look at those very simple and specific things, like "*Vertrag*" [contract], who is "*Käufer*" [buyer], "*Datum*" [date], "*Miete*" [rent], and what is the "*Gebäude*" [building] [. . .] When will [the contract] start, begin, end? [. . .] But it's good enough. It's enough to audit.

(I#15, Junior, Chinese)

In that respect, individuals "make use of any available linguistic resources that enable and ease mutual communication" (Karhunen, Kankaanranta, Louhiala-Salminen, & Piekkari, 2018, p. 999). A particularly important resource was online translation tools, which were emphasised in most of our interviews, such as when providing information to a client who speaks another language:

In those cases, I use Google Translate to translate [text]. And I only tell the manager who is on the engagement and who speaks French: "Can you at least check whether grammar, punctuation, and things like that are fine?"

(I#8, Senior, German, TR)

By following the credo of "we will make it work" (I#12, Senior manager, Filipino), individuals exhibit agency, which can be enhanced by communicating in writing. Individuals may then respond at their own chosen speed, reflect on their communication, and use dictionaries for help. Consequently, individuals display a linguistic competence they would not have achieved in verbal interactions. Although they doubtlessly feel empowered, such an approach "does not overcome language barriers, but circumvents them by partitioning translation tasks into what is perceived as accessible portions" (Detzen & Loehlein, 2018, p. 2041). It also shows an unproblematised understanding of language and communication, such as when a Chinese junior (I#15) considers herself "the only, kind of, German-speaking junior" in a particular team.

Yet, by *adapting*, individuals can participate in their team's conversations. Successful cases of this strategy show that the discomfort of people is reduced, suggesting that understanding one's team language is a "nice bonus" (I#22, Junior, Russian). However, this strategy does not fully eliminate the feeling of awkwardness that results from being constantly reminded that one is not fluent in the team language. For example, when a Luxembourger junior (I#5) joked in German that his employer did not know how good his German was, he used a grammatically awkward expression. All this suggests that the *adaptation strategy* is much about one's willingness to communicate in another language (I#8, Senior, German), which is stimulated by one's creativity to resort to other communicative means (Kassis-Henderson, 2005). By mitigating the language asymmetry, individuals enable team communication and positively affect their level of comfort in the team. As they may also enhance their language skills in the process, there may not be a distinct boundary to our next strategy, where individuals deploy their language skills more effectively.

## Activation

Individuals who follow an *activation* strategy display high language skills and high language reflexivity. Prior literature (Marschan-Piekkari et al., 1999; Śliwa & Johansson, 2014) shows that these individuals are capable to adapt strategically to distinct linguistic settings and actively mobilise their skills. This becomes most apparent when considering the language versatility of Luxembourger staff members, who tend to speak all four main languages and so have a distinct as well as visible advantage in the firms:

> You have these internal profiles, where it is shown what you special-ise in, which other professional qualifications you have, which lan-guages you speak. And, as a Luxembourger, you immediately have the four languages flagged up.
>
> (I#5, Junior, Luxembourger, TR)

Given that they are able to mobilise a range of language resources, "people say Luxembourgers are above everyone" (I#10, Senior, US). Combined with their familiarity with the local context, culture, and cus-toms, this language versatility enables them to interact with local clients and state authorities, and, on a senior level, to obtain and manage local audit engagements. For example, a Luxembourger interviewee (I#20, Junior) recognises from a client's welcoming or accent which language they prefer and adapts accordingly. Likewise:

> If [clients] know that you're a Luxembourger, they continue in French. That's their native language to which I can adapt—because I also speak French fluently.
>
> (I#6, Intern, Luxembourger, TR)

Inside the organisations, these individuals are able to move freely across different language teams, and they communicate freely with the main language groups. Local staff members are thus seen as "very smart people" who are needed in this market (I#17, Junior, Greek), highlighting that language skills are an indicator of competence (Śliwa & Johansson, 2014):

> If people can speak German, French, and, of course, English at the same time, it's good, really great for them. And it would be easier for them to adapt and to connect with people. [It] would really help.

[. . .] And I think it's necessary as well for the social environment because people can feel like robots if you only speak English.

(I#1, Intern, Turkish)

Notably, the interviewee describes an ideal that he considers worth striving for but that currently does not seem within reach. His status as an expatriate may enhance this impression where he recognises the benefits of language adaptability, without himself being able to access them. This suggests that *activation* is not commonly achieved. Yet, as interviewees see the opportunities that this strategy yields, they perceive language skills as a proxy for other, audit-related skills.

In summary, high language skills—paired with high reflexivity—enable free communication in any local audit team, allowing the individual to participate in both job-related discussions and social interactions. Language thus becomes a resource that is actively and creatively used to enhance one's position in the team, but that also facilitates unrestricted access to the corporate experience (Marschan-Piekkari et al., 1999; Śliwa & Johansson, 2014). The sense of comfort that is produced by the *activation strategy* suggests that individuals understand the far-reaching career prospects that communication allows them, and they invoke both language skills and language reflexivity strategically to realise these opportunities.

## Discussion and Conclusion

In this chapter, we have argued that it is the interplay of individuals' language skills and reflexivity that determines their responses to language asymmetries in multilingual organisations. Whereas our findings in the preceding present the four responses as distinct strategies, we note that our framework is not static. The context of multinational accounting firms implies that individuals' assignments to audit engagements are temporary, such that their responses need to be renegotiated as soon as they join another team. In this way, we suggest that individuals deploy distinct strategic positions, both across work assignments and time. As they repeatedly face language asymmetries of different natures, they likely become somewhat apt to deal with such situations and may thus acquire some level of reflexivity over time.

Although studying this dynamic character of the responses requires a longitudinal analysis, we can offer some thoughts based on our interview material. Primarily, it seems that individuals with low language skills and reflexivity tend to be passive actors who face exclusion from their teams due to their *avoidance strategy*. Although they are aware of their inferior position, they are as yet unable to exert the reflexivity necessary to regain access to the team. It seems likely to us though that some level of reflexivity can be acquired, specifically when and as individuals realise that they can lower their anxiety and discomfort by following a *confrontation strategy*. While not being explicit about this, some interviewees in that strategy seemed uncertain about how subtly or directly to *confront* their colleagues, suggesting that they had yet to find out how to adequately deploy their discursive strategy. This implies that reflexivity can indeed be learned or developed, at least to some extent, and presumably as individuals gain experience in an organisation. We further argue that individuals with medium levels of language skills and reflexivity may use the *adaptation strategy* to develop more adequate responses and, over time, they may *activate* increasing language skills. That is, by exerting reflexivity, they practice their language skills and thus become more apt to deal with language asymmetries. We thus posit that the boundaries between *avoidance* and *confrontation* and, respectively, *adaptation* and *activation* are malleable, as individuals are likely to develop some level of reflexivity over time. In turn, the boundaries between these sets of responses seem more rigid and require efforts from the individual to develop language skills.

As further evidence of individuals' evolving responses to language asymmetries, we can point to the distinct organisational experience that individuals are exposed to in the course of their careers. We particularly noted that junior auditors experienced language issues on the firms' work floors more immediately and more strongly. Senior staff, in turn, rather discussed the firms' language policies and management of language diversity. Whereas some insisted that language was not a significant issue at the firms, others demonstrated more awareness of the role of language, both when staffing audit teams and in the daily work of their teams. Yet these interviewees did not display much anxiety due to language asymmetries, which may indicate that these become less salient as individuals progress through the ranks. As such, they may have developed the reflexivity necessary to deal with language asymmetries, possibly also because, being hierarchically superior, they may impose their communicative preferences on others. Alternatively, they may be fluent in the team language and can thus activate their skills more readily, both in team conversations and in discussions with the client.

We have also suggested that our strategies are intertwined with the sense of comfort they trigger in individuals, and how the latter experience the team environment and organisational context. The strategies thus seem to have consequences for individuals' organisational and career trajectories. All interviewees emphasised communication skills, also because their post-engagement feedback evaluates their communication with the client, team members, and superiors. Interviewees hence agreed that "you need to communicate. If you don't, you will not survive" (I#13, Junior, French). Language thus enables teamwork and demonstrates commitment

(Detzen & Loehlein, 2018), as it helps auditors to listen in and learn, and be "a good team player" who is able to "help others out" (I#9, Intern, German, TR). In this way, communication becomes a proxy for showing interest, intellectual curiosity, and commitment. Making oneself heard, interacting with superiors, and building an organisational network are essential factors of one's "communicative competence" that ensures an individual's corporate success. Whereas interviewees suggested language skills as the one defining characteristic of an "ideal candidate" for the Big Four in Luxembourg, it is rather this communicative ability that needs to be developed (Karhunen et al., 2018). As team members increase their competence to deal with language asymmetry, they develop reflexivity and are enabled to move from one type of response to the next. As communicative ability complements linguistic competence, it affects individuals' responses to language asymmetries and they may effectively mobilise colleagues or online tools as language resources. Future research could investigate in more depth the repertoire of communicative resources, such as cultural, semiotic, or visual signals, which individuals draw on as part of their communicative competence.

In our study, we have limited ourselves to an investigation of individuals' reaction to language asymmetries, thus neglecting important self-other relations that take place in collaborative teams. That is, the individual's response will necessarily trigger a reaction from fellow team members, both on the discursive level and in the actual work. Presumably, the strategies affect subsequent collaboration between team members, which in turn likely has an impact on the team's work outcome. Likewise, as one of our interviewees alluded to, individuals' post-engagement feedback could be affected by language asymmetries, and the subsequent response of the individual and team. It is a limitation of our study that we did not explore in more depth others' reactions, but we hope to have made a first step in studying individuals' responses to language asymmetries. Future research is invited to build on our work and connect (responses to) language asymmetries to work outcomes.

Finally, we maintain that the multilingual context of the Big Four firms in Luxembourg offers a promising setting for language-sensitive research, as it is characterised by a mesh of distinct languages, which continuously change, overlap, and complement each other. The changing team structures and dynamics lend themselves to further discourse-based studies, but also to examine how individuals' corporate impressions are affected by the blend of their knowledge, skillset, and reflexivity, which shape their responses to the multilingual experience. Whereas our interviewees have acknowledged that language skills enhance their career opportunities, it remains for future research to examine the interplay between language and other work-related skills to further our understanding of the role of language in multilingual professional service firms.

# Appendix

Table 7A.1 List of interviewees

| # | Gender | Nationality | Position | Experience* |
|---|--------|-------------|----------|-------------|
| 1. | Male | Turkish | Intern | 1 month (5 years) |
| 2a. | Male | German | Senior Manager | 7 years |
| 2b. | Male | Luxembourger | Senior | 4 years |
| 2c. | Male | Italian | Junior | 2.5 years |
| 3. | Male | Lebanese | Manager | 6 months (9 years) |
| 4. | Male | Luxembourger/ French/Italian | Former Director | 12 years (2.5 years) |
| 5. | Male | Luxembourger | Junior | 9 months |
| 6. | Male | Luxembourger | Intern | 3 months |
| 7. | Male | French | Manager | 8 years |
| 8. | Female | German | Senior | 3 years |
| 9. | Female | German | Intern | 3 months |
| 10. | Female | US | Senior | 1 year (2 years) |
| 11. | Female | Chinese | Intern | 6 months |
| 12. | Female | Philippine | Senior Manager | 8 years (4 years) |
| 13. | Male | French | Junior | 4 months |
| 14. | Male | French | Senior | 10 months |
| 15. | Female | Chinese | Junior | 4 months |
| 16. | Male | Russian | Junior | 3 months (1 year) |
| 17. | Male | Greek | Junior | 1 year |
| 18. | Female | Chinese | Junior | 5 months |
| 19. | Female | Chinese | Junior | 3 months |
| 20. | Male | Luxembourger | Junior | 3 months |
| 21. | Male | Greek | Junior | 6 months |
| 22. | Female | Russian | Junior | 1.5 years |
| 23. | Male | Cameroonian | Intern | 3 months |

* Experience in Big Four in Luxembourg (outside of Luxembourg)
Note: Interview #2 was administered as group interview; positions were homogenized across firms.

# References

Aichhorn, N., & Puck, J. (2017). "I just don't feel comfortable speaking English": Foreign language anxiety as a catalyst for spoken-language barriers in MNCs. *International Business Review*, 26(4), 749–763.

Angouri, A., & Piekkari, R. (2018). Organising multilingually: Setting an agenda for studying language at work. *European Journal of International Management, 12*(1–2), 8–27.

Bellak, N. (2014). *Can language be managed in international business? Insights into language choice from a case study of Danish and Austrian multinational corporations (MNCs)* (PhD thesis). Copenhagen Business School, Denmark.

Bordia, S., & Bordia, P. (2014). Employees' willingness to adopt a foreign functional language in multi-lingual organizations: The role of linguistic identity. *Journal of International Business Studies, 46*(4), 415–428.

Detzen, D., & Loehlein, L. (2018). Language at work in the Big Four: Global aspirations and local segmentation. *Accounting, Auditing & Accountability Journal, 31*(7), 2031–2054.

Dor, D. (2004). From Englishization to imposed multilingualism: Globalization, the internet, and the political economy of the linguistic code. *Public Culture, 16*(1), 97–118.

Fredriksson, R., Barner-Rasmussen, W., & Piekkari, R. (2006). The multinational corporation as a multilingual organization: The notion of a common corporate language. *Corporate Communications: An International Journal, 11*(4), 406–423.

Gaibrois, C. (2015). *Power at work: The discursive construction of power relations in multilingual organizations* (PhD thesis). Universität St. Gallen, Switzerland.

Gaibrois, C., & Steyaert, C. (2017). Beyond possession and competition: Investigation cooperative aspects of power in multilingual organizations. *International Journal of Cross-Cultural Management, 17*(1), 69–84.

Harzing, A. W., & Feely, A. J. (2008). The language barrier and its implications for HQ—Subsidiary relationships. *Cross Cultural Management: An International Journal, 15*(1), 49–60.

Hinds, P. J., Neeley, T. B., & Cramton, C. D. (2014). Language as a lightning rod: Power contests, emotion regulation, and subgroup dynamics in global teams. *Journal of International Business Studies, 45*(5), 536–561.

Karhunen, P., Kankaanranta, A., Louhiala-Salminen, L., & Piekkari, R. (2018). Let's talk about language: A review of language-sensitive research in International Management. *Journal of Management Studies, 55*(6), 980–1013.

Kassis-Henderson, J. (2005). Language diversity in international management teams. *International Studies of Management & Organization, 35*(1), 66–82.

Kassis-Henderson, J., Cohen, L., & McCulloch, R. (2018). Boundary crossing and reflexivity: Navigating the complexity of cultural and linguistic identity. *Business and Professional Communication Quarterly, 81*(3), 304–327.

Klitmøller, A., & Lauring, J. (2013). When global virtual teams share knowledge: Media richness, cultural difference and language commonality. *Journal of World Business, 48*(3), 398–406.

Klitmøller, A., Schneider, S. C., & Jonsen, K. (2015). Speaking of global virtual teams: Language differences, social categorization and media choice. *Personnel Review, 44*(2), 270–285.

Kulkarni, M. (2015). Language-based diversity and faultlines in organizations. *Journal of Organizational Behavior, 36*(1), 128–146.

Lauring, J., & Klitmøller, A. (2015). Corporate language-based communication avoidance in MNCs: A multi-sited ethnography approach. *Journal of World Business, 50*(1), 46–55.

Logemann, M., & Piekkari, R. (2015). Localize or local lies? The power of language and translation in the multinational corporation. *Critical Perspectives on International Business, 11*(1), 30–53.

Lønsmann, D. (2014). Linguistic diversity in the international workplace: Language ideologies and processes of exclusion. *Multilingua, 33*(1–2), 89–116.

Lønsmann, D. (2017). Embrace it or resist it? Employees' reception of corporate language policies. *International Journal of Cross-Cultural Management, 17*(1), 101–123.

Marschan-Piekkari, R., Welch, D. E., & Welch, L. S. (1999). In the shadow: The impact of language on structure, power and communication in the multinational. *International Business Review, 8*(4), 421–440.

Neeley, T. B. (2013). Language matters: Status loss and achieved status distinctions in global organizations. *Organization Science, 24*(2), 476–497.

Ripamonti, S., Galuppo, L., Gorli, M., Scaratti, G., & Cunliffe, A. L. (2016). Pushing action research toward reflexive practice. *Journal of Management Inquiry, 25*(1), 55–68.

Śliwa, M., & Johansson, M. (2014). How non-native English-speaking staff are evaluated in linguistically diverse organizations: A sociolinguistic perspective. *Journal of International Business Studies, 45*(9), 1133–1151.

Steyaert, C., Ostendorp, A., & Gaibrois, C. (2011). Multilingual organizations as 'linguascapes': Negotiating the position of English through discursive practices. *Journal of World Business, 46*, 270–278.

Suddaby, R., Viale, T., & Gendron, Y. (2016). Reflexivity: The role of embedded social position and entrepreneurial social skill in processes of field level change. *Research in Organizational Behavior, 36*, 225–245.

Tenzer, H., & Pudelko, M. (2015). Leading across language barriers: Managing language-induced emotions in multinational teams. *The Leadership Quarterly, 26*(4), 606–625.

Tenzer, H., Pudelko, M., & Harzing, A.-W. (2014). The impact of language barriers on trust formation in multinational teams. *Journal of International Business Studies, 45*(5), 508–535.

Welch, D. E., & Welch, L. S. (2008). The importance of language in international knowledge transfer. *Management International Review, 48*(3), 339–360.

# 8 Learning in a Multilingual and Multicultural Business Setting

## Polish Expatriates' Stories of Critical Incidents in China

*Michał Wilczewski, Anne-Marie Søderberg and Arkadiusz Gut*

Despite new forms of global mobility, such as short-term assignments and virtual global teamwork, and despite the trend of appointing local managers in overseas subsidiaries (Ditchburn & Brook, 2015), many companies still find long-term expatriation an efficient strategy to benefit their overseas business operations (Brewster, Bonache, Cerdin, & Suutari, 2014). Expatriates, that is, highly qualified individuals who temporarily reside and work in another country (McNulty & Brewster, 2017), face cultural challenges occurring as a result of changing a living and working environment and, thus, leaving their "comfort zones" (Hemmasi & Downes, 2013). To better adjust in the new environment and maintain successful interactions with cultural others, they need to develop various cross-cultural competencies (Briscoe, Hall, & Frautschy DeMuth, 2006). Whereas the new knowledge and skills determine expatriates' career development, sharing new knowledge across national, cultural and language boundaries is also vital for multinational companies' (MNCs') success (Adler & Gundersen, 2008).

Prior studies (see a review by Manuti, Pastore, Scardigno, Giancaspro, & Morciano, 2015) show that expatriates' ability to learn how to navigate cross-cultural business contexts is a strategic asset for the company's competitiveness. Although the literature offers conceptual research into cross-cultural competencies (Caligiuri & Tarique, 2012), instruments to measure cultural intelligence (Ang et al., 2007; Thomas et al., 2008) and prescriptions for developing required skills and acquiring cultural knowledge through cross-cultural training programs (Caligiuri & Tarique, 2012), few context-sensitive empirical studies have explored how the capacity to function in multicultural and multilingual contexts is created with a focus on *what* expatriates learn from cross-cultural collaborations and *how* they learn from critical incidents. Furthermore, prior international business and international human resource management literatures have focused on the determinants of expatriate success/failure as seen from the organisational level, thereby neglecting the expatriates' individual perspectives (Guttormsen, Francesco, & Chapman, 2018). The issue of expatriates' actual performance and whether they consider the expatriation experiences as successful or challenging has largely been ignored.

This exploratory empirical study responds to the calls of more context-specific studies of cross-cultural collaborations in international business (Gertsen, Søderberg, & Zølner, 2012; Guttormsen et al., 2018). It expands on previous narrative research on collaborations between Western expatriate managers and Chinese professionals (e.g. Søderberg & Worm, 2011; Guttormsen et al., 2018). It aims to explore, at the individual level, what and how Polish expatriates, designated by a Western European MNC on an assignment to China between 2011 and 2015, have learned through their interactions with local staff in a highly demanding business setting—a multicultural and multilingual workplace involving 1,500 locals and over 150 international expatriates from Europe, the Americas and Asia.

We draw on narrative inquiry to deepen our understanding of how the expatriates learned from their interactions in a multilingual workplace. Our approach stands out by providing context-sensitive case studies of a group of under-researched Polish expatriates in China. We discuss their learning through the lens of a recently proposed "four-fold taxonomy of intercultural learning processes" (Morris, Savani, Mor, & Cho, 2014), which integrates and extends previous learning frameworks.

We pose three research questions: How did the expatriates retrospectively interpret their encounters with Chinese staff, and what did their stories reveal about their cultural learning? How did they apply the newly acquired knowledge to better function in the multilingual and multicultural business context? How did they position themselves in relation to the local staff as a result of intercultural collaborations?

First, we present the theoretical framework of our study. Second, we describe the research context and methodology. Next, we present narrative analyses of the empirical material. The study concludes with a discussion of the most important findings.

## Theoretical Framework

### Learning Culture

We take a social constructionist approach to culture and view it as a constantly negotiated phenomenon (Brannen & Salk, 2000) whereby knowledge is created and sustained through social interactions (Burr, 2006). Social interactions also underlie the process of learning, that is, creating and transforming knowledge to more effectively respond to new situations (cf. Armstrong & Li, 2017). Such knowledge may be explicit (easily articulated through language use such as assertions, generalisations or stereotypical opinions about cultural others) or implicit—acquired through direct experience and, hence, highly contextual and difficult to articulate (Lenartowicz, Johnson, & Konopaske, 2014).

Based on the preceding, we view expatriate cultural learning as both a process of creating explicit and implicit knowledge in an encounter between an expatriate and culturally different organisational members (Bird & Mendenhall, 2016) and transforming assumptions and perceptual skills as a result of such an encounter (Nardon, Steers, & Sanchez-Runde, 2011). The transformation is often triggered by a critical interaction that serves as an occasion for the expatriate's (self-)reflection and allows for better attributions of the cultural other's and expatriate's own behaviours, assumptions and emotions (Mezirow, 1991; Yan Lo-Philip et al., 2015). The social aspect of learning is emphasised in social learning theory (Bandura, 1986), which views learning as adjusting one's behaviours through reciprocal interactions with the environment (including other people). Experiential learning theory (Kolb, 1984) views learning as the process of transforming concrete experience through reflection that gives rise to new ideas/concepts that can be applied to the world around them to see what is happening.

### Integrative Approach to Expatriate Cultural Learning

Prior research has linked successful functioning in cultural situations and adjustment (i.e. how comfortable one feels in such situations) with cross-cultural competencies (e.g. Ang et al., 2007; Bücker, Poutsma, & Monster, 2016) and personality traits (e.g. Black, Mendenhall, & Oddou, 1991; Caligiuri, 2000; Tucker, Bonial, & Lahti, 2004). However, numerous studies of cross-cultural competencies, adjustment or personality focus on conceptualisations and are based on self-completed surveys collected from students (e.g. Brady-Amoon & Fuertes, 2011; Hanna, Crittenden, & Crittenden, 2013), which limits the possibility of gaining a deeper insight into expatriate learning in the host subsidiary as a result of social interaction and during a retrospective interpretation of events.

To overcome this limitation, we will apply M. W. Morris et al.'s (2014) "four-fold taxonomy of [expatriate] intercultural learning", which encompasses four learning processes: (1) *studying*—(explicit) internalizing explicit knowledge (e.g. learning from books or training programs); (2) *attributional reasoning*—(explicit) learning by attributing observed behaviours to the cultural other's motives, beliefs and intentions; (3) *social learning*—(implicit) learning by imitating others' behaviours; and (4) *conditioning*—(implicit) learning by looking for an optimal approach to intercultural interactions. The model recognises two learning processes that are particularly important for an expatriate, but which are downplayed either in the social or experiential learning approach. The first (explicit) process is studying which is vital for the expatriate's preparation for an international assignment. The second (implicit) process is social learning through imitation which, although present and central in social learning theory, is qualitatively different from learning by transforming the encountered experience in experiential learning theory, where observation is a reflective process. Accordingly, the four-fold taxonomy of intercultural learning shows off as an integrative approach that combines learning through experience and observation and, thus, recognises qualitatively different learning processes.

Using the model described earlier, we aim to situate and understand the learning processes that triggered changes in the Polish expatriates' behaviours and attitudes, as well as their perceptions of their own and others' identities.

## Methodology

### Material and Methods

This study is qualitatively oriented to enable the exploration of expatriates' intercultural experiences and learning (Spencer, 2011). We chose narrative inquiry as a research approach because it may trigger a reflexive understanding of experiences, which is pivotal in cultural learning. The empirical material encompasses stories collected in 2016 through narrative interviews with six Polish assigned expatriates who participated (for two and a half years on average) in building the MNC's subsidiary in Shenyang between 2011 and 2015. Interviewees were accessed using personal contacts.

For this study, we selected three stories to illustrate the learning processes entailed by the learning framework applied. These significant cases constitute timelines, plots and constructions of expatriates' own and cultural others' identities. We read through the material to identify any turning points and discoveries (Gertsen & Søderberg, 2011) that indicated an increase of expatriates' cultural (self-)awareness and the creation of cultural knowledge of local communication and organisational processes in the local context. Having assessed which stories best showed expatriates' learning over time, we arranged the material on a primary timeline (during expatriation in China) and secondary timeline (critical incidents, collaboration successes vs. failures as a result of applying newly acquired knowledge). We also collected additional information concerning the context of Polish interviewees' expatriation, their professional profiles and their preparation for the international assignment in China.

### The MNC

The MNC is an automotive component manufacturer based in Western Europe with a market share of about 20%. It has several dozen factories in over 15 countries on four continents. Many car manufacturers based in China equip their vehicles with this brand's products because of their high quality. Responding to the growing domestic demand for high-performance components in China and in other emerging countries, the MNC decided (around 2010) to build new factories in Brazil, Mexico, India and China. The Chinese subsidiary was built between 2011 and 2015 in Shenyang. The MNC already had one subsidiary in Shenyang and one in Shanghai. However, the "old" Shenyang factory had operated for about 10 years and lacked the production potential that would satisfy the rising demand for high-quality products. Therefore, launching the new factory was strategically important for the company's growth in the Chinese market. The MNC decided to modernise the old Shenyang factory and build one more factory there. Due to the new machinery parks and production and technological processes implemented in both factories, new approaches to production management were introduced and higher production standards were set. This is why the business venture required the support of about 150 Western managers and specialists with experience from factories using the same production processes and technologies. Accordingly, the scene for expatriate-local staff interactions was highly multicultural.

### Polish Expatriates and Local Staff

The Polish specialists' main assignment was to support local staff and share with them specialised knowledge acquired in the Polish subsidiary. Table 8.1 shows brief characteristics of three expatriates whose stories were chosen for analyses. It shows they were internationally experienced with the ability to speak two foreign languages: French, which is the company language in European subsidiaries; and English, which is the most commonly spoken foreign language in Poland ("Europeans and Their Languages", 2012) and the company language in the MNC's Chinese subsidiary.

About one-third of the Chinese staff had intercultural experiences working with foreigners in another MNC's factory in Shenyang and other MNCs in China. The company's policy required that all higher-level staff working in the new subsidiary should be proficient in English and the level of proficiency was checked by a native speaker of English during the recruitment process.

Although, complying with the language policy, expatriates communicated with Chinese technologists and managers in English, we have showed elsewhere (Wilczewski, Søderberg, & Gut, 2018, 2019) that communication with locals was hampered by the expatriates' little knowledge of the local language (the MNC provided them with a basic 120-hour Mandarin course to better deal with everyday matters rather than for use at work). Thus, we assume here that insofar as English proficiency to a certain degree enhanced expatriate-locals interactions,

Table 8.1 Interviewees' characteristics

| Fictitious name | Function (years) in Polish subsidiary | Function (years) in Chinese subsidiary | Assignment in China | Previous international experience (time) | Foreign language L1/L2 |
|---|---|---|---|---|---|
| Wladyslaw | Constructor (2) | Specialist (2.5) | • To design and develop training matrices for functional staff<br>• To coach five product managers at the local level | Scotland (5 years), France (2 years) | English/French |
| Stefan | Maintenance specialist (7) | Engineering supervisor/coach/ specialist (3) | • To supervise, advise and coach seven Chinese technologists and engineers<br>• To implement company methods and conduct internal audits | USA (4 months), France (2 weeks) | French/English |
| Janusz | Manager/product industrialisation engineer (9.5) | Process technologist/ specialist (2) | • To coach and support the head of quality assurance department | Thailand (2 years) | English/French |

the insufficient Mandarin proficiency limited the Poles' participation in the local communication processes, social networks (Zhang & Harzing, 2016) and interactions with locals, which, in turn, may have inhibited their cultural learning.

## Interview Procedure

The first author conducted semi-structured narrative interviews in yet another former expatriate's place of residence in Poland in 2016. Interviewees were given a broad topic "Please, tell me (a story) about your experiences with your co-workers in China". Next, they were asked focused questions to further stimulate the storytelling: "Can you think of something particularly surprising/frustrating/difficult/positive/thought-provoking/challenging?" The interviews were audio-recorded and transcribed verbatim, and the selected stories were translated by the first author from Polish into English, to be further analysed by all three authors.

### The Interviewer as a Co-author of Narratives

The interviewer should be viewed as a co-author of meanings shared by interviewees. The interviews were conducted on his initiative and he asked some focused questions, which may have influenced interviewees' narratives. Being aware of the participative role in the storytelling, he restrained himself from interruptions and rather encouraged the interviewee to carry on the storytelling. Moreover, the shared nationality, language and cultural background may have influenced the perspective taken on the experiences related. On the one hand, telling stories in Polish allowed interviewees to freely express their thoughts and emotions. On the other, however, relating intercultural experiences to a compatriot may have imposed an ethnocentric perspective and produced "living stories" that were comprehensible for a Pole and responded to his expectations (Boje, 2014).

## Empirical Analysis

We will analyse how interviewees related their experiences to present their perspective on collaboration incidents. We will identify the focal points and challenging situations that offered them opportunities for cultural learning by seeking what the narrators highlight as turning points and discoveries.

### "I did a mistake"—How a Critical Incident Leads to Learning

Władysław is a chemist with a PhD and seven years of international experience. In China, he worked in a team of 20 local constructors supervised by a European manager. As part of his preparation, Władysław learned about Shenyang from other expatriates. He went to China with his Polish wife and two small children.

In one of his stories, he recalled a critical incident with a local colleague, which was caused by misunderstandings:

> I was performing a test. I had made an arrangement with a technologist who would do the test on the machine. It's a lunch break . . . I'm taking the measurements and I realise there is not a single Chinese by my side. They all went for lunch. . . [pause]. They ruined the whole test. I had to start it over again, as my measurements were rubbish. No information . . . whatsoever. Finally, I got angry and went for lunch, too.
>
> A female Chinese employee came back from lunch. I told her something harsh. She responded with a laugh. But I know that it wasn't just a laugh . . . I made a mistake then, although we spoke normally later on . . . I apologised to her because I scolded her in front of other staff. She made me so angry because I lost several hours because of her, you know? And we were short of the material testing sample, so at that time we could not. . .
>
> When I had another test and I knew it was lunch time, I let her go, but I . . . explained to her that she should first come to me and tell me that she is leaving so that I can finish quicker or I can think what I can do next, right?
>
> Later, they informed me about when they would leave me there on my own because we learned how to communicate and avoid ruining each other's work. She simply went for that lunch, because others went, too. These were her priorities. . . . And I explained what her priorities should be, but in front of others, unfortunately. And she said,
>
> "So what? I did nothing wrong, I just left. Did you have any problem?"
>
> "Yes, my test is useless".
>
> "And you have a problem with that?"
>
> I will never forget these questions asked with a smile on her face. . . . But it was clear to me that she asked them in big stress. And that was typical of them that even when [I was] furious, they were always smiling. But that's an Asian mentality, I guess, because I've seen that in Japan as well. They could yell at each other or be angry with you, but always with a grin on their face. We have a different mentality, right? We use swearwords in every second sentence. But, anyway, that smile and her questions. . . . I think she was stressed very much and tried to save her face.

Władysław expected his team member to assist him with doing a quality test until its very end, but she left him to have a lunch break with local colleagues. He could not understand this behaviour and found it unacceptable, even if it seems to have been clear for the locals that a lunch break entitled them to leave the workplace. Because Władysław had not communicated that the team members should inform him about leaving the workplace when testing is performed, they simply could not fulfil his expectations.

The critical incident was a source of negative emotions for both the expatriate and his Chinese colleague. But these emotions served the expatriate as an incentive for better understanding her behaviour and triggered his cultural learning. Władysław showed a moment of self-reflection when recalling his reaction to the whole situation. He described how he scolded the colleague after the lunch break and that he could not understand her response to his allegations. But he also acknowledged that his reaction was reprehensible on cultural grounds, as he scolded his colleague in front of other team members. He explicitly referred to his behaviour as a "mistake". Most probably it was thanks to the strong emotions and the stress he observed in his local colleague's responses that he realised his behaviour did not fit culturally in that context. The short expatriate-local colleague conversation served as a turning point, which led to discovery. First, the critical situation increased his understanding of the importance of communicating his expectations explicitly toward cultural others. Second, it advanced his cultural awareness of the importance of the concept of face (*mianzi*) in communication in a Chinese business context, as threatening the interactant's face is a culturally inappropriate communication practice (Bond, 1991). Władysław's learning exerted a positive effect on intercultural collaboration, as he stressed that his colleagues would later inform him about them leaving the workplace. Having discovered his cultural *faux pas*, we assume he demonstrated more intercultural sensitivity in future intercultural interactions.

Władysław's learning was based on observations of local colleagues' behaviours and their reactions to his communication behaviours (reprimand) and on his cultural attributions. Władysław constructed the locals as professionals who, first, showed different priorities than Polish professionals. Second, extrapolating from his observations in Shenyang and his prior experiences in Japan, he constructed Asians as trying to hide their true emotions in critical situations vs. Poles as extroverts who do not hesitate to reprimand their colleagues at work. And even if this opposition was based on a generalisation, it explains to him a reason for the miscommunication related in the story.

### "There was a rule that you needed to get to people via the boss"—Learning Intra-subsidiary Communication Practices

The next story was told by Stefan—a mechanical engineer with international (short-term) experience from the MNC's US and French subsidiaries. He prepared for the expatriation by reading brochures about

Shenyang and by talking to other expatriates. Stefan relocated to China with his Polish wife and two small children.

Stefan told us about a communication strategy the expatriates developed in Shenyang to facilitate more contact with local colleagues:

> Communication was difficult to overcome . . . and it was difficult if you didn't get to people via their manager . . . then there was no progress. You couldn't push anything through if you hadn't talked to the manager of a given person. That was *difficult*.
>
> First, you go to the boss of the person you will collaborate with and you explain what needs to be done. The boss delegates certain duties to his subordinate and then you can approach that subordinate and explain what he needs to do, because any attempt to work directly with them, without the participation of their boss, usually failed—it only came down to a talk and they would say: "Yes, yes", and they would continue doing their own thing. So there was a rule that you needed to get to people via the boss. Even if you didn't want anything special from them, but only to give some recommendations, advice on doing something better. . . "Yes, yes", most of them said, "Everything is OK" . . . And, you know, they didn't give a damn about you.

Stefan described the relayed communication strategy that allowed him to establish contact with a Chinese co-worker. The strategy involved three steps: (1) approaching the superior of the target employee (in English); (2) letting his/her superior approach that employee (in Mandarin/English); and (3) approaching that employee (in English). Expatriates' attempts to communicate directly with locals, without their superior as a mediator, often failed insofar as their instructions were ignored.

It is likely that expatriates, having experienced communication difficulties and observed how hierarchy worked in that specific context, applied conditioning through which they modified their behaviours until they discovered what communication approach worked best in that context. As a result of this discovery, they devised a communication strategy which they articulated as a "rule" that encapsulated explicit knowledge about approaching a local colleague through his/her superior. This strategy may have been effective because, first, the local employee could feel obliged by the boss to communicate with the expatriate and follow his/her instructions. Second, having been informed about the problem in Mandarin, the Chinese employee had more time to prepare for discussing it in English with the Polish specialist.

Stefan perceived expatriate-local communication as being hampered by the strongly hierarchical organisational structure. It was challenging for him as an engineer whose role was to advise the locals, which entailed frequent communication. The perceived difficulties caused frustration and led to blaming the cultural other for poor collaboration and lack of respect for his recommendations, as implied by Stefan's negative perspective on locals' attitude toward him/expatriates ("they did not give a damn about you"). Accordingly, Stefan created his professional identity of an expatriate positioned somewhere outside the Chinese organisational structure. To participate in intra-subsidiary communication, at the level of technologists and engineers, he needed to "gain authorisation" from the Chinese managers.

### "Putting out fires"—Perceptions of Local Management and Working Styles

Janusz is an electrotechnician and external auditor. He had international experience from the MNC's Thai subsidiary where he worked as a control manager. He relocated to China with his Thai wife. Janusz said he did not pay much attention to preparation to live or work in China, because he expected he would mostly collaborate with other expatriates, as his direct superior was a European manager. However, his tasks also involved coaching and supporting a local head of a quality assurance department, so he interacted with locals on a daily basis.

Janusz told us about what he learned about management processes in Shenyang:

> I was a coach to a Chinese [male] on a managerial position—a technology team leader. He supervised the Chinese [employees], and I was on a parallel position to his, but my job was to teach him this . . . European thinking, so that he starts working . . . not in the Chinese style. The idea was to use my experience, but not to show him technical knowledge, but rather some ways of managing problems, in a more long-term perspective—how to manage results, indices and annual goals.
>
> The management style there [in Shenyang] wasn't so much. . . "forward-looking". That was . . . what you could observe in Poland in the past—"putting out fires", but not prevention. For example, we had a problem with one expired product . . . It took us about a year to develop a system that monitored products, controlled cold stores and pulled out products before expiration dates. Because in China . . . when there was a big problem, they started to act and "put out fires" in order to ensure production. So it was a juggling act for us to continue production.
>
> There was one manager who did everything his own way, a *weird* way . . . but he had [good] results. But when he ordered something, he soon changed that. He often changed the planning process when he planned something himself. Generally, he messed up a lot, but still had [good] results. Nevertheless, after a few years, some guy

[a Polish engineer] once said that he couldn't stand all that any more [laughter]. So when they had to implement something, then that [Polish] guy couldn't do his thing because he [the Chinese manager] had already changed something. He [the Chinese manager] also demanded hard work after hours, which was sometimes unnecessary . . . so the atmosphere was tense. And when he [the Polish engineer] wanted something [from his co-workers], nobody listened, because the manager had just changed the arrangement. There was chaos. . .

I wouldn't generalise about all the Chinese, but there were many, many cases when they did things their own way. I don't mean to evaluate it and decide if it's right or wrong. They just always acted . . . taking up a different logic. In Poland, we tend to somehow deal with the problem, and there [in China] they "put the blinders on", "Ok, there's a problem, but I don't see anything, I'm moving on, in another direction, which is comfortable". But later, there are fires, though it was nice and pleasant for a while.

Janusz projected the "Chinese" management style as short-term oriented and different from the style exhibited by Poles or other Europeans. That projection was modelled by his interpretation of the locals' approaches to solving problems. Unable to understand the local practices, he concluded that the locals avoided facing problems. Janusz's observations of local managers in Shenyang was reinforced by stories from other expatriates who found it difficult to adjust to the hierarchical structure in China and appreciate the local management style, which they perceived as odd and chaotic. However, although incomprehensible to him, Janusz acknowledged that it allowed local managers to obtain satisfactory results.

Janusz's exposition of his supportive role in Shenyang unfolded reflections on intercultural collaboration and culture-specific working styles and employee management. He described them through comparison to the style he considered typical of Poles, which allowed him to render his observations comprehensible for the interviewer. He made a reference to socialist times in Poland before 1989, which are remembered by Poles as times of mass employment and little organisation at work. In effect, Janusz framed Chinese management and working styles as leading to similar problems.

Janusz described local management and working styles using general and ambiguous expressions. In his view, the locals acted "their own way", "taking up a different logic". He thought about their behaviours in terms of "putting out fires" and underpinned his narration on the metaphor CRISIS IS FIRE. This discursive device allowed him to construct his role as a coach who shared knowledge about how crisis situations are dealt with in the Polish subsidiary.

Janusz's learning was dominated by attributional reasoning. Trying to understand locals' behaviours, he compared them to behaviours presented by Polish and European professionals and, hence, attributed the former to the specificity of Chinese culture. Through this process, he constructed cultural knowledge of European management and working styles, which he viewed as "forward-looking" vs. Chinese style as "short-sighted". Unable to understand the local time management and task scheduling, he viewed the processes as odd and chaotic. This indicates that his learning was limited because, seeing that the processes led to satisfactory production results, he still found it difficult to function in that business context by transforming his own approaches. For example, he failed to discern that what he perceived as changing arrangements may have been perceived by locals as flexibility. Nevertheless, Janusz's story also indicates that he tried to act in different ways to function in that context (cf. "it was a juggling act for us to continue production"), so it seems that he learned through conditioning, although the results of it are obscure based on the story alone.

Janusz constructed his professional identity as an expatriate who was a coach to a local manager. He viewed their relationship through a cultural lens, blaming cultural differences for unsuccessful collaborations. This construction suggests a limited ability to cross his ethnocentric perspective on intercultural collaboration, which the story confirmed by showing the lack of understanding of the logic of locals' behaviours.

## Conclusions

Expatriate empirical research shows that culturally intelligent individuals perform and adjust better in culturally complex business contexts and make better behavioural attributions (Lee & Sukoco, 2010; Templer, Tay, & Chandrasekar, 2006). To be more successful in culturally diverse situations, benefit from personal and career development and contribute to a company's competitiveness, expatriates need to develop cross-cultural competencies to enhance understanding of cultural others' behaviours, appreciate cultural differences and foster intercultural collaborations. Although scholars agree that cross-cultural competencies are developed in the process of life-long learning (Briscoe et al., 2006), little attention has been paid to what expatriates learn through intercultural interactions in a multicultural and multilingual workplace, how the learning actually happens and what its outcomes are.

With this qualitative case study into learning processes of Polish expatriates in a Chinese subsidiary of a Western European MNC, we responded to recent calls to conduct context-specific research (Lenartowicz et al., 2014; Manuti et al., 2015; Morris et al., 2014) that advances our understanding of how expatriates develop a capacity to function in a multicultural and multilingual business context. By analysing the Polish expatriates' narratives, we gained insight into (1) how and what they learned through their intercultural collaborations, (2) how they applied the newly acquired knowledge to better navigate in the multicultural and multilingual business context and (3) how they positioned themselves in relation to cultural others. We drew on the "four-fold taxonomy of intercultural learning" (Morris et al., 2014) to investigate qualitatively different learning processes.

The three preceding narrative analyses revealed that critical incidents of expatriate-local staff collaboration resulted from the expatriate's unclear expectations toward the cultural other. Critical incidents were also a source of negative emotions which, nevertheless, stimulated the expatriates' desire to understand the reasons for unsuccessful interactions and, thereby, engage in cultural learning processes. They could, for example, learn about the importance of the concept of face, effective communication in the extremely hierarchical structure, culture-specific approaches to time management, employee management and working styles. Having discovered that culturally inappropriate behaviours caused critical events, the expatriates could thus raise their cultural awareness and sensitivity, modify their behaviours and, thereby, better address culturally challenging situations.

The three Polish expatriates linked in their storytelling communication and collaboration difficulties with a strongly hierarchical organisational structure in the Chinese subsidiary. Their position as specialists advising the locals was unclear, which, combined with their low command of the local language and some problems in communicating in English, were obstacles to their everyday interactions with the local managers, technologists and engineers.

The Polish expatriates' learning was predominated by direct interactions with the locals and observations of their behaviour. Based on those, they created explicit knowledge by making attributions to the locals' motives, intentions, beliefs and cultural differences—which exemplifies *attributional reasoning* (Morris et al., 2014). Moreover, they used the knowledge acquired through *studying* as an important framework to interpret their intercultural interactions.

We showed a critical role of these two explicit processes in expatriate learning, as they determined its trajectory. We found that the Polish expatriates' negative perceptions of the local organisational processes, caused by their cultural (mis)attributions and/or their limited ability to cross the ethnocentric perspective, prevented them from engaging in those processes. This decreased their exposure to intercultural interaction and, hence, inhibited new understandings and further cultural learning. Accordingly, we found that not all cultural knowledge expands the individual capacity to navigate multicultural and multilingual contexts, especially when it is stereotypical or based on generalisations (e.g. "[It is typical of] Asian/Chinese mentality/thinking").

We also captured the involvement of *conditioning* and *social learning* in the expatriates' learning processes. For example, the expatriates surmounted difficulties in approaching their local peers by seeking alternative approaches to communication (e.g. through their local colleagues' superiors), which is an example of learning through transforming communication behaviours.

Finally, this study showed that the Polish specialists, who collaborated closely in teams with local technologists/engineers, were exposed to communication and collaboration problems on a much more frequent basis than their expatriate counterparts who occupied managerial positions (see, e.g., Guttormsen et al., 2018). Therefore, we suggest that future research focuses more on intercultural experiences, knowledge sharing and learning of expatriates at lower positions in the company hierarchy.

# References

Adler, N. J., & Gundersen, A. (2008). *International dimensions of organizational behavior* (5th ed.). doi:10.1002/tie.5060280112

Ang, S., Van Dyne, L., Koh, C., Ng, K. Y., Templer, K. J., Tay, C., & Chandrasekar, N. A. (2007). Cultural intelligence: Its measurement and effects on cultural judgment and decision making, cultural adaptation and task performance. *Management and Organization Review*, 3(3), 335–371. doi:10.1111/j.1740-8784.2007.00082.x

Armstrong, S. J., & Li, Y. (2017). A study of Anglo expatriate managers' learning, knowledge acquisition, and adjustment in multinational companies in China. *Academy of Management Learning and Education*, 16(1), 1–22. doi:10.5465/amle.2013.0335

Bandura, A. (1986). *Social foundations of thought and action: A social cognitive theory*. Englewood Cliffs, NJ: Prentice Hall.

Bird, A., & Mendenhall, M. E. (2016). From cross-cultural management to global leadership: Evolution and adaptation. *Journal of World Business*, 51(1), 115–126. doi:10.1016/j.jwb.2015.10.005

Black, J. S., Mendenhall, M. E., & Oddou, G. (1991). Toward a comprehensive model of international adjustment: An integration of multiple theoretical perspectives. *Academy of Management Review*, 16(2), 291–317. doi:10.5465/AMR.1991.4278938

Boje, D. M. (2014). *Storytelling organizational practices: Managing in the quantum age*. London: Routledge.

Bond, M. H. (1991). *Beyond the Chinese face: Insights from psychology*. Hong Kong: Oxford University Press.

Brady-Amoon, P., & Fuertes, J. (2011). Self-efficacy, self-rated abilities, adjustment, and academic performance. *Journal of Counseling and Development*, 89(4), 431–438. doi:10.1002/j.1556-6676.2011.tb02840.x

Brannen, M. Y., & Salk, J. E. (2000). Partnering across borders: Negotiating organizational culture in a German-Japanese joint venture. *Human Relations*, *53*(4), 451–487. doi:10.1177/0018726700534001

Brewster, C., Bonache, J., Cerdin, J.-L., & Suutari, V. (2014). Exploring expatriate outcomes. *International Journal of Human Resource Management*, *25*(14), 1921–1937. doi:10.1080/09585192.2013.870284

Briscoe, J. P., Hall, D. T., & Frautschy DeMuth, R. L. (2006). Protean and boundaryless careers: An empirical exploration. *Journal of Vocational Behavior*, *69*(1), 30–47. doi:10.1016/j.jvb.2005.09.003

Bücker, J., Poutsma, E., & Monster, H. (2016). How and why does expatriation management influence expatriates' employability? *Journal of Global Mobility: The Home of Expatriate Management Research*, *4*(4), 432–452. doi:10.1108/JGM-11-2015-0058

Burr, V. (2006). *An introduction to social constructionism*. London and New York: Routledge.

Caligiuri, P. M. (2000). Selecting expatriates for personality characteristics: A moderating effect of personality on the relationship between host national contact and cross-cultural adjustment. *Management International Review*, *40*(1), 61–80. doi:10.2307/40835867

Caligiuri, P. M., & Tarique, I. (2012). Dynamic cross-cultural competencies and global leadership effectiveness. *Journal of World Business*, *47*(4), 612–622. doi:10.1016/j.jwb.2012.01.014

Ditchburn, G., & Brook, E. R. (2015). Cross-cultural adjustment and fundamental interpersonal relations orientation behaviour (FIRO-B). *Journal of Global Mobility*, *3*(4), 336–349. doi:10.1108/JGM-05-2015-0017

Europeans and Their Languages. (2012). *Special Eurobarometer 386*. Retrieved from http://ec.europa.eu/public_opinion/archives/ebs/ebs_386_en.pdf

Gertsen, M. C., & Søderberg, A.-M. (2011). Intercultural collaboration stories: On narrative inquiry and analysis as tools for research in international business. *Journal of International Business Studies*, *42*(6), 787–804. doi:10.1057/jibs.2011.15

Gertsen, M. C., Søderberg, A.-M., & Zølner, M. (2012). *Global collaboration: Intercultural experiences and learning*. New York: Palgrave Macmillan.

Guttormsen, D. S. A., Francesco, A. M., & Chapman, M. K. (2018). Revisiting the expatriate failure concept: A qualitative study of Scandinavian expatriates in Hong Kong. *Scandinavian Journal of Management*, *34*(2), 117–128. doi:10.1016/j.scaman.2018.03.005

Hanna, R. C., Crittenden, V. L., & Crittenden, W. F. (2013). Social learning theory: A multicultural study of influences on ethical behavior. *Journal of Marketing Education*, *35*(1), 18–25. doi:10.1177/0273475312474279

Hemmasi, M., & Downes, M. (2013). Cultural distance and expatriate adjustment revisited. *Journal of Global Mobility: The Home of Expatriate Management Research*, *1*(1), 72–91. doi:10.1108/JGM-09-2012-0010

Kolb, D. A. (1984). *Experiential learning: Experience as the source of learning and development*. Englewood Cliffs, NJ: Prentice Hall.

Lee, L.-Y., & Sukoco, B. M. (2010). The effects of cultural intelligence on expatriate performance: The moderating effects of international experience. *The International Journal of Human Resource Management*, *21*(7), 963–981. doi:10.1080/09585191003783397

Lenartowicz, T., Johnson, J. P., & Konopaske, R. (2014). The application of learning theories to improve cross-cultural training programs in MNCs. *International Journal of Human Resource Management, 25*(12), 1697–1719. doi:10.1080/09585192.2013.860384

Manuti, A., Pastore, S., Scardigno, A. F., Giancaspro, M. L., & Morciano, D. (2015). Formal and informal learning in the workplace: A research review. *International Journal of Training and Development, 19*(1), 1–17. doi:10.1111/ijtd.12044

McNulty, Y., & Brewster, C. (2017). Theorizing the meaning(s) of 'expatriate': Establishing boundary conditions for business expatriates. *International Journal of Human Resource Management, 28*(1), 27–61. doi:10.1080/09585192.2016.1243567

Mezirow, J. (1991). *Transformative dimensions of adult learning*. San Francisco, CA: Jossey-Bass.

Morris, M. W., Savani, K., Mor, S., & Cho, J. (2014). When in Rome: Intercultural learning and implications for training. *Research in Organizational Behavior, 34*, 189–215. doi:10.1016/j.riob.2014.09.003

Nardon, L., Steers, R. M., & Sanchez-Runde, C. J. (2011). Seeking common ground: Strategies for enhancing multicultural communication. *Organizational Dynamics, 40*(2), 85–95. doi:10.1016/j.orgdyn.2011.01.002

Søderberg, A.-M., & Worm, V. D. (2011). Communication and collaboration in subsidiaries in China—Chinese and expatriate accounts. *European Journal of Cross-Cultural Competence and Management, 2*(1), 54–76. doi:10.1504/ejccm.2011.042677c

Spencer, A. (2011). Americans create hybrid spaces in Costa Rica: A framework for exploring cultural and linguistic integration. *Language and Intercultural Communication, 11*(1), 59–74. doi:10.1080/14708477.2010.517847

Templer, K. J., Tay, C., & Chandrasekar, N. A. (2006). Motivational cultural intelligence, realistic job preview, realistic living conditions preview, and cross-cultural adjustment. *Group and Organization Management, 31*(1), 154–173. doi:10.1177/1059601105275293

Thomas, D. C., Elron, E., Stahl, G., Ekelund, B. Z., Ravlin, E. C., Cerdin, J.-L., . . . Lazarova, M. B. (2008). Cultural intelligence: Domain and assessment. *International Journal of Cross Cultural Management, 8*(2), 123–143. doi:10.1177/1470595808091787

Tucker, M. F., Bonial, R., & Lahti, K. (2004). The definition, measurement and prediction of intercultural adjustment and job performance among corporate expatriates. *International Journal of Intercultural Relations, 28*(3–4), 221–251. doi:10.1016/j.ijintrel.2004.06.004

Wilczewski, M., Søderberg, A.-M., & Gut, A. (2018). Intercultural communication within a Chinese subsidiary of a Western MNC: Expatriate perspectives on language and communication issues. *Multilingua: Journal of Cross-Cultural and Interlanguage Communication, 37*(6), 587–611. doi:10.1515/multi-2017-0095

Wilczewski, M., Søderberg, A.-M., & Gut, A. (2019). Storytelling and cultural learning—An expatriate manager's narratives of collaboration challenges in a multicultural business setting. *Learning, Culture and Social Interaction, 21*, 362–377. doi:10.1016/j.lcsi.2019.04.007

Yan Lo-Philip, S. W., Carroll, C., Li Tan, T., Ann, O. Y., Heng Tan, Y., & Hwee Seow, S. (2015). Transforming educational practices: Cultural learning for short-term sojourners. *International Journal of Intercultural Relations*, *49*, 223–234. doi:10.1016/j.ijintrel.2015.10.006

Zhang, L. E., & Harzing, A. W. (2016). From dilemmatic struggle to legitimized indifference: Expatriates' host country language learning and its impact on the expatriate-HCE relationship. *Journal of World Business*, *51*(5), 774–786. doi:10.1016/j.jwb.2016.06.001

# Section 3

# The Role of Language in International Business Education

*Editor: Sierk Horn*

# A New Look at the Role of Language in Business Education

*Sierk Horn*

Why do learning and teaching practices of language in business schools deserve our attention? Historically, international business scholarship has sought to transcend disciplinary boundaries and almost by definition has regularly come into contact with, and has in the process become informed by research from diverse linguistic backgrounds *as long as this is pre-packaged in the English language* (Horn, 2017). Over twenty years ago, the eminent IB scholar John Dunning called for affirming the importance of foreign language know-how in business education when he wrote that "the effectiveness of our efforts to study and teach international business is entirely dependent on our capability to marshal and organise the necessary human and other assets" (Dunning, 1989, p. 411). However, educational institutions today often struggle to clearly define what exactly the study of language can do for business students (Moore, 2006). Some scholars go so far as to argue that discounting the impact of language on business activities has created hierarchies of knowledge creation (Tietze & Dick, 2013). These ensure that the Anglophone monopoly of management thought leadership and approaches to management research (and, by extension, its dissemination) are not compromised (see Holtbruegge, 2013). Holden and Michailova (2014, p. 10) note that

> in the world of IB we are dealing, literally and metaphorically, with the cross-border interplay of entire terrains of corporate contexts and experiences among multiple mental and social frames of reference. This, in itself, requires a more expansive perspective on the delicacies of translation if we are to advance our current thinking and practices.

All too often, 'language' is usually used synonymously with 'culture,' whereby 'culture,' then, can be dealt with in modules on intercultural communication or country- or region-specific briefings (without the explicit mention of language). Although many business schools have established programmes that combine general business courses with foreign language training (Sacco, 2014), a seamless implementation that brings these two domains together is not so simple. This section is going to make the case that there is no reason why foreign language study should not play a more central role in business education.

The scale and scope of commercial activities across national borders make linguistic expertise more, rather than less, precious in the future. Scholars, too, have responded to this growing need for communication skills with intensive research exploring the role of language in international business from a variety of perspectives (for on overview see Tenzer, Terjesen, & Harzing, 2017). Less attention, however, has thus far been given to how to make excellent research on the interplay between language and management relevant to business education and practice. This is surprising not least because of a rapidly expanding international student mobility (ICEF, 2015). In the UK, for instance, about a third of business studies cohorts are now made up of international students (OECD, 2018). Arguably, resultant classroom diversity is an ideal breeding ground for the next crop of skilled professionals.

Language diversity in organisations and groups, the experience of people while at work (using their own or second languages) and the role they occupy because of their proficiency all affect what happens in and around modern multinational corporations. Potentially painful disruptions occur inside organisations (e.g. distortions of processes, performance, and knowledge production) and outside organisations (e.g. attraction, selection and retention of employees, and engagement with customers). In short, language diversity influences all sorts of decision-making processes, even the extent to which firms internationalise. No wonder that firms are increasingly seeking to attract internationally fluent students and retain multilingual employees. The question then becomes what business schools can do to prepare students for a future where cultural and linguistical diversity shape almost every aspect of work lives. This section builds on the extensive work on language in international business as portrayed in the preceding chapters of this book. It explores in three chapters how and to what extent learning and teaching practices in business schools have evolved while the world's companies adapt to an increasingly multilingual environment. They are, collectively, looking for ways to help business schools to take active responsibility in preparing students to be effective in international business contexts.

Much of the findings in research on language in international business has been decoupled from what happens in educational institutions and how they prepare students for working in a culturally and linguistically diverse work environment (at home and abroad). If language is a key component of making sense in internationally operating organisations, shouldn't management education promote communication skills and, in doing so, spur willingness to engage with the knowledge contained in other languages than English? The chapters in this section bring attention to the challenges and opportunities of integrating language diversity in business classrooms. They provide first-hand insight into learning and teaching practices, including student expectations and experiences and the design and implementation of innovative training methods. They also explore ideas about how programmes can marry essential business expertise with more pragmatic aspects of language (e.g. behavioural adaptability, cross-cultural awareness, etc.). At the same time, the contributions highlight impediments scholars might face under business school regiments. The absorption of linguistic expertise in curricula mandates a willingness to seek interdisciplinary dialogue. But language-sensitive initiatives are oftentimes deemed too soft and, hence, not meaningful enough for training the next crop of business leaders. Also, language training, especially ab initio courses, is time- and resource-intensive. Such opportunity costs also meet worries about language elements, not adding real value or even undermining the cohesiveness of business programmes. Such hegemonic undercurrents can be so strong that even programmes that have successfully integrated language into management training are being robbed of some if not all their language elements.

The chapters in this section offer new approaches to languages in international business education, first by making clear that there is practical importance attached to language in business training. In today's time and age proficiency in a language other than one's own is not a 'nice to have' but a 'must-have' skill; second, many higher education institutions may engage in international student exchange programmes. However, the three chapters are going to argue that although these are necessary measures to broaden intercultural horizons, by themselves, they are not enough to create value from linguistic and cultural diversity. The contributions explicitly or implicitly suggest that there is much to gain from the willingness and confidence of resolving diversity (thus, letting go of commonplace conceptions of culture and language as sources of conflict).

## Practical Importance of Language Training

Our knowledge about the critical role of languages in international business is relatively advanced. In spite of mounting evidence (e.g. Piekkari, Welch, & Welch, 1999; Brannen, Piekkari, & Tietze, 2014) this is not echoed in the curricula of many international business programmes. One of the reasons for this dissatisfying status quo is the popular view of culture and language as being up and foremost a source of conflict ('culture shock') and disruption (for instance, of information flows). The chapter by Mughan cautions against an overly excessive and perhaps irrational commitment to proficiency (in foreign languages) and exactitude (in translation practice). Fetishising foreign language use in business environments provokes misconceptions around differences in outlook, action, and values. Assessment of skilled language use as being costly and impractical (especially in environments where one has to act quickly) is a result of that. In the same vein, Kassis-Henderson and Cohen argue that language training in higher education institutions is usually motivated by the development of in-depth expertise concerning one language (which is, in turn, tied to specific geographies). Such emphasis of the local, according to the authors, no longer reflects the need to think of language skills as mobile and flexible resources. Both chapters go on to explore ways of how management education can think of language skills in more reflective and more constructive ways. They suggest that 'unthinking' classic distinctions of linguistic have and have nots may ameliorate the tendency of seeing a multilingual workplace as a nuisance or barrier to smooth information flows. Gaibrois and Piekkari, too, explore how educators may overcome negative reactions of language diversity. Instead of looking at changes in institutional environments, they challenge conceived wisdom of linguistic boundaries in the classroom (i.e. where more often than not, the 'gold-standard' is being based on the native-speaker model). Their work suggests that the stimulation of curiosity and self-reflexivity opens up space for the student's own questions and interests. In this way, students leave behind their cultural and linguistic 'comfort zone.' They are thus more likely to take a fresh look at what language skills can do for them.

## Bringing to Light the Positive Sides of Linguistic Diversity

Speaking and using the same language adds credibility. As a consequence, a common corporate language creates pervasive social pressure (Neeley, 2012), not least because language diversity is commonly viewed as something negative. Miscommunication is just one of the awkward effects of a linguistically diverse workplace. Language or accents help us interpret how close we feel to others. People tend to be less willing to display integrative behaviour if they perceive cultural similarity to decrease (Wiswede, 1994). Emphasis on ingroup cohesion, then, brings about some form of 'groupthink' ('Me'—'Us'—'Them'). Blatant or hidden discrimination (Ng, 2007), resistance to diversity (e.g. Feely & Harzing, 2003), unhealthy competition (Neeley & Dumas, 2016) or an atmosphere of political correctness (von Bergen, Soper, & Foster, 2002) is often the result of that.

All three contributions ask how we can make people more positive about linguistic diversity. The authors discuss how business schools can help students develop some defense mechanisms that inoculate them to entirely focus on the negative effects of language diversity. Kassis-Henderson and Cohen challenge us to rethink language skills being tied to a specific country or national culture. They argue that professional skills that come with language learning, most notably adaptability, sensitivity, or navigating in-between cultures, are often underappreciated.

Against this backdrop, the goal of business schools may then be to foster an understanding of language as a mobile capability. Mughan goes one step further in urging business schools to develop a language-general curriculum. Similar to Kassis-Henderson and Cohen, the starting point of his contribution is that nobody really focuses on the added value foreign language learning can bring to the world of business. He suggests a competency-based approach to language learning more mindful about positive social interactions at work. Finally, Gaibrois and Piekkari offer us insights into how this emphasis of honing language intelligence could look like in the classroom. Their contribution strongly suggests that business school students usually wonder about (or even rebel against) learning about the strategic importance of foreign languages as part of their programme. The authors then take us on a journey of how they step-by-step reduced negative attitudes towards linguistic diversity and refocused students' attention on the positive aspects of multilingual contexts. Although students expanded knowledge and skills by exploring new territory largely independently, the authors highlight that learners must not be left alone. There is a complex interplay between students' and module convenors' experiences. Such co-creation of knowledge seems crucial for making a difference in how language teaching is integrated into business curricula.

# References

Brannen, M. Y., Piekkari, R., & Tietze, S. (2014). The multifaceted role of language in international business: Unpacking the forms, functions and features of a critical challenge to MNC theory and performance. *Journal of International Business Studies, 45*(5), 495–507.

Dunning, J. H. (1989). The study of international business: A plea for a more interdisciplinary approach. *Journal of International Business Studies, 20*(3), 411–436.

Feely, A. J., & Harzing, A. W. K. (2003). Language management in multinational companies. *International Journal of Cross-Cultural Management, 10*(2), 37–52.

Holden, N. J., & Michailova, S. (2014). A more expansive perspective on translation in IB research: Insights from the Russian handbook of knowledge management. *Journal of International Business Studies, 45*, 906–918.

Holtbruegge, D. (2013). Indigenous management research. *Management International Review, 53*(1), 1–11.

Horn, S. (2017). Non-English-nativeness as social stigma in academic settings. *Academy of Management Learning and Education, 16*(4), 579–602.

ICEF. (2015). *ICEF monitor.* Retrieved from http://monitor.icef.com/2015/11/the-state-of-international-student-mobility-in-2015/

Moore, T. (2006). Foreign language requirements for business students: An update. *Journal of College Teaching & Learning, 6*(3), 65–68.

Neeley, T. (2012). Global business speaks English. *Harvard Business Review, 90*, 116–124.

Neeley, T., & Dumas, T. L. (2016). Unearned status gains: Evidence from a global language mandate. *Academy of Management Journal, 59*, 14–43.

Ng, S. H. (2007). Language-based discrimination: Blatant and subtle forms. *Journal of Language and Social Psychology, 26*, 106–122.

OECD. (2018). *Education statistics.* Retrieved from www.oecd-ilibrary.org/education/data/education-at-a-glance/share-of-international-students-enrolled-by-field-of-education_e86f4692-en

Piekkari, R., Welch, D. E., & Welch, L. S. (2014). *Language in international business: The multilingual reality of global business expansion.* Cheltenham: Edward Elgar.

Sacco, S. J. (2014). Integrating foreign languages and cultures into U.S. international business programs: Best practices and future considerations. *Journal of Teaching in International Business, 25*(3), 235–249.

Tenzer, H., Terjesen, S., & Harzing, A.-W. (2017). Language in international business: A review and agenda for future research. *Management International Review, 57*, 815–854.

Tietze, S., & Dick, P. (2013). The victorious English language: Hegemonic practices in the management academy. *Journal of Management Inquiry, 22*(1), 122–134.

Von Bergen, C. W., Soper, B., & Foster, T. (2002). Unintended negative effects of diversity management. *Public Personnel Management, 31*(2), 239–251.

Wiswede, G. (1994). *Einführung in die Wirtschaftspsychologie* [Introduction to business psychology]. Munich: UTB.

# 9 "At the Beginning, I Thought the Topic Was Boring"

## Educating Business Students in Language Diversity Through Transformative Learning

### Claudine Gaibrois and Rebecca Piekkari

The topic of multilingualism in companies remains marginal in management education to date, despite the fact that the era of globalisation and migration has inevitably turned companies into "multilingual realities" (Brannen, Piekkari, & Tietze, 2014, p. 496). This, however, is contrary to teaching in the field of cross-cultural management, which has a long tradition in management education. Few programmes at business schools devote an entire course or even a session to this topic despite its obvious relevance for managerial praxis. This is a reflection of the "Englishization" (Dor, 2004) of management education, where "management gospel" is spread in English, although neither English nor the management discourse are neutral (Tietze, 2008). The teaching models of business schools were exported from the United States to Europe and beyond in the 1950s and 1960s (Sahlin-Andersson & Engwall, 2002), and because the United States is an officially monolingual—although *de facto* multilingual—country, it is not surprising that especially MBA programmes offered by business schools have traditionally neglected multilingualism. In addition, business schools tend to adopt a functionalist perspective, or as Ghoshal (2005) puts it, they focus on the social costs arising from human imperfections instead of addressing the complexity of human nature, of which multilingualism is a part.

When considering the learners in management education, the fact that language diversity is neglected is even more puzzling, as the past three decades have witnessed significant growth in a linguistically and culturally diverse student population (Zhang, Xia, Fan, & Zhu, 2016). Consequently, "teaching to monocultural audiences will be less and less frequent" (Szkudlarek, McNett, Romani, & Lane, 2013, p. 491) over time. In addition, international students bring skills and experiences to the classroom, which provide ample opportunities for intercultural learning (Zhang et al., 2016) and make "management education itself a cross-cultural activity" (Joy & Poonamallee, 2013, p. 397). However, instead of responding to the unprecedented cultural heterogeneity in the contemporary classroom, management education still follows the US business school model (Joy & Poonamallee, 2013). Even when teaching cross-cultural management, the discussion of language(s) is "woefully limited" (Holden, Michailova, & Tietze, 2015, p. xlvii).

In order to enhance the standard cross-cultural management curriculum, scholars in cross-cultural management education suggest a transformative approach to teaching and learning (Szkudlarek et al., 2013; Zhang et al., 2016). This approach focuses on shifts in mindsets, welcomes multiple perspectives and critically reflects on both the dominant and the non-dominant cultures in the classroom (Zhang et al., 2016). Students should be encouraged to "develop a new pair of eyes through which they can perceive the world" (Szkudlarek et al., 2013, p. 489). Joy and Poonamallee (2013) have offered a set of teaching practices that challenge the dominance of the US and Western paradigm underlying management education. Rather than being experts with answers and explanations, teachers are invited to create opportunities for students to bring in phenomena that interest them and issues that they want to solve. Also, one of the aims of management education should be to encourage students to create their own vocabulary for articulating knowledge or explaining phenomena instead of using the established vocabulary of their discipline. Another practice that Joy and Poonamallee (2013) suggest is to introduce non-Western countries and companies in case-based learning because most of these cases currently report on experiences of Western multinational corporations in various host countries.

This chapter analyses a transformative educational and learning experience at the London School of Economics in 2017. From a reflexive approach, we draw on our collective experience of running a one-week intensive seminar called "Managing Multilingual Companies" for an international group of MSc students. The seminar turned out to be a learning process both for students and faculty. The students were invited to bring their wealth of experiences in multilingual professional contexts to the class. In order to facilitate learning, students were tasked to explore self-chosen research questions through case studies (Cassell, 2018). We argue that there is a need to include management of multilingualism as a core element of management education, as this would truly prepare learners for the multicultural element of contemporary managerial positions.

## Conceptual Background: Transformative Learning Theory

As mentioned earlier, a transformative approach to teaching and learning has been suggested as an alternative to the standard curriculum (Szkudlarek et al., 2013; Zhang et al., 2016). Transformative learning refers to "processes that result in significant and irreversible changes in the way a person experiences, conceptualizes, and interacts with the world" (Hoggan, 2016, p. 71). Conceptually, the transformative learning approach rests upon the basic premise that "a defining condition of being human is that we have to understand the meaning of our experience" (Mezirow, 1997, p. 5). Over time, individuals acquire frames of reference—or structures of assumptions—through which they understand their experiences (Mezirow, 1997). They tend to reject ideas that do not fit their preconceptions and label these ideas as unworthy of consideration. Transformative learning is a process of effecting change in such a frame of reference. Transformative learners "move toward a frame of reference that is more inclusive, nuanced, self-reflective, and integrative of experience" (Mezirow, 1997, p. 5). We transform our frames of reference through critical reflection on the assumptions—our own or those of others—upon which our interpretations are based. This might, for instance, happen through engaging in task-oriented problem solving (objective reframing) or self-reflectively assessing our own ideas and beliefs (subjective reframing), which develops autonomous thinking. Thus, Mezirow (1997) suggests that educators should set objectives that explicitly promote autonomous thinking and recognise that this requires experiences designed to foster critical reflexivity.

Transformative learning theory, as it has evolved over the years, aims at achieving a variety of learning outcomes. Hoggan (2016) offers a typology of transformative learning outcomes, of which particularly the following three are relevant for education on managing language diversity: (i) changes in worldview (e.g., more comprehensive or more complex worldview; becoming aware of something new); (ii) the capacity for greater complexity in seeing, interpreting and functioning in the world (e.g., higher awareness that expands beyond oneself); and (iii) significant shifts in learners' sense of self (e.g., heightened sense of responsibility). Because managing language diversity is not included in the conventional canon—analogous to Mezirow's (2000, p. 8) "cultural canon"—of management education, business students cannot be expected to be aware of the significant implications of using English as a corporate language on e.g., team members' contributions to meetings, or the challenges of transmitting information from the headquarters to subsidiaries located in different language environments. Rather, the subject is likely to be perceived as marginal, a 'nice to have' subject related to human resource management (HRM) or diversity management. Fundamental learning outcomes of placing language diversity centre stage in management education, therefore, consist of helping students to become aware of the complex implications of multilingualism in professional contexts and to create a heightened sense of responsibility in their future roles as managers of linguistically diverse teams. This can be achieved by, for example, making students increasingly aware of the existence of social, economic and political contradictions or the role of power, privilege and oppression in society (Hoggan, 2016, p. 66).

In transformative learning contexts, the educator is a "collaborative learner" (Mezirow, 2000, p. 15) who facilitates learning rather than being an authority. The objective is to create an environment in which learners learn from each other and help each other to learn in problem-solving groups (Mezirow, 1997). An appropriate learning set-up requires the absence of outside coercion, equal opportunities for all participants to contribute and the possibility for everybody to be critically reflective (Mezirow, 2000). Transformative learning outcomes can be achieved through an appropriate range of educational activities, which include group projects, role plays and case studies. Especially case studies engage students in task-oriented problem solving, which is one way to stimulate critical reflection on underlying assumptions (Mezirow, 1997).

## The Seminar Set-up and Design

### Participants

We delivered the one-week seminar to a group of 45 international students as an element of their CEMS (The Global Alliance of Management Education, www.cems.org) Master's in International Management programme hosted by the London School of Economics. The programme brings together professors and students from various CEMS institutions. The seminar is a mandatory element of the programme, and students are automatically assigned to the seminar of the host school where they will spend their exchange term. Thus, most of our students were going to stay at the London School of Economics for the autumn term and were therefore enrolled in this seminar. In addition, given the availability of places, a small number of students applied themselves to attend the seminar because of its unconventional topic and attractive location.

The cultural and linguistic diversity in the classroom was significant. There were students from emerging markets such as Brazil, Chile, China and India sitting next to students from post-communist countries such as Hungary and Poland, or students from Northern (e.g., Denmark or Norway), Middle (e.g., the Netherlands or Germany) and Southern (e.g., Portugal or Italy) Europe. Interestingly, there were only very few native English speakers among the students, one of which was from the UK and another who was from the United States. These students were also bilinguals (e.g., English and Urdu). In general, many students had hybrid identities (Bhabha, 1994) with several nationalities and native tongues. With 21 female and 24 male students, the gender-mix was relatively balanced.

It was expected that the topic of language diversity would be unfamiliar to a significant part of our audience, because it is not a part of the CEMS schools' standard curricula. We were also aware that language diversity might be perceived as a gendered, 'feminine' topic, as it is frequently associated with human resource management. CEMS students major in diverse disciplines ranging from finance, information systems, accounting, marketing and strategy to creative sustainability and industrial engineering. These students are known for being demanding, because they go through a very strict selection process and the CEMS programme enjoys an elite status in many CEMS schools. The programme has consistently been ranked in the top 10 of the Financial Times Global Masters in Management ranking every year since it first appeared (www.cems.org).

### Instructors

Our team of instructors consisted of three female teachers who represented different ages, career stages and cultural backgrounds (Switzerland, Finland and Belgium). Whereas we were responsible for the course design and delivery, the third teacher was in charge of the input on the relationship between language and culture. She also acted as an observer of the learning process and supervised student groups on their case studies. The first author was working as a journalist before returning to academia and starting to work as a lecturer and researcher on language and cultural diversity. She was socialised in more formal and hierarchical teacher-student relationships than the second author, who is a Professor of International Business and had a classic academic career path. She was trained in Finland but spent several years abroad teaching and doing research in English-speaking universities, which exposed her to US-style interactive case-based teaching and learning. The third teacher is a Professor Emerita with extensive experience in teaching international groups of BSc, MSc, MBA and executive MBA students in the field of cross-cultural management.

Language-wise, the faculty was as diverse as the audience. All instructors spoke various languages and were from bilingual families. Also, they all originated from countries which are officially multilingual (Switzerland has four official languages; Finland and Belgium have two each). The first author grew up bilingually with German/Swiss-German and French in the German-speaking part of Switzerland. She also had excellent proficiency in English, good proficiency in Spanish and Italian, and an elementary proficiency in Portuguese. The second author was born in Germany but moved as a baby to Finland with her Swedish-Russian speaking family. She was also fluent in English and had a good understanding of French and Spanish. The third lecturer was from Belgium, and her native languages were Dutch and French. In addition, she spoke excellent English and some Thai. Thus, none of the lecturers were native speakers of English, the language of instruction in the CEMS programme.

Our language trajectories made us very much aware of the potential challenges associated with using English as the language of instruction in an educational setting characterised by power asymmetry and grading. The students possessed various degrees of fluency in English and spoke it using different accents which were likely to affect their level of comfort in the classroom and their willingness and ability to actively participate in discussions and debates. We, therefore, paid particular attention not to react negatively to differences in English proficiency or accents, and we always tried to summarise students' statements when we were unsure about the intended meaning. Occasionally, we also supported students by suggesting words or expressions that might be helpful for them.

However, the fact that the faculty was entirely composed of non-native speakers of English meant that everybody in the class—except for the very few native speakers—were on more or less "equal terms" (Canagarajah, 2007, p. 926). Because English was used as "a language for communication" (House, 2003, p. 556) rather than as "a language for identification" (House, 2003, p. 556), the participants were more at ease. The presence of non-native English-speaking faculty also signalled that contributing to class discussions in a meaningful way did not require 'perfect' English. In this context, the native English standard was abandoned for a "let it pass" principle according to which the speakers' communicative competence was not evaluated as incomplete or deficient (House, 2003, p. 558). This contributed to a sense of psychological safety in the classroom. The variety of educational and professional backgrounds among the faculty members also allowed us to reflect upon whether some students' limited participation in class was due to lack of interest, or a result of being socialised in an educational system in which the professor is always 'right'.

## Educational Methods

In the spirit of a transformative approach to teaching and learning, which focuses on shifts in mindsets and welcomes multiple perspectives (Zhang et al., 2016), we opted for a broad variety of educational methods. We balanced theory- and practice-driven sessions with experiential exercises. First and foremost, from the beginning we established a learning atmosphere based on the sharing of experiences and reflections. As Joy and Poonamallee (2013) argue, teachers should refrain from primarily acting as experts. Table 9.1 gives an overview of the adopted curriculum elements and the related learning goals.

In the following, the educational methods mentioned in Table 9.1 will be unpacked.

*Table 9.1* Overview of curriculum elements, reasons for inclusion and learning goals

| Curriculum element | Reason for inclusion in curriculum | Learning goals |
| --- | --- | --- |
| Coming up with a metaphor about "What language diversity means to me?", visualising and discussing the metaphor in groups | Use of an unexpected, non-traditional educational method | (Self-)awareness of the new topic of language diversity that allows students to share experiences and emotions |
| Faculty input on the 'English empire', language strategies, power effects of multilingualism, various 'Englishes' and accents, the role of English in spreading the 'management gospel' | Introduction to a research-based perspective on language diversity that goes beyond the functionalist view | Problematising the notion of language diversity and the common view that English is the 'golden solution'; rendering students aware of the power effects of language diversity |
| Self-chosen real-life case studies in groups | Personal involvement of the students in the topic by having them conduct research on language diversity in real-life professional contexts | Appreciation of the complexities related to language diversity by engaging students in task-oriented problem solving and critical reflection |
| Workshops with guest speakers | Bringing practical challenges and opportunities of language diversity from various organisational, geographical and industry contexts into the classroom | Development of a more nuanced understanding of language diversity and alternative ways of facilitating communication in multilingual contexts based on real-life experiences |
| Role play "Negotiating HRM practice transfer across borders" | Providing students with an experiential exercise in the classroom; one role required students to simulate limited language skills which significantly affects the negotiation dynamics | Development of a heightened sense of responsibility for individuals whose language proficiency is limited |
| Migration walk in London | Placing language diversity in the broader societal, historical and spatial context of London and the UK; learning outside the classroom | Development of a more comprehensive and situated understanding of language diversity |

*Awareness-Raising and Faculty Inputs*

In order to help students develop awareness of the new topic (Hoggan, 2016) of language diversity, they were asked to visualise what language diversity means to them at the start of the seminar week (see Table 9.1). The students were encouraged to draw metaphors with coloured pens, which they shared in groups and presented on a flipchart. The risk of this unconventional method was that it might have been regarded as 'too soft' and childish, especially by business students. However, we noticed that most students seemed very motivated to engage with this exercise.

Another important learning goal was to problematise the notion of language diversity and develop a more complex perspective (Hoggan, 2016) that challenges the commonly held view of English being the 'golden solution'. We therefore familiarised the students with research findings on the role of language diversity in professional contexts that go beyond the functionalist perspective business students are used to (see Table 9.1). These more traditional expert inputs were delivered in a very interactive mode, always inviting students to answer questions first and share their own thoughts before presenting the research-based view. Faculty inputs covered topics such as HRM-related challenges in multilingual organisations, the "English Empire" (The Economist, 2014) and its many facets (e.g., Steyaert, Ostendorp, & Gaibrois, 2011), language strategies and the effects of introducing corporate languages, and the relationship between language and culture. We also addressed critical perspectives on multilingualism, which focused on power issues at multiple levels of analysis. These included the micro level (the decisive role of language skills for influence and participation, e.g., Angouri, 2014; Marschan-Piekkari, Welch, & Welch, 1999; Vaara, Tienari, & Piekkari, 2005), the meso level (language competence and societal/organisational status, e.g., Bourdieu's, 1991, "linguistic capital") and the macro level (e.g., Phillipson's, 1992, "English linguistic imperialism"). We also sensitised the students to the 'world of Englishes' by showing them various videos in which accents of non-native English speakers and dialects within English played a role. The critique of English as the language in which "management gospel" (Tietze, 2008) is spread was another topic that was covered. We demonstrated that neither English nor the management discourse is neutral, but rather is situated in socio-historical contexts which only privilege some and create a unifying system of knowledge (Tietze, 2008).

*Case Studies in Groups*

After the initial awareness-raising exercise and short faculty inputs offered in an interactive mode, students were introduced to the core assignment of the week. As transformative learning theory highlights, case studies engage students in task-oriented problem solving, which is one way to stimulate critical reflection on underlying assumptions (Mezirow, 1997). We therefore asked student groups to qualitatively investigate a self-chosen research question on language diversity through a research-based case study (see Table 9.1). In a business school context, the use of qualitative methods takes the vast majority of the students beyond their "comfort zone" (Cassell, 2018, p. 119), which is precisely one of the strengths of this research method. As Cassell (2018, p. 131) highlights, a qualitative approach offers business students the opportunity to learn to manage and structure real-life complexity and to "challenge existing mindsets in a creative manner." This is very much in line with the desired outcomes of transformative learning, namely to develop a more complex worldview, to become aware of something new, to build the capacity to appreciate complexity and tolerate uncertainty in the world and to develop a heightened sense of responsibility (Hoggan, 2016).

Because the self-chosen, research-based case studies represented the core element of the seminar, students were granted a significant number of hours for supervised and unsupervised group work on their projects. This culminated in a final presentation on the last seminar day and a final report that had to be delivered at the end of the seminar. The evaluation of the case study represented 80% of the final grade in total (with 40% for the final presentation on the last seminar day and 40% for the final report). The rest of the total grade consisted of an individual pre-assignment and a student evaluation of the final presentations (each worth 10%). Over the week, the faculty members acted as coaches during the students' research, supporting them in solving their self-chosen puzzles by asking them guiding questions and by offering additional references. The groups were formed by the faculty in order to ensure diversity in terms of country origin, university affiliation, language background and gender. With respect to the choice of topic, the students drew on the faculty and guest speakers' inputs, their existing professional and personal contacts, and knowledge of the language environment in their respective home countries. The final topic was a compromise and an outcome of a rather lengthy negotiation process during which the students weighted the various research interests within the group, the availability of relevant data and what was doable within the limited time frame of the seminar.

In designing the group work, we purposefully did not come up with a set of case studies or a list of possible cases, because we wanted to give the students the flexibility to bring in phenomena that were of interest to them and represented issues that they wanted to solve (Joy & Poonamallee, 2013). Also, we intended to draw upon the wealth of experiences of language diversity in the classroom that such an international group of students possessed (Zhang et al., 2016). Furthermore, because we had many students from emerging and post-communist countries as well as students with hybrid identities (Bhabha, 1994), we intended to create an opportunity for them to introduce perspectives from non-Western countries or non-national languages as part of their case-based learning. To give the students some orientation and inspiration for the development of their research questions, we introduced two types of multilingual organisations (NGOs and public organisations such as hospitals) as alternatives to the traditional multinational corporation, various interactional settings (e.g., job talks, written communication and skype conferences), research orientations and perspectives (focus on policies vs. focus on practices; functional, political or relational perspective) and possible data sources (e.g., interviews, blogs, personal experiences and observations).

We also gave the students a short methodological introduction by addressing how to develop research questions (e.g., use 'How' or 'Why' questions; see Booth, Colomb, & Williams, 2003) and how to analyse the case from multiple viewpoints with the help of various data sources. We explained that the students should both aim to explain the case, but also to answer the question of what their study was 'a case of' in more abstract, theoretical terms. This encouraged students to distance themselves from their case during the research process. By defining originality as one criterion of the evaluation of the case study, we further encouraged the students to move beyond what they might consider 'safe' research questions based on conventional management courses or textbook approaches.

Conducting qualitative case studies made students realise how many factors might come into play when people of various language backgrounds come together for communication and work purposes. The issues they covered ranged from hierarchies between languages (Hua, 2014) on a societal level, to questions of participation versus exclusion in conversations or organisations, to advantages of native speakers and the effects of using English as a language of instruction in higher education (see Table 9.2 for an overview of research-based case studies and their contribution to transformative learning). More specifically, one student group took on a case study on Uber drivers of Ukrainian origin in Poland. Their findings not only showed how limited language skills of non-native service deliverers can create customer frustration, but they also highlighted the public polemics and the (re)production of cultural stereotypes to which such problems might lead.

Another case study showed that the governmental language policy in South Tyrol, which requires its teenage citizens to choose one linguistic community, either German- or Italian-speaking, has significant effects on the labour market. The students found that Italian and German occupied different roles, with German being the language perceived as the language predominantly used in business contexts, which affects both teenagers' choice of linguistic community and the likelihood of being recruited. The study also showed that native Italian speakers are occasionally discriminated against, whereas German native speakers enjoy considerable

*Table 9.2* Overview of research-based case studies and their contribution to transformative learning

| Main learning outcomes | Focus | Contribution to transformative learning |
| --- | --- | --- |
| Appreciating the impact of political and societal issues on business (e.g., governmental language policies and hierarchies of languages) | Relevance of the broader context in which management of language diversity takes place | Moving away from a narrow view to a more comprehensive view of managing language diversity in business contexts |
| Understanding the relationship between limited language skills and the reproduction of cultural stereotypes (e.g., 'culture' viewed as excuse and explanation for miscommunication instead of lack of language proficiency) | Under-addressed role of language in intercultural communication | Increasing the awareness of the connections between language diversity and the use of 'culture' as an all-encompassing explanatory factor of behaviour |
| Becoming aware of language-based exclusion and inclusion | Heightened self-awareness and sense of responsibility for management of language diversity | Moving away from a functionalist perspective to a more self-reflexive view of managing language diversity |
| Understanding the advantages that native English speakers have when English is used as a lingua franca (not only in business, but also e.g., in higher education) | Downsides of adopting English as a common corporate language | Moving away from a neutral, instrumental view to a more critical view of language that underscores power imbalances and asymmetries in organisational life |
| Viewing the advantages of 'broken English' as a common platform for non-native speakers | Awareness of using 'imperfect' language skills as individual and organisational resources for communication | Moving away from a deficit-oriented view to a resource-oriented view of 'broken English' that does not consider it a limitation |
| Appreciating the challenges of language differences in service-oriented interactions (e.g., customers or patients) | Context-specificity of language use | Moving away from an instrumental to a more nuanced and complex view of managing language diversity in professional settings |

advantages in business. Similarly, issues of participation and access to services were raised in two case studies on the medical sector.

While one group addressed the problems of non-native English speaking immigrants in the UK healthcare system, another investigated the challenges in interactions between patients and medical volunteers who did not share a language in developing countries. Yet another group investigated the effects of non-native English speaking faculty teaching in English on master's students. As the group wrote in their final report, contrary to their pre-conceived expectations, the lecturers' lack of fluency did not represent an obstacle for students, but rather prepared them for the job market, where the common language is a 'broken' or 'multilingual' version of English.

### Guest Speakers

In order to support students in developing a more complex perspective (Hoggan, 2016) on language diversity based on real-life experiences from various industries and geographical contexts, we complemented our educating trio with a set of guest lecturers who acted as 'voices from practice', as Table 9.1 shows. These guest lecturers were carefully chosen with respect to a number of criteria. First of all, in order to counterbalance the female dominance of the instructors, two out of the three guest speakers were male. Second, we invited a Human Resources Vice President who originated from an emerging country and worked at the headquarters of a European multinational corporation (a CEMS corporate partner). In doing so, we responded to Joy and Poonamallee's (2013) call to explicitly introduce non-Western countries and voices from the periphery in management learning. A related consideration was to confront the stereotype that all human resource managers are females. Third, we chose the guest speakers from a broad variety of industry sectors, ranging from consumer goods and private equity to toy manufacturing. This demonstrated to the students that language diversity matters across industries, even in a tough 'numbers industry' such as private equity. Finally, the invitation of a language manager from a European toy manufacturer showed that at least in some companies, top management considers language diversity so important that it allocates a specific management position to this activity.

The three guest speakers from the professional world demonstrated the relevance of language diversity across several industries. Two of them (the HRM Vice President from a multinational corporation and the language manager of a toy producing firm) first introduced the students to 'real-life' problems related to language diversity in their companies and then asked the students to come up with solutions. These proposed solutions were then discussed together with the visiting managers. The co-founder and partner of a private equity firm presented and discussed leadership in a multicultural private equity organisation. Furthermore, an academic guest lecturer addressed the underestimated role of language diversity in SMEs, and the participants of a round table debated recruitment, translation challenges and management in multilingual environments.

## Experientially Oriented Educational Methods

The seminar also included experientially oriented educational methods. A role play was developed which was inspired by a real managerial situation (see Table 9.1) and simulated the negotiations of transferring HRM practices across borders in a Swiss multinational corporation. It involved three actor roles and an observer, who gave feedback to the fellow students in actor roles and reflected on the role play in class. One role description involved poor fluency in English. The roles also differed in terms of career stage, nationality, leadership style and organisational status (corporate headquarters, regional headquarters and local subsidiary). Together these roles created a complex scenario for the meeting on HRM issues for the actors to simulate. The use of a role play as an educational method aimed at making students *experience* the consequences of limited language skills on the process and outcome of negotiations. In line with the transformative learning approach, we thus aimed at developing a heightened sense of responsibility (Hoggan, 2016) in class for individuals whose language proficiency is limited. For the simulation, we thus purposefully reversed the roles of the acting students in order to maximise the effect of the experience. For example, those who were in reality very proficient in English played the role of the manager with the weakest English skills, female students took on male roles, and the rather reserved students played the role of the vocal manager.

Another experiential educational method took place outside the classroom, as Table 9.1 shows. One afternoon, the whole class and the faculty went on a guided migration walking tour through London, which ended in the culturally very diverse neighbourhood of Brixton. This represented a strong contrast to the 'safe' classroom. The walk embedded the language topic into the wider societal, historical and spatial context of migration and thus contributed to the students' development of a more comprehensive view (Hoggan, 2016) on language diversity. Also, by taking the students and faculty out of the classroom into the 'real' world and the various neighbourhoods of London, another more physical, material and sensual way of engaging with the topic was provided.

## Discussion and Conclusion

In this chapter, we have discussed the key insights gained from educating business students in managing language diversity in a one-week seminar at the London School of Economics through a transformative learning approach (Hoggan, 2016; Mezirow, 2000; Mezirow, 1997). We aimed at guiding students—and future managers—to become aware of the significance of this unfamiliar topic. Our purpose was to develop a more complex perspective on language diversity beyond the common view of English as a 'golden solution' as well as a heightened sense of responsibility for individuals whose language proficiency is limited in interaction. As our title suggests, many students did not consider the topic very relevant or exciting at the beginning of the seminar, which they revealed in the feedback session on the last seminar day. However, over the course of the week, they had changed their perspective, as several of them stressed. One student even approached us after the end of the seminar to confess to us that at the beginning, he had thought the topic was boring, but that he was now fascinated by it.

The introduction to critical perspectives on language diversity, which highlighted power issues, played an important role in supporting students to move beyond a functionalist and even simplistic perspective on language diversity. During the course of the seminar, students returned to the critical perspectives, especially in their research-based case studies. Students mentioned as a key takeaway that language is not only an instrument of communication but that it also has social implications for e.g., trust building in organisational settings. They also named the complexity and the multi-layeredness of language as an important insight. Others stressed that a mandated common corporate language does not represent the only way to address multilingualism, with some even questioning whether the much evangelised "Englishization" (Dor, 2004) is as important a trend as is often assumed.

In this seminar, we opted for qualitative case studies in groups as a core element of the curriculum. They proved to be an excellent method because it made students engage with the complexity of language diversity. Business school students tend to be trained from a functionalist worldview, which emphasises the social costs arising from human imperfections (Ghoshal, 2005) and often goes hand-in-hand with a mechanistic and instrumental understanding of language. These fundamental assumptions are rarely questioned in the classroom. As an educational method, case studies provide an avenue for generating alternative explanations about phenomena, to contextualise them and to reflect on practitioners' understanding of their world.

We are aware that asking students to conduct qualitative case studies that are based on self-developed research questions is demanding. Our experience shows, however, that with adequate support and coaching sessions dedicated to working on case studies in groups, students were able to live up to this task. Importantly, this freedom of choice noticeably contributed to students' sense of fulfilment and identification with their projects as well as receptiveness of the seminar topic at large. As previous research shows, linking learning to students' own interests can improve motivation (Schunk & Mullen, 2013). We therefore believe that asking students to conduct research-based case studies that are guided by self-developed research questions could also be used in other higher education settings, both at universities and in applied sciences contexts. In the latter case, students' strong grounding in practice and first-hand experience of language diversity in professional contexts might even be an advantage, leading to the development of more managerially relevant research questions. Successfully conducting such a challenging project may also have had an empowering effect on students.

During the seminar, we acted as coaches rather than experts in order to support the students' learning process. This faculty role proved very useful as it assisted us in remaining open to new insights and enhanced student-centred learning processes. At the same time, giving selected research-based inputs to stimulate thinking at the beginning of the seminar proved important, especially in the case of neglected topics, whose relevance might not be immediately obvious to students.

The guest speakers also offered the students a set of unexpected insights and thus opportunities for transformative learning (Szkudlarek et al., 2013; Zhang et al., 2016). Both male speakers (the HRM Vice President of the multinational corporation and the co-founder of the private equity firm) stressed the importance of being humble in communication across linguistic and cultural borders. One of them even self-critically reflected upon having made fun of people with limited English skills earlier in his career. The representative of the private equity sector, a tough 'numbers industry', surprised the participants with his sensitive, self-established rules for leading meetings with linguistically diverse participants. He shared his practice to always make the 'weakest', e.g., the non-native speaker at the table, speak up first, and never to ask people with limited language skills 'yes' or 'no' questions because they might answer 'yes' for insecurity or conformity reasons. The students were very impressed when hearing these confessional tales and personal reflections—perhaps also because they were told by two male practitioners, countering the cliché that language issues are 'feminine'.

Working with experiential education methods such as role plays proved to be a powerful method to make students, who may be initially sceptical towards the topic, engage with it. Some business students, who have travelled widely and who are fluent in many languages, may never have personally experienced how it feels to be handicapped because of limited language fluency. Assigning them this unfamiliar role might be an effective way to address this.

Engaging in self-reflexivity (Cunliffe & Jun, 2005) about our experiences as educators in the seminar, we realised that the cultural and linguistic diversity of students represented a precious resource of insight and thus learning opportunities (Zhang et al., 2016). The large number of students from emerging and post-communist countries offered many opportunities to introduce non-Western countries and non-traditional companies in case-based learning (Joy & Poonamallee, 2013). In a joint learning process, the 45 students and the three faculty members alike benefited from the wealth of experiences that came together in the classroom. We therefore strongly encourage faculty to aim at having a broad mix of language backgrounds and countries of origin in the classroom and aim at creating a safe atmosphere for learning. Actively mixing students from very different backgrounds—for instance by 'forcing' them to work in teams with students of other nationalities and native languages, as we did in this seminar—is one way of achieving this. Students from 'the periphery' are particularly inclined to bring additional perspectives assuming they possess sufficient skills in the language of instruction.

## Suggestions for Educators

In terms of suggestions for educating business students in the future, we found students with bicultural (Brannen & Thomas, 2010) or multicultural (Pekerti & Thomas, 2016) identities or from the periphery to be genuinely interested in language diversity as a topic. They represent valuable resources in terms of motivating students who are less interested in the topic at the outset. Faculty could thus consider purposefully mixing students with diverse profiles in discussions as well as projects conducted in groups.

Finally, the multilingual reality that students experienced in the classroom was not an explicit part of the original seminar. Although students talked about the relevance of language diversity in their home countries (e.g., linguistically very diverse countries such as India vs. de facto monolingual countries such as the UK) and shared experiences of multilingualism in professional contexts throughout the seminar, we did not explicitly ask them to reflect on the effect of using English as a language of instruction on their class participation or group work. Although many students articulated how much their view on language had changed in the course of the seminar, we did not explicitly invite students to reflect on this. Therefore, we suggest introducing reflexivity (e.g., Cunliffe, 2009, 2016; Cunliffe & Jun, 2005; Kassis-Henderson, Cohen, & McCulloch, 2018) as a fundamental part of the learning outcomes and delivery of future seminars on managing multilingual companies. When students and faculty start questioning what they take for granted (Cunliffe, 2016), they get closer to the goals of transformative learning, and thus to the irreversible changes in their way of experiencing, conceptualising and interacting with the world around them (Hoggan, 2016). Instead of being understood as a hindrance to the smooth transmission of seemingly neutral information, language diversity becomes part of the complexities of human nature (cf. Ghoshal, 2005) that has significant implications for managers and employees. This is something every well-rounded educator and practitioner should be aware of.

## Acknowledgments

We thank two anonymous reviewers for their valuable comments on a previous version of this book chapter and the responsible editor, Sierk Horn, for his valuable suggestions. We would also like to acknowledge Jane Kassis-Henderson and Wilhelm Barner-Rasmussen for their suggestion to include reflexivity in the seminar curriculum, as well as Peter Daly for his highly valuable literature suggestions. Furthermore, we thank Jason Roger Parry for carefully proofreading this chapter. Finally, we are grateful to the CEMS team at the London School of Economics for their support and approval of this contribution as well as to the many CEMS students whom we were privileged to teach.

## References

Angouri, J. (2014). Multilingualism in the workplace: Language practices in multilingual contexts. *Multilingua, 33*(1–2), 1–9.

Bhabha, H. (1994). *The location of culture*. London: Routledge.

Booth, W. C., Colomb, G. G., & Williams, J. M. (2003). *The craft of research* (2nd ed.). Chicago: The University of Chicago Press.

Bourdieu, P. (1991). *Language and symbolic power* (Gino Raymond and Matthew Adamson, Trans.). Cambridge: Polity Press.

Brannen, M. Y., Piekkari, R., & Tietze, S. (2014). The multifaceted role of language in international business: Unpacking the forms, functions and features of a critical challenge to MNC theory and performance. *Journal of International Business Studies, 45*(5), 495–507.

Brannen, M. Y., & Thomas, D. C. (2010). Bicultural individuals in organizations: Implications and opportunity. *International Journal of Cross Cultural Management, 10*(1), 5–16.

Canagarajah, S. (2007). Lingua franca English, multilingual communities, and language acquisition. *The Modern Language Journal, 91*, 923–939.

Cassell, C. (2018). "Pushed beyond my comfort zone": MBA student experiences of conducting qualitative research. *Academy of Management Learning & Education, 17*(2), 119–136.

Cunliffe, A. L. (2009). The philosopher leader: On relationalism, ethics and reflexivity—A critical perspective to teaching leadership. *Management Learning, 40*(1), 87–101.

Cunliffe, A. L. (2016). "On becoming a critically reflexive practitioner" redux: What does it mean to be reflexive? *Journal of Management Education, 40*(6), 740–746.

Cunliffe, A. L., & Jun, J. S. (2005). The need for reflexivity in public administration. *Administration & Society, 37*(2), 225–242.

Dor, D. (2004). From Englishization to imposed multilingualism: Globalization, the Internet, and the political economy of the linguistic code. *Public Culture, 16*(1), 97–118.

The Economist. (2014, February 15). The English empire: A growing number of firms worldwide are adopting English as their official language. *The Economist*. Retrieved September 15, 2015, from www.economist.com/business/2014/02/15/the-english-empire

Ghoshal, S. (2005). Bad management theories are destroying good management practices. *Academy of Management Learning & Education, 4*(1), 75–91.

Hoggan, C. D. (2016). Transformative learning as a metatheory: Definition, criteria, and typology. *Adult Education Quarterly, 66*(1), 57–75.

Holden, N., Michailova, S., & Tietze, S. (2015). Editorial introduction. In N. Holden, S. Michailova, & S. Tietze (Eds.), *The Routledge companion to cross-cultural management* (pp. xlv–xlix). London: Routledge.

House, J. (2003). English as a lingua franca: A threat to multilingualism? *Journal of Sociolinguistics, 7*(4), 556–578.

Hua, Z. (2014). Piecing together the 'workplace multilingualism' jigsaw puzzle. *Multilingua, 33*(1–2), 233–242.

Joy, S., & Poonamallee, L. (2013). Cross-cultural teaching in globalized management classrooms: Time to move from functionalist to postcolonial approaches? *Academy of Management Learning & Education, 12*(3), 396–413.

Kassis-Henderson, J., Cohen, L., & McCulloch, R. (2018). Boundary crossing and reflexivity: Navigating the complexity of cultural and linguistic identity. *Business and Professional Communication Quarterly, 81*(3), 304–327.

Marschan-Piekkari, R., Welch, D., & Welch, L. (1999). In the shadow: The impact of language on structure, power and communication in the multinational. *International Business Review, 8*(4), 421–440.

Mezirow, J. (1997). Transformative learning: Theory to practice. *New Directions for Adult and Continuing Education, 74*, 5–12.

Mezirow, J. (2000). Learning to think like an adult: Core concepts of transformation theory. In J. Mezirow (Ed.), *Learning as transformation: Critical perspectives on a theory in progress* (pp. 3–33). San Francisco, CA: Jossey-Bass.

Pekerti, A. A., & Thomas, D. C. (2016). n-Culturals: Modeling the multicultural identity. *Cross Cultural & Strategic Management, 23*(1), 101–127.

Phillipson, R. (1992). *Linguistic imperialism*. Oxford: Oxford University Press.

Sahlin-Andersson, K., & Engwall, L. (2002). *The expansion of management knowledge: Carriers, flows and sources*. Stanford, CA: Stanford University Press.

Schunk, D. H., & Mullen, C. A. (2013). Motivation. In J. Hattie & E. M. Anderman (Eds.), *International guide to student achievement* (pp. 67–69). London: Routledge.

Steyaert, C., Ostendorp, A., & Gaibrois, C. (2011). Multilingual organizations as 'linguascapes': Negotiating the position of English through discursive practices. *Journal of World Business, 46*(3), 270–278.

Szkudlarek, B., McNett, J., Romani, L., & Lane, H. (2013). The past, present, and future of cross-cultural management education: The educators' perspective. *Academy of Management Learning & Education, 12*(3), 477–493.

Tietze, S. (2008). *International management and language*. London: Routledge.

Vaara, E. Tienari, J., & Piekkari, R. (2005). Language and the circuits of power in a merging multinational corporation. *Journal of Management Studies, 42*(3), 595–623.

Zhang, M. M., Xia, J., Fan, D., & Zhu, J. C. (2016). Managing student diversity in business education: Incorporating campus diversity into the curriculum to foster inclusion and academic success of international students. *Academy of Management Learning & Education, 15*(2), 366–380.

# 10 Language Management in the Global Firm

## Transforming Research Into Education

*Terry Mughan*

In the time since the publication of special issues on language in the *Journal of World Business* (Piekkari & Tietze, 2011) and the *Journal of International Business Studies* (Brannen, Piekkari, & Tietze, 2014), the productivity and visibility of scholars working in the field has increased significantly. For two leading journals to dedicate space to language in this way was considered to constitute entry to the mainstream of business and management scholarship (Mughan, 2015). The appearance of this current volume in the Routledge Companion Series supports this view.

Prior to this date, challenging questions about language were also raised by eminent international business scholars for whom language is not their primary field of interest. Johanson and Vahlne (1977) and Luo and Shenkar (2006) acknowledged that research in international business that ignored language as a core dimension of international operations is fundamentally flawed. On the other hand, since then, we have seen a massive decline in the numbers of students in English-speaking countries studying languages at both secondary and higher education levels (Tinsley, 2019). At the same time, the number of people learning English as a second language has mushroomed and many of them have sought employment in the global workforce, either in companies in emerging economies, in subsidiaries of global organisations or as migrants (Goby & Nickerson, 2015). Some of the world's largest corporations, which now have easier access to this multilingual workforce, have decided to declare English as their official corporate language (Neeley, 2012). In addition, technological solutions to the language problem, such as freely available translation and voice recognition software have multiplied. If we look at the world through the rose-tinted spectacles of English native-speakers the language problem has largely disappeared. Maybe it has in some respects, and in others it has just morphed into something less visible. What does contemporary research in the international business community tell us about these changes?

Of course, language is the primary means by which human beings formulate and communicate their most complex thoughts and ideas, so it would appear reasonable to use this chapter to review progress. Its purpose is to ask whether this scholarly activity has progressed in such a way as to embed language as a core theme in the study of international business and its associated fields, such as management, organisational behavior and communication in the new global economy. In particular, we will consider whether this body of research has generated knowledge and tools to improve the broader domain of business and management in its primary activities of research and education. In other words, can all managers, linguists or not, find here something they can act on? From a scholarly point of view, are we communicating with our peers in strategy, operations, marketing and organisational behavior etc., or are language-sensitive researchers communicating mainly with each other and our respective networks in a comfortable collective mindset?

The structure of this chapter will consist of a review of relevant litera-ture, in the first instance of several recent field-wide reviews. Then there will be a closer focus on the 'competing' perspectives of lingua franca and multilinguality (the practice of multiple language use) in international business, under the general heading of 'policy.' This will then be elabo-rated on in a review of the work on 'language strategy' emanating mainly from the United Kingdom and the heavy policy focus on languages as a key asset in the internationalisation of small and medium-sized enter-prises from roughly 1977 to the present day, a field massively under-acknowledged in the view of the author.

In discussing these contributions, reference is made to important pub-lications in the journals and collections mentioned earlier, as well as to data more broadly sourced by the author that is pertinent to this review. This discussion is grounded in a general reflection on the field of language in international business at this stage, which is critical and constructive. I will argue that the model of language education based mainly on con-cepts of proficiency (in foreign languages) and exactitude (in translation practice) is no longer sufficient to reflect business realities or address the needs of managers.

The chapter will go on to do more than review literature. It will also make a proposition. This proposition will stem from the preceding review and discussion and will take the form of an outline plan for a future direction that follows logically from a commitment to education as well as research. It will address the question "What do linguists and international business educators need to do to advance to the next level of the integration of language research findings into international busi-ness research and education?"

## Literature Review

The field of language in international business is intrinsically broad because it draws on associated fields of linguistics, cultural studies, psychology and education to understand phenomena in trade, firms, organisation, production, sales and negotiations. Rather than attempt to capture all the relevant articles, books and perspectives that have been published over the last 10, 20 or 30 years, I will focus in this first part of the review on pieces that have endeavored to take a bird's eye view of the field and identify their key characteristics and themes as they pertain to the aforementioned question.

Piekkari and Tietze wrote the introduction to and edited the *Journal of World Business*, Special Issue (2011). The purpose of this collection, which attracted 11 submissions of which six were selected for publication, was to "set the agenda" for language-sensitive research around something of a focus on the concept of language-standardisation, the attempt by senior management to "instill a common corporate language" (p. 267). A range of associated themes such as translation, multilinguality, the language barrier, language competence of managers, human resource strategies and the role of language in cross-cultural research provided empirical substance with real business relevance to the debate about organisational approaches to the language problem. In this respect, the issue crystalised the desire on the part of corporations to impose universal solutions across their global operations and saw that as somewhat at odds to the broader commitment to communication with local markets that remains central today to global strategy in most such organisations. The quality of the articles selected for this special issue and its framing were very influential in opening up new doors for discussion and research in the years following its publication.

Brannen et al. wrote the introduction to and edited the *Journal of International Business Studies*, Special Issue (2014). This dedicated issue of the top-ranked international business journal had as its purpose "to encourage the development of new and emerging theoretical domains that originate from an explicit focus on language and thereby render the IB field more sophisticated in its understanding of the multifaceted role of language in today's global business realities" (p. 2), whilst considering concepts like semiotics, gender and power to be of relevance to IB research. The result was a wide range of articles published over two issues of the journal on subjects as diverse as gender and post-colonial perspectives to the more conventional type considering language and its relationship with culture, MNCs and research methods. This special issue attracted 78 submissions, of which 14 were published in *JIBS*. Even in comparison with other special issues in this leading journal, these figures are strikingly high and reflect a true awakening of a scholarly community.

In their book, *Language in International Business*, Piekkari, Welch, and Welch (2014) take a mainly functional approach to the place of languages in firms' international expansion, whilst assembling a broad picture of the exposure to language on all levels of the organisation and its markets. An incontrovertible case for the place of language at the heart of international business strategy, drawing on several decades of distinguished research and authorship, is made. Much of this data and theory draws on collaboration with Scandinavian companies and the ensuing findings that a strong command of the English language by managers does not exclude the use and value of other languages in the modern business organisation. The authors conclude that "managerial action has to be in concert with individual action in order for language to be seen as a distinctive part of the firm's international capabilities." This perspective of the relationship between management and language capability crystalises the power and value of this book.

The dedicated section on language assembled and edited by Mughan (2015) "Language and languages: moving from the periphery to the core" in the Routledge Companion to Cross-cultural Management (eds. Holden, Michailova, & Tietze, 2015) was the first of its kind in a cross-cultural collection. It contained chapters covering a wide range of perspectives on the subject. In adopting a lens from the field of cross-cultural management (culture-general, culture-specific), it sought to give prominence to the separate but connected and sometimes confused domains of specific (usually national) language codes on the one hand and general phenomena crossing languages (drawn from linguistics, psychology and philosophy) on the other. The section contained theoretical and empirical pieces with fascinating studies of multilingual communities in Switzerland and the United Arab Emirates, demonstrating how language differences are manifested and tackled in contemporary communities and projects.

In their review of 264 academic articles in the area of language and international business, Tenzer, Terjesen, and Harzing (2017) present a view of the subject informed more by perspectives of disciplinary diversity beyond business and management and its units of analysis. In noting ". . . that the field remains fragmented, with serious knowledge gaps in theory, data, methodology, and content" (p. 28), the authors call for more "integration of insights from different academic disciplines as an opportunity to gain a deeper understanding of language complexity in international business" (p. 29).

Brannen and Mughan (2016), as part of a special collection of books on key international business themes, conducted a review of articles on language published in the *Journal of International Business Studies* between 1976 and 2017. They identified four key themes within which language had found a fit with other scholars in the area of international business; language as an instrument, language and culture, language and strategy and language as a central construct in IB. They also identify four emerging challenge areas in IB where language will play an integral part: language policy and the MNC, migration and human mobility, big data and multilinguality. They conclude that the growth in language research has not had a great impact on the domain of firm strategy and call for more focus on the core areas of business by linguists.

This review of recent reviews is necessarily brief but is illustrative of the scale, complexity and depth of the challenges facing researchers and innovators in this area. The wide range of concepts, many of which have antecedents in disciplines other than languages and are necessarily dependent on or connected with other concepts and theories, makes the challenge of lucidity and impact even harder to achieve. The breadth and relevance of recently published research inspired by sociolinguistics, gender studies or post-colonial theory have been an important part of the growth in the field in the last decade, and it is not the purpose of this chapter to doubt its relevance or integrity. My impulse, however, is to return to the call made in Brannen and Mughan (2016) for greater focus to be laid on the deeper integration of language awareness and theories into the core field of international business strategy and management operations. This objective is not uncommon in our field. Jack (2015) maps out the challenge for the field of cross-cultural management as being about research, education and inclusivity. In the next section, I will identify some key contributions made by language researchers in this field that constitute managerial knowledge. What do we know about language in international business organisations that managers in those organisations (as well as students) need to know?

## Language-Sensitive Research

One of the main debates among scholars has been around the issue of language policy in the international organisation. Advocates of the lingua franca model as a solution for communicative failures in the multicultural organisation vie with proponents of multilinguality who see it as a resource for innovation and identification. Neeley (2012) put a stake in the ground for the English language, stating that adopters (of it) "will find significant advantages" (p. 2). In analysing the process of policy development, Dhir and Goke-Pariola (2002) pointed out the complexity and risk facing corporate leaders. "The process that constrains a company to a standard language may actually deny it access to critical resources unique to the members' own diverse training and experiences" (p. 242). Sanden (2018) identifies ten areas of risk in the process, including employee performance, reallocation of power, non-compliance of employees and lack of alignment with the overall business plan. She proposes that the selection of a single language is not an end in itself and that language management strategies need to be put in place.

Harzing, Koster, and Magner (2011) identify and categorise language problems that emerge in global organisations and the in praxis solutions (such as code-switching) found by managers. Angouri (2013) stresses the limitations of the top-down policy approach and the enduring importance of 'rapport' between employees that drives the continuing use of native languages. Janssens and Steyaert (2014) delve into the process of communication in culturally complex organisations and propose three models of language policy, monological lingua franca, monological multilingualism and multilingual franca. They see language use as a complex, hybrid process and a form of social practice. Many scholars have called for more empirical work to map language practice, although important studies already exist. Yanaprasart (2016) describes an extensive project carried out in Swiss organisations which, from the state-level down, have a high degree of multilinguality enshrined in their policies. In this defined policy environment, the emphasis is on the *management* of languages in the workplace and identifying a multilingual model "that better values plurilingual speakers, recognizes their achievements, strengthens their uniqueness for collective goals by providing them diverse, creative, hybrid forms of linguistic tools" (p. 103). Goby and Nickerson (2015) explore the reciprocity of language use between Arabic and English in their study of workplace communication in Dubai. Their call for more micro-level research to explore co-operative behavior reinforces models of social practice and rapport building found elsewhere. Moreover, it demonstrates how the field of cross-cultural management now applies to all levels of the workforce, not just expatriates. Barner-Rasmussen, Ehrnrooth, and Koveshnikov (2014) develop the concept of 'boundary-spanners,' people in the organisation who can "engage in and facilitate significant interactions between . . . two groups" (p. 887) in the MNC. They find that these individuals play a crucial role in inter-unit relationships, even when their skills and actions are not officially recognised by the employer. Human resource policy in this area is the prime focus of Peltokorpi and Vaara (2014). In examining the effects of language-sensitive recruitment on knowledge transfer in MNCs, they found that they are related to concepts of identity, power, networks and communicative competence and can be both productive and counter-productive. Here again, the importance of a customised, non-binary approach to language policy and practices is advocated. Church-Morel and Bartel-Radic (2016) view the language construct from a diversity perspective and see the concepts of skills, identity and power as being innately associated with both. Their findings "point to the need to decouple language skills from language attitudes and examine the precise relationships between them" (p. 22). Cohen, Kassis-Henderson, and Lecomte (2015) also see diversity as a key concept, particularly as it relates to language environments. They argue that multilinguality promotes receptiveness to cultural nuance and that a new dimension of language education that promotes a new form of skills (akin to what I refer to here as language-general skills) is needed to equip future managers to prosper in the new global environment. Lauring and Klitmøller (2017) approach the language issue from the point of view of inclusion and creativity and discuss ways in which language-users and groups may be ostracised for reasons of low competence in a given language. This study reinforces the message that managing specific language competences on their own needs to be accompanied by the management of the social dimensions of language use in the organisation.

An exciting and valuable supplement to the idea of complexity and multi-linguality is provided by Ronen et al (2014). He studied translated texts on the World Wide Web, specifically the media of books, Wikipedia and Twitter. Whilst English emerged as a global hub, it was inextricably inter-related with 'intermediate languages' which include Spanish, French, German, Russian, Portuguese and Chinese. The salient point here is that English is not an independent global language, distinct from other languages. Where data appear in English, it has often been fed in and translated from other languages in various sequences and processes and vice versa. The interplay between languages happens electronically, too, and sometimes invisibly.

To summarise, language-sensitive research into global organisations and phenomena does not support the idea of a rigid single lingua franca policy as a solution to the challenges of cross-border corporate communication. This research has identified a number of phenomena which are linked to the language problem in those organisations (see Table 10.1). These include:

*Table 10.1* Language-related phenomena in organisations

- (Absence/presence of) language policy
- (Absence/presence of) language strategy
- Absence of language management
- Capability
- Anxiety
- Diversity
- Creativity
- Identity
- Power
- Networks
- Social and linguistic hybridity and dynamic practice
- Inter-unit relations (Boundary-spanning)

These findings are based, for the large part, on research into language practice in international or multilingual organisations. There is some evidence of focused studies of the management of language as a strategic practice (particularly in human resource management), but it is mainly the *absence* of policy and strategy and the ad-hocism of problem-solving and decision-making across the entire organisation with regard to language that emerge from empirical studies.

## Management-Centred Research

Management (as a general concept) is distinct from many other social science disciplines to the extent that it focusses on solutions as much as it does on problems. In other words, the purpose of research into management is to improve management practice. This propositional dimension of research and development has yet to come to prominence in the language-sensitive part of the IB community. Despite the substantial progress in identifying the problems bedevilling their subject-area, which on a macro level include historical neglect, preference for quantitative, numerically based data and theory-building and the collapse of foreign language-learning in English-speaking universities, language researchers in IB have not yet sought to apply the empirical evidence they have obtained to the task of improving the quality of language management in global organisations or indeed universities. This historical journey from instrumentalism to interdisciplinary diversity, bypassing management learning, is described in the Brannen and Mughan (2016) review of the international business field. Significant contributions have been made by mainstream management scholars to integrate language into mainstream international and organisational theory. Brannen (2004), in an assessment of the internationalisation process of Disney obtained through an ethnographic study, uses the code model of communication and a semiotics framework to arrive at a theory of recontextualisation. The blend of semantic and strategic fit she adopts serves as an exemplar for linguists researching business process. Luo and Shenkar (2006) proposed an organisational strategy framework for the design of a language system. Brannen and Doz (2012) presented the multinational organisation as a generator of its own internal language and examined the extent to which that process might alternatively give rise or inhibit strategic agility in competitive international markets. This view of language, as a barometer of strategic health as opposed to a simple instrument reflecting practices and processes, is developed in a later piece which illustrates the importance of semiotics in the organisation more fully (Brannen & Mughan, 2018).

In this respect, it is incumbent to extend the reach of language research in IB not just to other social science disciplines but to associated communities closer to home. The mainstream of IB, as described in this review so far, represents a rather narrow scope of study mainly in the domain of multinational corporations (MNCs). It excludes a healthy body of literature pertaining to the internationalisation of small and medium-sized enterprises (SMEs) that is rarely cited in IB journals even though the concept of language is central to both the academic and policy studies of this community. Lloyd-Reason and Mughan (2002) describe the key features of this perspective as being a focus on the owner-manager, management of limited resources and the development of key skills in international operations, including the development of an international mindset to obtain and understand information and intelligence from multiple foreign markets.

This strand of literature is based on the rationale of government support for these companies justified by the concept of 'market failure.' Exporting is economically necessary, but for these companies, the costs and risks are prohibitive and deter owner-managers from going international. Government support in the areas of skills development and access to market information is therefore economically justified. In the United Kingdom, for example, this policy has been executed for several decades and universities became partners with government in the provision of these services, such as the Language for Export Scheme in the 1980s (Mughan, 1990).

The overall proposition emerging from these studies was termed a "Language Management Strategy" by Embleton and Hagen (1992) and in a later, large-scale study funded by the European Commission (Hagen, 2011) came to embody the following measures (p. 4) in Table 10.2:

*Table 10.2* A 'functional' language strategy

- Using local agents to solve language problems
- Creating culturally and/or linguistically adapted websites
- Using linguistic audits
- Using professional translators/interpreters
- Translating promotional, sales and/or technical material
- Offering language training and cultural briefing schemes, including online language learning
- Instituting a 'polyglot' employee selection and recruitment policy
- Encouraging cross-border staff mobility
- Adopting 'buddying' and secondment schemes
- Forging links with local universities, e.g. for taking students on foreign placement
- Encouraging native-speaker recruitment
- Planning e-commerce underpinned by multilingual operations (e.g. local currency and language

This suite of activities was designed to improve the management capability of the company. That means developing a language strategy that accompanies the practice of language training within the company, based on a needs analysis and language audit of existing personnel. The overarching principle is that skills in specific languages have to be developed in line with the company's international strategy and accompanied by a range of activities, both technical and social, to equip the company with the resources to build communications and relations with foreign partners, including agents, other representatives and potential clients. Later work (Hagen, 2011) sought to leverage the growth of cross-cultural studies by further linking language skills with cross-cultural knowledge and skills.

Reeves and Wright (1996) developed an exhaustive guide to language auditing in small and medium-sized enterprises that bears the germs of a language management model for larger companies, too. It took a thoroughly functional approach by applying standard strategic and operational principles to the concept of language. It proposed that preparing for international operations should entail as rigorous an assessment of the internal language capacity and capabilities of the organisations as would be applied to, say, production capacity. This entails a five-stage audit process of posts and postholders with the resulting data being mapped against target market data and strategic plans. This functionalist approach to international operations may serve as the basis for a language management strategy. Their target readership is very interesting because it does not focus on the language users but on those who manage and support those users (see Table 10.3).

So, this was a book about languages targeted at people who are not necessarily practicing linguists. It is a book for people who have to manage languages. Whilst this body of work has had significant impact on companies across the UK and Europe, it has received scant attention from the IB research community. Now, two decades later, the business environment has changed and we see more companies formed as a result of mergers, acquisitions and alliance and more emphasis on the global teams that have come about in response to new structures and markets, although exporting, subsidiaries and agents still play a big part in the operations of many companies. The work by Hagen and Reeves and Wright was policy and practitioner based and was implemented widely in the United Kingdom to support small companies in their entry into foreign markets. It has the twin virtues of positioning data about language as a central part of firm strategy and asserting that language needs to be managed on several levels of company structure and not just by linguists.

This collection of articles focusing on SMEs is different from the 'language-sensitive category' in two ways. First, they span a time-frame

*Table 10.3* Target readership for Reeves and Wright (1996)

1. General managers
2. Management consultants who are looking at overall strategy and who wish to identify the weaknesses in their organisation's chains of communication, especially where these chains cross language boundaries
3. Training managers who want to identify how their organisation communicates with speakers of other languages, who want to assess the skills that the workforce already possesses and who want to know what it will cost in terms of time and money to train staff and to improve their communication systems
4. Foreign language training providers who need to understand their role within the context of an organisation as a whole and who want the tools to plan and provide training programmes that truly satisfy the needs of their customers

and a business community which is wider than most of the publications in the first category. Second, and more importantly, they take a different approach from the others. Their primary purpose, for the most part, is to examine the overall business performance of the firm. Language is one contributory factor in that but is not the primary motivation of the authors. In that sense, they are relevant to our focus here on a broad definition and context of language in the international business organisation beyond the instrumental or proficiency based schools of thought.

## What Is a Language-General Curriculum?

Learning about language in international business is not the same as learning languages for international business. Linguists tend to be preoccupied by the concepts of proficiency and exactitude in specific language situations. Another level of consciousness and capability is required to design and run a language strategy. It rests on the development of a curriculum designed to provide language-general competence for all international managers. For example, in developing a language policy a company might decide to choose a language as its main corporate language. This could be any national language, maybe English, Chinese or Spanish. This is a language-specific choice and is usually driven by considerations of skills gaps, efficiency and added-value. In implementing this policy, the organisation may discover in the course of time that management turnover is increasing because managers in their 40s onwards who are not fluent in that corporate language are leaving the company. To stem the outward flow of expertise, the company decides to investigate a series of options involving discussions between human resources and production divisions and executives. This may involve changing recruitment and training strategies and communication and meetings management in affected areas. This is a language-general task which involves an understanding of the functioning and relations between several languages and specific challenges encountered across divisions and levels of the organisation. It cannot be made by linguists alone, but it is best made with the input of linguists.

Similarly, a division may have frequent communications with host clients, governments or business communities. This may involve the receipt, translation and production of documents in the native language of the host community. How this is carried out should be subject to normal task and process analysis like all other areas of operations design. It would be informed by capable linguists and would comprise procedures to ensure quality and monitoring of product and suppliers, cost management and authorisation processes. This rational and managed process is a good example of a language-general task in the organisation. It does not always happen this way, however, and the task is often delegated to a single individual deemed to be competent in the target language to handle. That is a language-specific solution that falls far short of the standards of professional excellence to which most international organisations aspire in all other business processes.

It is rare to find these concepts embodied in a coherent way in the business school curriculum, even in international business programs, but there are examples. At a Canadian university, a new global master's course was submitted for approval and ran into difficulties because it contained ab initio language learning as a mandatory course. The Validation Committee contained members from Social and Natural Science faculties whose view was that all learning at that level should be advanced and seen to add value to the intellectual and academic standing of the students. Ab initio language learning was seen at worst as little more than a hobby for mature students like these and at best as something practical and useful but not 'academic.' The author was asked to produce a special course illustrating to students a 'higher level' of knowledge and ability stemming from the process of foreign language learning. Table 10.4 is an extract from the course outline.

This syllabus contains both language-specific and language-general elements and contains individual and organisational levels of awareness. When combined with the results of the literature review, we have a

*Table 10.4* An outline language-general syllabus

This course is designed for students of international business learning a foreign language as part of their programme. It provides a framework for understanding differences between languages and the relationship between language and culture, subjects of great relevance to global companies. It explores the process of language interaction in global organisations and shows how foreign language learning can add value to businesses and careers when seen and considered as a multi-dimensional tool. Students will be expected to develop an awareness of language as an over-arching phenomenon in business and blend this with their emerging command of a foreign language to show how they can add value to organisations.

**Course Objectives**
This course is designed to provide business students learning a foreign language with the knowledge and insights to understand the role and impact of language and foreign language learning on culture and international business. The learning outcomes for this course allow students to:

- Identify ways in which language as a phenomenon varies across national settings
- Analyse the role of language in communication across cultures
- Assess the impact of language and foreign language skills on the nature and performance of teams and organisations
- Leverage their own language learning strategies to improve their employability and understanding of global business

**Topics**

- The Language 'problem'
- Language use in organisations (inc. lingua franca)
- Theories of language use in business
- Language acquisition and proficiency
- MNC teams and language challenges
- Managing language and adding value to MNCs

framework for a language-general curriculum and a language-management model.

## Language-General Competence (LGC) for All Managers

Language is part of overall business strategy and practice and should be integrated into both over-arching strategic design and implementation process and the detail of day-to-day management of operations in the organisation. So it follows that any program designed to make language function more effectively will need to be customisable in its design and application to the organisation and measurable in its outcomes. The LGC proposition made here does not go that far yet as it is preliminary in its design and will be subject to piloting, review and development. It is shared here as a way of initiating a discussion about language management.

### Why Is LGC Needed?

The long-standing view of language as an 'instrument' and little more has been disproven by the research summarised in this chapter which has been carried out into organisations in the global era (see Table 10.5).

*Table 10.5* Why is LGC needed?

---

- Global business organisations are de facto multilingual in their composition, markets and processes.
- Languages as specific codes (Spanish, Chinese) have high recognition in the management community but are considered as problems rather than solutions.
- Many supposedly 'cultural' problems and needs are, in fact, language problems. These problems are rarely dealt with thoroughly in cross-cultural learning or training.
- All global firms receive and transmit data which pass through numerous filters before being used as information for decision-making.
- Firms and managers need tools and skills for understanding the various forms language takes, the problems it can pose and the advantages it can offer when well managed.
- Language in multicultural organisations is a marker of identity and power that shows itself eventually as a critical factor in social relations in the organisation.
- Language management is essential and needs to be managed ethically and responsibly in the international organisation.
- A multilinguality strategy will establish a fairer environment for motivating employees to work together.
- Employees will be better prepared to contribute and thrive in the workplace, which values diversity and fairness.
- Managers in global firms are confronted every day with 'problems' rooted in language. This instrument will identify those who have the predisposition or ability to look beyond the 'lost in translation' response and discover what is really going on.
- Currently, no comprehensive, recognised model for LGC exists.

---

### Where Is LGC Needed in the Organisation?

In the contemporary, multinational organisation, language and multiple national languages are ubiquitous, whether used formally or socially by members of the organisation. All divisions and units of the organisation need to be connected by processes that ensure good understanding between individuals and units. Piekkari et al. (2014) identify human resources, international marketing, foreign operation modes and networks as the key locations for language management. Brannen and Mughan (2016) further identify key phenomena influencing corporate behaviors such as migration and mobility, big data (and now artificial intelligence) and language innovation as external factors impinging on corporate language strategy. To summarise, in business organisations, effective use of language is needed for the functions and purposes shown in Table 10.6.

*Table 10.6* Domains of language use in firms

- **(KA)** Knowledge-related actions (Strategy)
- Internal communication and document generation and processing
- Transforming digital, technical or aesthetic concepts into comprehensible, actionable artefacts across borders
- Intellectual property, innovation and I.T. processes
- **(LA)** Localisation-related actions (Marketing and CSR)
- Market intelligence
- Product adaptation
- Public and government relations
- **(MA)** Morale-related actions (Human Resources)
- Equity and diversity management
- Workforce and team management
- Talent recognition and development
- Incentives and rewards

### What Does LGC Consist Of?

If language is an issue for all members of the organisation, it should be embedded in all policies, routines and practices of the organisation. The language management strategy should be designed around and locked into key organisational strategy artefacts shown in Table 10.7.

*Table 10.7* The organisational context of the language management strategy

- A core strategy document (mission, vision and resources of the organisation vis-à-vis its products, markets, competitors and stakeholders)
- A statement of related language principles (terminology, contiguity and objectives)
- A list of learning objectives and competencies (language-specific and language-general)
- A training and evaluation strategy and plan

At this stage of the 21st century, LGC cannot be just a functional tool. It should reflect changes in society and what the 21st century citizen brings to the organisation. Its content reflects the benefits of recent interdisciplinary research into demographic, organisational and social change. That research has identified the multi-dimensional ways in which language in its diversity can influence and reflect behavior in organisations. These concepts were identified earlier in this chapter (see Table 10.8).

*Table 10.8* Key cultural markers established in the literature

- (Absence/presence of) language policy
- (Absence/presence of) language strategy
- Absence of language management
- Capability
- Anxiety
- Diversity
- Creativity
- Identity
- Power
- Networks
- Social and linguistic hybridity and dynamic practice
- Inter-unit relations (boundary-spanning)

## The Importance of Cultural Markers

The action plan and competences should be informed and shaped by the awareness that language is not just a tool in itself but a phenomenon that embodies and reflects concepts that condition the culture, i.e. the mindset and morale of the organisation and the human relationships within it. At this stage, I am proposing that the strategy model and the competence list should incorporate the four most well-established markers in the literature (see Table 10.9).

A competence framework built around the actions and values models is the best way to design a tool to transform these learning objectives into organisational practice.

*Table 10.9* Key cultural markers

- POWER (**P**)—the ways in which language policy and practice may establish wanted or unwanted tiers, zones and imbalances of power, influence and advantage in roles and relationships
- IDENTITY (**I**)—the extent to which language may represent dimensions of the personality (individual and collective) which are conducive or resistant to behavioral change
- CAPABILITY (**C**)—how language competence may or may not interface with or reflect other competences or expertise
- ANXIETY (**A**)—an organisation-level understanding of the effect communication has on self-esteem, performance and productivity

## Developing an Educational Syllabus

The strategy document and model need to be transformed into a framework that is actionable on the level of education and training in the organisation. The preferred way of doing this is to identify a set of competences that informs the priorities, methods and steps in the design and outcomes of education and training (see Table 10.10).

*Table 10.10* The LGC target competence list

1. **Target Competence: formulate a policy for language use:** lingua franca, multilingual or multilingual franca **(P,I,C,A)** (KA, LA, MA)
   Purpose: to create a sound basis for the management of language as a business tool
2. **Target Competence: language self-awareness (P,I,C,A)** (MA)
   Purpose: to promote a healthy attitude towards the individual and her ability to manage language
3. **Target Competence: process management. Which organisational scenarios are most susceptible to language-based disruption or failure? (P,I,C,A)** (KA, MA)
   Purpose: to identify processes most liable to give rise to manifestations of power distortion, communicative failure and personal or professional anxiety that will be harmful to the team and the organisation
4. **Target Competence: draw up your company's (or project) market and language map.** What are the languages and cultures of your current and future markets and how close are you to those markets? **(C)** (KA) (LA)
   Purpose: to map the exposure of the firm to foreign languages and assess the ability and readiness of the manager to identify the need for this data and go about obtaining it
5. **Target Competence: audit your own resources:** What skills and knowledge does your company have? Identify and empower your boundary-spanners I **(C,A)** (KA, MA)
   Purpose: to assess the extent to which management of a firm identify the strengths and weaknesses of their organisation in terms of communication in foreign languages
6. **Target Competence: build a program for specific language training of key personnel:** using your boundary-spanner resource, know what your organisation has to learn and build a language and knowledge inventory for the company **(P,C)** (KA, MA)
   Purpose: to proactively chart a language map of current and future markets
7. **Target Competence: integrate language-general competence into market knowledge processes (P,C)** (KA, LA)
   Purpose: to make sure your managers understand the challenges and opportunities posed by languages and markets and promote knowledge transfer about cultures and communication with markets between divisions, teams and individuals
8. **Target Competence: manage the language strategy (P,I,C,A)** (KA, LA, MA)
   Purpose: to build a team of managers able to design and evaluate language-specific and general learning by personnel and monitor language use as part of equity and diversity policy and business strategy
   The process of design and implementation of a language management strategy is represented in Figure 10.1.

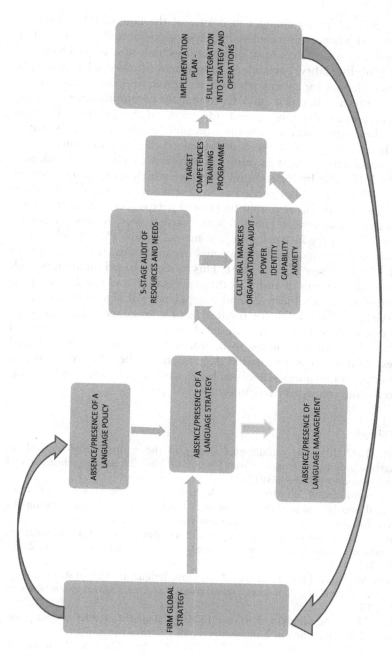

*Figure 10.1* The process of language management strategy design

## Conclusion

This chapter addresses changes in nature of the language 'problem' in international business in recent years. From a position of paucity of language skills in the 20th century, organisations have now moved to one of surfeit. Multilinguality, particularly in informal situations, has given rise to new challenges for executives and strategists, and some have turned to lingua franca policy as a quick fix to manage communications, despite the documented shortcomings and side effects of this practice. The purpose of the chapter was to develop a proposition that language-sensitive research has not yet directly contributed to the development of new international management learning or competence to help deal with new realities. It did this by focusing on literature which took an overview of recent work in the field or carried a direct reference to language management. Drawing on this research, functional perspectives on language use and strategy design were blended with cultural perspectives on power, identity and anxiety in workplace settings to outline the role played by language in contemporary international organisations. It then proposed a model for language management. This model is based on an approach consisting of a system of audits of the organisation and the development of a set of learning objectives and competencies designed to create an organisational framework for the design of a language strategy and its management. It is an organisation-level model which is both structural and humanist and is designed to be integral to the firm's international business strategy. It is anticipated that it can also be adapted for use in universities and business schools to bring worldly relevance and innovation to the international curriculum.

## References

Angouri, J. (2013). The multilingual reality of the multinational workplace: Language policy and language use. *Journal of Multilingual and Multicultural Development, 34*(6), 564–581.

Barner-Rasmussen, W., Ehrnrooth, M., Koveshnikov, A., & Makela, K. (2014). Cultural and language skills as resources for boundary spanning within the MNC. *Journal of International Business Studies, 45*(7), 886–905.

Brannen, M. Y. (2004). When Mickey loses face: Recontextualization, semantic fit, and the semiotics of foreignness. *Academy of Management Review, 29*(4), 593–616.

Brannen, M. Y., & Doz, Y. (2012). Corporate languages and strategic agility: Trapped in your jargon or lost in translation? *California Management Review, 54*(3), 77–97.

Brannen, M. Y., & Mughan, T. (Eds.). (2016). *Language in international business: Developing a field.* Cham, Switzerland: Palgrave Macmillan.

Brannen, M. Y., & Mughan, T. (2018). Strategic agility: The critical role of language. In C. Prange & L. Heracleous (Eds.), *Agility.X: How organisations thrive in unpredictable times.* Cambridge: Cambridge University Press.

Brannen, M. Y., Piekkari, R., & Tietze, S. (2014). The multifaceted role of language in international business: Unpacking the forms, functions and features of a critical challenge to MNC theory and performance. *Journal of International Business Studies, 45*(5), 495–507.

Church-Morel, A., & Bartel-Radic, A. (2016). Skills, identity, and power: The multifaceted concept of language diversity. *Management International Journal, 21*(1), 12–24.

Cohen, L., Kassis-Henderson, J., & Lecomte, P. (2015). Language diversity in management education: Towards a multilingual turn. In N. Holden, S. Michailova, & S. Tietze (Eds.), *The Routledge companion to cross-cultural management* (pp. 151–160). New York: Routledge.

Dhir, K. S., & Goke-Pariola, A. (2002). The case for language policies in multinational corporations. *Corporate Communications: An International Journal, 7*(4), 241–251.

Embleton, D., & Hagen, S. (1992). *Languages for business: A practical guide.* Sevenoaks: Hodder and Stoughton.

Goby, P., & Nickerson, C. (2015). Multicultural and multilingual: Workplace communication in Dubai. In N. Holden, S. Michailova, & S. Tietze (Eds.), *The Routledge companion to cross-cultural Management* (pp. 103–111). New York: Routledge.

Hagen, S. (2011). *Report on language management strategies and best practice in European SMEs: The PIMLICO project.* Brussels: European Commission.

Harzing, A.-W., Koster, K., & Magner, U. (2011). Babel in business: The language barrier and its solutions in the HQ-subsidiary relationship. *Journal of World Business, 46*(3), 279–287.

Holden, N., Michailova, S., & S. Tietze, S. (Eds.). (2015). *The Routledge companion to cross-cultural management* (pp. 79–84). New York: Routledge.

Jack, G. (2015). Cross-cultural management research and education. In N. Holden, S. Michailova, & S. Tietze (Eds.), *The Routledge companion to cross-cultural management* (pp. 183–188). New York: Routledge.

Janssens, M., & Steyaert, C. (2014). Re-considering language within a cosmopolitan understanding: Toward a multilingual franca approach in international business studies. *Journal of International Business Studies, 45*(5), 623–639.

Johanson, J., & Vahlne, J. E. (1977). The internationalization process of the firm—A model of knowledge development and increasing foreign market commitments. *Journal of International Business Studies, 8*(1), 23–32.

Lauring, J., & Klitmøller, A. (2017). Inclusive language use in multicultural business organization: The effect on creativity and performance. *International Journal of Business Communication, 54*(3), 306–324.

Lloyd-Reason, L., & Mughan, T. (2002). Strategies for internationalization within SMEs: The key role of the owner-manager. *Journal of Small Business and Enterprise Development, 9*(2), 120–129.

Luo, Y., & Shenkar, O. (2006). The multinational corporation as a multilingual community: Language and organization in a global context. *Journal of International Business Studies, 37*(3), 321–339.

Mughan, T. (1990). 1992: Is "languages for export" enough? *European Business Review, 90*(3), 24–28.

Mughan, T. (2015). Introduction: Language and languages—Moving from the periphery to the core. In N. Holden, S. Michailova, & S. Tietze (Eds.), *The*

*Routledge companion to cross-cultural management* (pp. 79–84). New York: Routledge.

Neeley, T. (2012). Global business speaks English. *Harvard Business Review*, *90*(5), 116–124.

Peltokorpi, V., & Vaara, E. (2014). Knowledge transfer in multinational corporations: Productive and counterproductive effects of language-sensitive recruitment. *Journal of International Business Studies*, *45*(5), 600–622.

Piekkari, R., & Tietze, S. (2011). A World of languages: Implications for international management research and practice. *Journal of World Business*, *46*(3), 267–269.

Piekkari, R., Welch, D., & Welch, L. S. (2014). *Language in international business: The multilingual reality of global business expansion*. Cheltenham: Edward Elgar.

Reeves, N., & Wright, C. (1996). *Linguistic auditing: A guide to identifying foreign language communication needs in corporations*. Clevedon: Multilingual Matters Ltd.

Ronen, S., Gonçalves, B., Hu, K. Z., Vespignani, A., Pinker, S., Hidalgo C. Z. (2014). Global language network. *Proceedings of the National Academy of Sciences*, *111*(52), E5616–E5622. doi: 10.1073/pnas.1410931111

Sanden, G. R. (2018). Ten reasons why corporate language policies can create more problems than they solve. *Current Issues in Language Planning*. doi:10.1080/14664208.2018.1553914

Tenzer, H., Terjesen, S., & Harzing, A. (2017). Language in International Business: A review and agenda for future research. *Management International Review*, *57*(6), 815–854.

Tinsley, T. (2019). *Language trends 2019. Language teaching in primary and secondary schools in England*. Survey Report. London: British Council.

Yanaprasart, P. (2016). Managing language diversity in the workplace: Between 'one language fits all' and 'multilingual model in action.' *Universal Journal of Management*, *4*(3), 91–107.

# 11 From the Multilingual Classroom to the Multilingual Workplace

## Learning to View Language Through a Different Lens

*Jane Kassis-Henderson and Linda Cohen*

Today's workplace is characterised by cultural and linguistic diversity. A major challenge in international organisations is how to deal with this diversity, for if left untended it can hinder work processes and lead to additional costs. It is therefore not surprising that when linguistic diversity is discussed it is most often perceived as problematic. When viewed through this negative lens, the multilingual workplace is seen as generating language barriers: how to understand others and be understood if people do not speak the same language(s) (Harzing, Köster, & Magner, 2011). In an effort to deal with the problems arising from this multilingual environment, MNCs have resorted to solutions which on the surface 'simplify' the complexity stemming from this diversity: translation and/or the use of a *lingua franca*, most often English. However, both of these so-called solutions—widely studied by business and management scholars—have proven to be sources of further problems which may themselves lead to the dysfunction of teams and operations. An important out-growth of these simplified solutions is the dominance of the English language in management education, which, in many countries, tends to reduce the motivation of students to learn other languages and ultimately deprive MNCs of an important potential resource: multilingualism.

Indeed, this simplified view overlooks the evidence which points to the benefits of a well-managed multilingual workplace. Research has shown that language diversity is a resource with potential added-value for organisations as it can enhance communication and increase performance (Jannsen & Steyaert, 2014; Barner-Rasmussen, Ehrnrooth, Koveshnikov, & Mäkkelä, 2014; Kassis-Henderson, 2005). If managed effectively, it can be a key factor contributing to team building and group cohesion (Holden, 2002; DiStefano & Maznevski, 2000). Future managers need to learn how to generate the full potential of this language diversity as well as to understand and anticipate the possible problems that may arise. Inadequately or inappropriately dealing with language diversity can have a negative impact on interpersonal relations, trust and the working atmosphere (Cohen & Kassis-Henderson, 2012; Griffith, 2002).

These findings deserve to be more fully addressed and incorporated into the curricula of business schools and management education as the following pages will show.

## Part I: Theoretical Background

### Redefining 'Language' Skills to Meet the Challenges of the Multilingual Workplace

Traditionally, language courses teach skill-sets linked to a specific national context or culture. This approach, rooted in the essentialist paradigm (Hofstede, 1980), views language and culture as a uniform block based on national identity (Ganesh, 2015). In other words, one country/one language/one culture is the mantra, ignoring the micro-variations that exist, as if all individuals fit into a specific country-based mold. Focusing solely on a linguistic code in this way tends to disregard the fact that there is not only one way of speaking or using a linguistic code; nor are there fixed, static contexts in which communication takes place. Individuals are far from being monolithic blocks; language and language usage is dependent on the multiple aspects of an individual's identity which cannot be reduced—as in the essentialist approach—to the stereotypes of the particular national culture which is stamped on their passport or in which they live (Holliday, 2011).

Sociolinguists and scholars in organisational behaviour, international business and critical cross-cultural management have analysed the ways in which different facets of an individual's identity—beyond national culture—condition reactions and expectations in social interactions. An individual cannot be reduced to being French/Irish/German as if all French/Irish/Germans speak the same way in every context. Identity is much more complex and multi-faceted: profession; rural/urban; gender; age . . . and each facet has a bearing on how language is used, on '*voice*' and on how an individual interacts with the other(s). Although not always consciously, a person changes their way of speaking depending on the facet of their identity that comes to the fore in a given interaction.

One useful approach for our purposes breaks down personal identity into three main categories—demographic, geographic and associative—forming a 'mosaic of tiles' (Chao & Moon, 2005) with each tile representing a different facet. This underscores the importance of thinking beyond essentialist dimensions when talking about identity and language usage. Although individuals may use the same linguistic code, they draw from different linguistic resources or *repertoires* based on the configuration—or mosaic—created from the 'tiles' that form their identity. These language 'tiles'—or personal repertoires or '*voices*'—are deployed depending on the needs of each encounter and on which '*voice*' a person chooses to use and with whom. '*Voice*' therefore echoes what socio-linguists have called the variations attributable to a national or ethnic identity or to a particular social class, generation or gender (Gumperz, 2003; Kramsch, 2012). Deconstructing identity in this way explains the micro-variation in the use of styles, accents and words within what is otherwise considered to be the same 'language' or linguistic code (Blommaert, 2005, 2010). In any given interaction, the way '*voice*' is used determines how the message is sent and received. This flexible aspect of language usage tends to be an automatic or unconscious reflex when using a native tongue in familiar contexts. However, the very competencies that allow for this flexibility are not sufficiently addressed in foreign language teaching, which prevents them from becoming an accessible resource or competence.

Language learning must therefore encompass, in addition to the specific linguistic code, the more general meta-cognitive skill-set linked to the functional approach to communication or the practical aspect of language usage. There is a need to change from thinking in terms of 'specific skills' linked to a country or national culture to thinking in terms of more flexible language usage linked to the awareness of the multiple identity markers of each individual and how these markers determine interaction in context. In order to adequately prepare students to deal with diversity in the mobile, multilingual workplace, there must be a shift from placing the emphasis solely on the specific, nation-based linguistic code to demonstrating how speakers use linguistic resources in context (Cohen & Kassis-Henderson, 2017; Jannsens & Steyaert, 2014; Makoni & Pennycook, 2012; Virkkula-Räisänen, 2010). This implies that teachers and students should not merely think about language as an objective competence in a homogeneous cultural and linguistic environment but as the capacity to use a repertoire of skills and personal linguistic resources appropriate to each interaction. As Blommaert claims, it is important "for linguists in the age of globalization to think in terms of mobile resources, framed as trans-contextual networks, flows and movements and to 'unthink' the classic distinctions and biases through which language has traditionally been viewed" (Blommaert, 2010, p. 1). Kramsch, a scholar who has significantly contributed to rethinking language education (Kramsch, 1993), talks of the need for students in second language acquisition to become aware of the importance of '*voice*' in order "to move between languages and to understand and negotiate the multiple varieties of codes, modes, genres, registers, and discourses" that will be encountered in the real world (Kramsch, 2012, p. 107). These aspects must be formalised and incorporated into the business school curricula in order to transform the complexity of dealing with linguistic diversity into a valuable resource for the individual in the multilingual workplace.

## Beyond Essentialism: Dealing with Diversity and Giving Voice to Our Multiple Identities

In order to lay the groundwork to derive the full potential from language diversity, the 'language' component in the educational process must have a dual focus: 'language-specific' skills linked to a specific linguistic code corresponding to a specific country or region, and 'language-general competencies' (Mughan, 2015; Brannen & Thomas, 2010) incorporating the functional or pragmatic aspects of language usage in context. Today, the former has set the agenda when it comes to second-language acquisition. The easily measurable language-specific skills are ideal for selecting, testing and recruiting, but do not cover the range of skills that determine if language is used effectively in a given interaction. These 'language-general' skills, which are more difficult to identify and measure and therefore overlooked in the educational process and insufficiently addressed by the testing industry, are indeed indispensable in the multilingual workplace. 'Language-general' competencies have been defined as "a set of dynamic interacting dimensions consisting of knowledge, cross-cultural abilities, behavioural adaptability and cross-cultural communication skills, linked by cultural frame switching and cultural metacognition" (Mughan, 2015, p. 109). For efficient language usage in context, one must go beyond the oft-cited intercultural skills such as open mindset, cross-cultural awareness and adaptability to new working contexts. Developing the qualities allowing for a more subtle understanding of language usage, which also incorporate the values of interculturality, is crucial in international business education. Among such qualities are the ability to appropriately contextualise interactions; the propensity to take into account other perspectives; and the readiness to adopt translingual practices and to hold a benevolent attitude to linguistic asymmetry (Barner-Rasmussen et al., 2014).

The combination of 'language-specific' and 'language-general' skills is similar to the qualities found in bi-cultural/bi-lingual individuals. Cross-cultural management researchers have found these individuals to be a rare and valuable resource as they assume the role of 'boundary-spanners' in MNCs (Barner-Rasmussen, 2015; Hong & Doz, 2013; Brannen & Thomas, 2010). From this perspective, language diversity in the workplace has the potential to become—if the actors are adequately prepared—a cohesive element, rather than a divisive or discriminatory factor. We argue that the development of these qualities can and should be included in curricula so as not to remain the exclusive domain of those bilingual/bicultural individuals alone. By birthright, bi-cultural individuals are inherently in touch with at least some aspects of the multiple facets of their identity and therefore have an advantage when it comes to developing these language-general competencies, such as changing *voice* in function of each interaction. As said earlier, language usage is dependent on which aspect of identity becomes salient in a given context and therefore an individual does not use the same *voice* in every interaction. As identity encompasses more than national background, students—of all backgrounds—have to become aware of the importance of the multiple aspects of identity in order to use language effectively in context.

## Part II: Learning How to View Language Through a New Lens—Pedagogical Insights

### Redefining Competencies for the Multilingual Workplace

The marketing discourse around published teaching material and testing for language learning, or "second language acquisition", tends to be couched in terms of 'effective' or 'successful' communication in a specific language based on the ideal native speaker model as they interact in stereotypical contexts. In the case of Business English, studies show the gap between language as used in the workplace and prescribed patterns of usage as found in commercially produced texts. We argue that the formulaic approach advocated by "marketing mythologies of purportedly universal forms of language use" (Nair-Venugopal, 2015, p. 38) does not adequately address the complex and changing situations of the multicultural and multilingual workplace. Research has shown that standardised tests fail to determine whether a student has the ability to study or work in a given language when the language is divorced from a specific academic or professional setting (Pilcher & Richards, 2017). As we argue throughout this chapter, gaining formal 'language-specific' proficiency of the type that can be tested in a vacuum should not be the sole aim of language teaching in business schools. It is equally important for students to understand the value of contextualised communicative language practice in order to develop the 'language-general' competence we are advocating. Business students deserve a more nuanced approach to language learning based on an understanding that using language appropriately in context is more adapted to the requirements of the professional world than demonstrating what are recognised to be impeccable language skills (Rogerson-Revell, 2008; Kankaanranta, 2006; Nickerson, 2005) as if language is used in a vacuum and context is irrelevant. Scholars studying recruitment and assessment standards for language ability also point to the shortcomings of solely adopting a language-specific model and recommend evaluating how language is used in context (Charles & Marshan-Piekkari, 2002).

The key to using language appropriately in context is an awareness of the importance of, coupled with the ability to draw upon, contextual elements in the course of interaction. These aspects, which include the situation of the encounter, the topic addressed and the relationship between speakers (Gudykunst, 1991), determine the structure, type and style of message and therefore must be taken into account for successful interaction. Understanding how the multiple facets of identity can affect the relationship between speakers is therefore an important first step in learning how to use language effectively. Individuals—like contexts—are not one-dimensional and must be viewed in their complexity. In addition to knowing an individual's nationality and language—often one of the first pieces of information one can glean at the start of an encounter—an awareness of the other party's profession, ethnicity, gender or age for example may be as useful to further the encounter as they give clues for the appropriate style of interaction and '*voice.*' This calibrating phase in turn helps build the relationship itself as well as the manner in which individuals relate to each other as this is co-constructed in the course of interaction.

This means that a teaching model must demonstrate the limitations of and go beyond the essentialisation of languages, cultures and identities. Relying on fixed categories of national languages creates the unnecessary and indeed artificial cleavage of native/non-native speakers. The process of relating to the other requires complex communication skills beyond deploying grammatically correct units of speech. It follows that students need to learn what matters in interactions and how to deal with new and unpredictable contexts. Knowing a specific language and its related national culture—the stated objective in language learning—although part of the process, is insufficient preparation for the multilingual workplace. It is therefore necessary to reformulate objectives in course descriptions by including 'interacting in multilingual/multicultural contexts,' along-side what has long been the primary focus of language learning: attaining native-speaker competence and acquiring country-specific knowledge.

## Language Matters: An Institutional 'Problem' and the Fallacy of Easy Solutions

International educational institutions are often no different from other multinational organisations when it comes to (*mis*)handling their own language-related issues in multilingual contexts. There too, when 'language' related issues arise, the focus tends to be on overcoming the 'problems' associated with practical matters. One example is how the translation of documents and slides is dealt with. In the same way as in MNCs, the problems arising from the overreliance on automatic translation which provides an easy solution to translation issues would be prevented if a more subtle understanding of language-related issues and usage prevailed. Another 'problem' concerns the negative reaction of students or faculty to lack of fluency or strong accents, revealing their blind adherence to the 'gold-standard' based on the native-speaker model. Here again can be noticed the negative impact of the essentialist model when it comes to dealing with language diversity both as an institutional matter as well as an object of study. Hence the interest of rethinking language competency by including the language-general skills throughout the business studies curricula.

One common symptom of the neglect concerning language-related issues is seen in the widely held assumption among program directors of business schools that language skills will improve by 'osmosis'—the process of gradual or unconscious assimilation—through study or internships abroad or regular contact with 'international' students or faculty in the home university. Communication competence and intercultural sensitivity are also purported to be developed in this way. However, if intercultural experiences are not incorporated into a pedagogical framework—in the form, for example, of preparation and debriefing in the classroom—students fail to reflect on them and to gain in competence (Ledwith & Seymour, 2001).

There is also the assumption—among programme managers and business school deans—that the presence of native English speaking management faculty in non-English speaking countries can lead to less investment in 'language' faculty and 'language' classes (thereby killing two birds with one stone). However,—and this applies to all languages, although it is more often a question of English in business schools—language skills cannot be passively acquired by students listening to a lecture in a foreign language. Although listening comprehension may be improved, merely hearing a language does not provide functional or pragmatic competencies. Given this institutional quest for easy solutions to language matters, it therefore comes as no surprise that the essentialist model has remained at the heart of second-language acquisition and a more subtle approach to pedagogy has been neglected.

Viewing language diversity through a different lens and seeing language-related issues as opportunities rather than problems can lead to creative solutions to better incorporate multilingualism into the classroom, solutions which will later carry over into the workplace. For example, when it comes to presentations, different scenarios can be explored to deal with the language barrier: slides can be in one language and the oral presentation in another; discussion can be bilingual as some students and faculty have the ability to understand a language but prefer to express themselves in another. Again, such flexible solutions mirror workplace practices where code-switching and other ways of integrating multiple languages in a workgroup—or *multilingual franca* practices—have been observed (Kassis-Henderson, 2005; Canagarajah, 2007; May, 2013; Jannsens & Steyaert, 2014; Cohen & Kassis-Henderson 2017). However, such behaviour does not arise automatically and needs to be specifically addressed in the classroom. Courses devoted to managing language diversity and the multilingual workplace will allow students to reframe incidents arising in interactions in order to transform what could be considered problematic situations into value-enhancing experiences.

The discussion that follows provides examples of the various ways such language-related issues and values of interculturality can be incorporated into the classroom.

### The Pedagogical Framework—Leveraging the Multilingual Learning Context

Language-general competencies are not explicitly addressed in language studies curricula, which have been primarily (if not exclusively) devoted to language-specific objectives. And in the same vein, courses on cross-cultural management tend not to address the language dimension beyond the classic essentialist country/culture specific dimensions as espoused by Hofstede and Hall, for example.

If recognised and valued rather than quashed, working with manifestations of diversity offers a rich learning opportunity. Indeed, the diverse student body and faculty of today's universities and business schools create an ideal learning environment for preparation for the multilingual workplace.

A starting point for leveraging this potential in all taught courses and group/project work is to compose groups of diverse nationalities and varied levels of language proficiency (with the proviso that all students have already attained a minimal acceptable level in the language/s of instruction). In such contexts they can learn that 'successful communication' is possible in spite of academically 'weak' language skills and that 'native-speaker' does not necessarily equate with effective communication: the native-speaker may not be understood because of their rapid over-confident speech whereas the intermediate-level foreign speaker may deliver a clear, although grammatically imperfect, message. Here, the role of the teacher is to 'orchestrate' and highlight the different contributions to class or group discussions to turn them into learning opportunities.

### The Pedagogical Virtue of 'Critical Incidents'—Or Learning to Make Sense of Personal Experience

In a multilingual academic or professional environment there is always potential for learning from experience by promoting the self-reflexive use of personal 'critical' incidents in the classroom. But this potential is too often wasted—or remains underexploited—if an adapted framework is not provided to help make sense of this experience. The examples we present in the following show the value of systematically leveraging—or exploiting—certain incidents which have occurred to turn what would otherwise be considered insignificant events into transformational learning experiences.

'Critical incidents' can, for example, lead to addressing crucial problems such as, for instance, not taking into account cultural context in the meaning of certain terms and translation, the use of English as a *lingua franca* in multilingual settings, or incidents concerning identity and self-presentation in terms of nationality or language profile. Speakers using their non-native language in the classroom may also lead to undesirable effects (therefore becoming a 'critical incident') when professors or students react negatively to each other's language and communication skills. Speaking with a strong accent, or in a style that does not correspond to a person's expectations, or not having a 'native speaker' level can lead to stigmatisation and rejection as considered to be a sign of incompetence (Rogerson-Revell, 2007)—a discriminatory attitude that risks being carried over into the workplace (Neeley, 2012).

A critical incident related to this attitude provoked an 'aha moment' for one of the authors—at the time under the influence of the essentialist model which, as discussed earlier, has long been the dominant discourse—when she suggested a student going to study in the UK should tone down their heavy German accent to better emulate a native English speaker. The student replied: "But I don't want to sound like an English person, I want people to know I am German!" This remark led to a discussion about the unjustified preeminence of the native-speaker model and the empowering or stigmatising effects of accents. And thanks to self-reflexivity, this incident—among others—contributed to an understanding of the need to reappraise the fundamentals of language pedagogy (Cohen & Kassis-Henderson, 2012; Cohen, Kassis-Henderson, & Lecomte, 2015; Kassis-Henderson, Cohen, & McCulloch, 2018).

Our argument demonstrates that if these issues are not adequately addressed within a pedagogical framework they remain problematic for the people who are stigmatised, and, furthermore, a learning opportunity is lost. Exposure to diversity in learning situations and life experiences can lead to sensitivity and non-judgmental behaviour in multilingual contexts, but as some individuals have had little or no exposure to diversity it is all the more important to address and frame these issues in an educational environment which is *de facto* diverse (Cohen et al., 2015).

### The Dominance of English: Silencing Voices

As institutions are the product of the environment in which they have been created and evolve, business schools reflect the economic environment in which they are embedded which has led to English becoming the dominant language in management education (Tietze, 2008). The other languages taught, if any, are the ones which mainstream decision-makers deem 'useful.' This narrow utilitarian vision has resulted in business schools overlooking the benefits stemming from multilingualism and cultural diversity and the fact that all languages—be they oral or written, national or local—add value through the competencies that come with speaking more than one tongue. Mirroring this utilitarian vision, bi-cultural students from former colonised countries or non-Western cultures aspiring to integrate this dominant model tend to censor their linguistic and cultural heritage if it falls outside of what is considered 'useful.' Such students tend to silence aspects of their linguistic profile, for example when preparing a CV or on job application forms, and fail to mention the languages and skills that fall outside of the mainstream radar. They therefore do not capitalise on the fact that the interplay of languages and dialects, both written and oral, contributes to the development of the language-general skills which facilitate the ability to use language in context and that have proven their value in the multilingual workplace.

### Understanding 'Communication' and 'Culture' Through a New Lens

Next we present an example of the way a course can be re-designed to enable the development of language-general skills. This course entitled 'Communication and Culture' is delivered in a Master in Management Program in a European business school with an international faculty and student body. The course was initially country-based, describing national business practices through the essentialist model. Although this approach is helpful to become acquainted with the common values and behaviours that characterise each specific national culture, it overlooks the diverse factors that determine identity construction as explained earlier. This course was therefore redesigned to develop broader intercultural competencies and to promote the value of interculturality as well as to introduce the concept of language-general communication skills in order for our students to become more effective members of multilingual/multicultural organisations.

The principle objective of the course 'Communication and Culture' is to incite students to question the common assumptions associated with these two concepts. They do this through an inductive process and are plunged into multicultural/multilingual group-work with the task of analysing cases given by the professor or critical incidents they have experienced individually. After this collective exercise—followed by theoretical input—they reflect by writing personal logs—or journals—after classroom sessions to record what they have learnt from the experience. We ask students to focus on key elements related to 'communication'—for example what facilitated or hindered it—and to 'culture'—questioning national stereotypes often wrongly attributed to other students (Kassis-Henderson et al., 2018). Throughout such exercises they discover the value of reflexivity and the importance of repositioning when confronted to expectancy disconfirmation based on incorrect preconceived ideas (Rosenblatt, Worthley, & MacNab, 2013). Their written observations show the transformation in their thinking when they make comments such as:

STUDENT LOG: this did really revolutionize my treatment of stereotypes, cultural patterns and clichés in that way that I try to avoid them even more than up to now.

### Problem of 'English'—and Presumed Similarity, Hiding Other Voices

Students are incited to reflect on the consequences of the use of English as a *lingua franca* and to question whether it results, as is widely believed, in the convergence of communication styles. When operating in English, young Chinese professionals are reported to communicate in an increasingly direct way resembling that of 'Westerners' and diverge from expected stereotypical modes (Kankaanranta & Lu, 2013 in Saarinen & Piekkari, 2015, p. 428). This behaviour is said to blur national cultural communication traits. Although this finding is helpful to move beyond national stereotypes it is important, as discussed earlier, to see the individual beyond this sole dimension. Observations made by our students show they have understood the risk of overestimating these supposed similarities which are thought to arise through the mere use of English, which hide the importance of other 'tiles' or *voices* hidden further below the surface:

STUDENT LOG: (Non-Asian commenting on working with Asian students): "We had overestimated common global business similarities and overlooked the risk of miscommunication and misunderstanding." He adds: "There is a richness of diversity of origin and at the same time there is unity which could be found in speaking the same language or sharing similar university experiences."

Another student shows an understanding of the value of reflecting on their own culture in comparison with others, and of adopting a dialectical approach (Martin & Nakayama, 2015) to effectively interact in social encounters:

STUDENT LOG: It is difficult to see my own culture alone; it is easier to understand it when comparing with a different one. By seeing similarities but also differences makes one appreciate both and I think that it is very useful to have this type of knowledge.

### Working in Multilingual Groups

Experience in multilingual student groups working on projects or case studies provides an opportunity to anticipate the experience of working in international teams in MNCs. However, as said earlier, a pedagogical framework—with preparation beforehand and regular debriefing—is necessary to enable students to benefit fully from the experience and to enhance the learning process.

For the preparation phase, one method is to build a seminar around empirical insights from research conducted on international management teams (Kassis-Henderson et al., 2018). Students are asked to discuss the following questions: (a) In which language or languages will they be working? (b) What consequences do they anticipate from this choice ? (c) What are the merits and demerits of different communication channels, methods and styles? For the debriefing phase they reflect on the impact of language practices on the cohesion and working atmosphere in the group. Learning is often at its height when students realise that an interaction results in or provokes the contrary of their expected outcome. Such expectancy disconfirmation is involved when they see from experience that the most productive participants are not necessarily those with the best academic level in the working language but those who have the capacity to value the different language capabilities and divergent styles of the group members. As faculty and students are biased by their own cultural context, it follows that an important starting point for this, as any, learning process is to become aware of the weight of these subjective expectations and to gain an understanding of the value of different practices in a diverse setting.

Beyond reflecting on the language issue, working in multilingual/cultural groups allows students to become aware of the added-value of interculturality as they realise that similar mindsets tend to lead to quick and easy solutions (Ledwith & Seymour, 2001; Jensen, 2001). Having learnt from experience that multicultural groups generally bring about more creative, flexible attitudes and perspectives, students will be better prepared to play a constructive role when part of a multilingual and/or multicultural team in the workplace.

*Learning to Know the 'Other': Building Rapport*

Other pedagogical initiatives provide an opportunity to develop these valuable language-general competencies. The tandem program, for example, allows students to reflect on the process of interaction with international partners. This program consists in the forming of partners—or 'tandems'—from diverse language and cultural backgrounds who meet regularly in informal contexts of their choice. Initial guidelines are given by faculty with suggestions of topics to help orientate the discussion around intercultural themes and incite expectancy disconfirmation (such as their educational experience and what shocks or surprises them in an unfamiliar context). They are informed that this program was designed to help integrate different student populations, to enable students to use language in a natural context and to gain intercultural awareness by stimulating interaction. At the end of each semester students were asked, in interviews and questionnaires, to reply to the question "*What has this experience taught you about interaction in an international context?*" This feedback process allowed the students to reflect on and render explicit aspects of the interaction process that otherwise would have not been dealt with. Most students had assumed that language affinity would suffice to establish a constructive relationship. However, their answers showed they had become aware that they needed to learn how to interact in international groups and that knowing a language or culture is insufficient preparation. They also reflected on the *misplaced* performance anxiety they initially felt based on the widely held misconception of the need to attain an ideal language level approximating that of the native speaker. Their replies showed that the tandem experience led to a reflexive learning process and indicate the value of specifically addressing these issues in a pedagogical framework (Cohen & Kassis-Henderson, 2012).

## Conclusion: The Added-Value of Multilingualism

In this chapter we have highlighted the importance of looking at language through a broader lens in order to reassess the competencies necessary for enhanced performance in today's international, and increasingly diverse intra-national, work settings.

Language diversity is commonly understood as the co-existence of speakers of different languages, and it is in this sense that the multilingual workplace tends to be portrayed. Although the actors in today's workplace have to deal with the challenges of increasing multilingualism where the interplay of languages has been identified as one of its key features, the language-specific model in language teaching and language assessment remains dominant. Languages are viewed as distinct entities and taught as separate academic disciplines in separate classrooms, leaving little room for teaching or learning about real life communication between people who speak different languages.

Debate on business and professional communication has also been influenced by the language-specific approach when the conclusion is to implement one 'common' working language for diverse workplace settings—and this practice is, as we have seen, replicated in business education. Although convenient, a *lingua franca* solution (often English) raises ethical issues concerning not only power and status but the ramifications on organisational and individual performance due to marginalising diverse *voices* and points of view. Language and intercultural communication studies tend to reflect the shortcomings of this simplistic approach where the objectives are defined in terms of learning one specific language and culture. We have demonstrated the need to include the competencies of a general nature which incorporate the values of interculturality (Borghetti,

2017)—identified as language-general skills—required for interaction in a multicultural/multilingual workplace. Based on a critical and self-reflexive stance, these include an awareness of context, sensitivity to the interplay of languages, and a broader understanding of identity and *voice*. A more ethical approach to learning how to interact with others lies at the core of our argument. We therefore claim that in order to facilitate the understanding of identity and culture as dynamic and socially constructed rather than essentialist and static, there is a need for a more nuanced and complex pedagogy with teachers selecting approaches and methods for the insights they will evoke in learners about interculturality (Holmes, 2015; Szkudlarek, 2009).

By building on the work of scholars who have pointed to the mismatch that exists between language teaching material and actual discursive practices, the pedagogical insights presented earlier indicate ways to better prepare students for the situations they are likely to encounter in their future careers. By shifting the focus to the competencies that come with 'language-general' skills, we are adding other dimensions beyond what has been formally recognised as competence in a specific language which, we argue, enhance communication practices and lead to increased performance in professional contexts. As our chapter shows, teachers of languages and intercultural communication should veer away from 'recipes for success' and easily measurable criteria to focus on the values, critical attitudes and behaviours that foster positive interaction in the multilingual workplace.

# References

Barner-Rasmussen, W. (2015). What do bicultural-bilinguals do in multinational corporations? In N. Holden, S. Michailova, & S. Tietze (Eds.), *The Routledge companion to cross-cultural management* (pp. 79–85). London and New York: Routledge.

Barner-Rasmussen, W., Ehrnrooth, M., Koveshnikov, A., & Mäkkelä, K. (2014). Cultural and language skills as resources for boundary spanning within the MNC. *Journal of International Business Studies, 45,* 886–905.

Blommaert, J. (2005). *Discourse.* Cambridge: Cambridge University Press.

Blommaert, J. (2010). *The sociolinguistics of globalization.* Cambridge: Cambridge University Press.

Borghetti, C. (2017). Is there really a need for assessing intercultural competence? Some ethical issues. *Journal of Intercultural Communication, 44.* ISSN:1404-1634.

Brannen, M.-Y., & Thomas, D. (2010). Bicultural individuals in organizations: Implications and opportunity. *International Journal of Cross Cultural Management, 10*(1), 5–16.

Canagarajah, S. (2007). Lingua franca English, multilingual communities and language acquisition. *The Modern Language Journal, 91*(1), 923–939.

Chao, G. T., & Moon, H. (2005). The cultural mosaic: A meta theory for understanding the complexity of culture. *Journal of Applied Psychology, 90*(6), 1128–1140.

Charles, M. L., & Marshan-Piekkari, R. L. (2002). Language training for enhanced horizontal communication: A challenge for MNCs. *Business Communication Quarterly, 65*(2), 9–29.

Cohen, L., & Kassis-Henderson, J. (2012, July–August). Language use in establishing rapport and building relations: Implications for international teams and management education. *Revue Management et Avenir, 55*, 185–207.

Cohen, L., & Kassis-Henderson, J. (2017). Revisiting culture and language in global management teams: Toward a multilingual turn. *International Journal of Cross Cultural Management, 17*(1), 7–22.

Cohen, L., Kassis-Henderson, J., & Lecomte, P. (2015). Language diversity in management education: Towards a multilingual turn. In N. Holden, S. Michailova, & S. Tietze (Eds.), *The Routledge companion to cross-cultural management* (pp. 151–161). London and New York: Routledge.

DiStefano, J. J., & Maznevski, M. L. (2000). Creating value with diverse teams in global management. *Organizational Dynamics, 29*(1), 45–61.

Ganesh, N. (2015). A non-essentialist model of culture: Implications of identity, agency and structure within multinational/multicultural organizations. *International Journal of Cross Cultural Management, 15*(1), 101–124.

Griffith, D. A. (2002). The role of communication competencies in international business relationship development. *Journal of World Business, 37*, 256–265.

Gudykunst, W. B. (1991). *Bridging differences: Effective intergroup communication*. Thousand Oaks, CA: Sage.

Gumperz, J. (2003). Interactional sociolinguistics: A personal perspective. In D. Schiffrin, D. Tannen, & H. E. Hamilton (Eds.), *The handbook of discourse analysis* (paperback ed., pp. 215–228). Oxford: Blackwell Publishing.

Harzing, A.-W., Köster, K., & Magner, U. (2011). Babel in business: The language barrier and its solutions in the HQ-subsidiary relationship. *Journal of World Business, 46*(3), 279–287.

Hofstede, G. (1980). *Culture's consequences comparing values behaviors, institutions and organizations across nations*. Thousand Oaks, CA: Sage.

Holden, N. J. (2002). *Cross-cultural management: A knowledge management perspective*. London: Financial Times/Prentice Hall.

Holliday, A. (2011). *Intercultural communication and ideology*. London: Sage.

Holmes, P. (2015). Intercultural encounters as socially constructed experiences: Which concepts? Which pedagogies? In N. Holden, S. Michailova, & S. Tietze (Eds.), *The Routledge companion to cross-cultural management* (pp. 237–247). London and New York: Routledge.

Hong, H.-J., & Doz, Y. (2013). L'Oréal masters multiculturalism. *Harvard Business Review, 91*(6), 114–118.

Jannsens, M., & Steyaert, C. (2014). Re-considering language from a cosmopolitan understanding: Toward a multilingual franca approach in international business studies. *Journal of International Business Studies, 45*, 623–639.

Jensen, K. (2001). International business. In B. Macfarlane & R. Ottewill (Eds.), *Effective learning & teaching in business & management* (pp. 123–137). London: Kogan Page.

Kankaanranta, A. (2006). "Hej, Seppo, could you pls comment on this!" Internal email communication in lingua franca English in a multinational company. *Business Communication Quarterly, 69*, 216–225.

Kankaanranta, A., & Lu, W. (2013). The evolution of English as the business lingua franca: Signs of convergence in Chinese and Finnish professional communication. *Journal of Business and Technical Communication, 27*(3), 288–307.

Kassis-Henderson, J. (2005). Language diversity in international management teams. *International Studies of Management and Organisation*, 35(1), 66–82.

Kassis-Henderson, J., Cohen, L., & McCulloch, R. (2018). Boundary crossing and reflexivity: Navigating the complexity of cultural and linguistic identity. *Business and Professional Communication Quarterly (BPCQ)*, 81(3), 304–327.

Kramsch, C. (1993). *Context and culture in language teaching*. Oxford: Oxford University Press.

Kramsch, C. (2012). Authenticity and legitimacy in multilingual SLA. *Critical Multilingualism, an Interdisciplinary Journal*, 1(1), 107–128.

Ledwith, S., & Seymour, D. (2001). Home and away: Preparing students for multicultural management. *International Journal of Human Resource Management*, 12(8), 1292–1312.

Makoni, S., & Pennycook, A. (2012). Disinventing multilingualism: From monological multilingualism to multilingual franca. In M. Martin-Jones, A. Blackledge, & A. Creese (Eds.), *The Routledge handbook of multilingualism* (pp. 439–453). Abingdon: Routledge.

Martin, J. N., & Nakayama, T. K. (2015). Reconsidering intercultural (communication) competence in the workplace: A dialectical approach. *Language and Intercultural Communication*, 15(1), 13–28.

May, S. (2013). *The multilingual turn, implications for SLA, TESOL and bilingual education*. New York: Taylor & Francis.

Mughan, T. (2015). Language and languages: Moving from the periphery to the core. In N. Holden, S. Michailova, & S. Tietze (Eds.), *The Routledge companion to cross-cultural management*. London and New York: Routledge.

Nair-Venugopal, S. (2015). Issues of language and competence in intercultural business and contexts. *Language and Intercultural Communication*, 15(1), 29–45.

Neeley, T. B. (2012). Status loss and achieved status distinctions in global organizations. *Organization Science*, 24(2), 476–497.

Nickerson, C. (2005). English as a lingua franca in international business contexts. *English for Specific Purposes*, 24(4), 367–380.

Pilcher, N., & Richards, K. (2017). Challenging the power invested in the International English Language Testing System (IELTS): Why determining 'English' preparedness needs to be undertaken within the subject context. *Power and Education*, 9(1), 3–17.

Rogerson-Revell, P. (2007). Using English for international business: A European case study. *English for Specific Purposes*, 26, 103–120.

Rogerson-Revell, P. (2008). Participation and performance in international business meetings. *English for Specific Purposes*, 27, 338–360.

Rosenblatt, V., Worthley, R., & MacNab, B. (2013). From contact to development in experiential cultural intelligence education: The mediating influence of expectancy disconfirmation. *Academy of Management Learning & Education*, 12(3), 356–379.

Saarinen, J., & Piekkari, R. (2015). Management is back! Cross-cultural encounters in virtual teams. In N. Holden, S. Michailova, & S. Tietze (Eds.), *The Routledge companion to cross-cultural management* (pp. 420–430). London and New York: Routledge.

Szkudlarek, B. (2009). Through western eyes: Insights into the intercultural training field. *Organisation Studies, 30*(9), 975–986.

Tietze, S. (2008). *International management and language: Studies in international business and the world economy.* London: Routledge.

Virkkula-Räisänen, T. (2010). Linguistic repertoires and semiotic resources in interaction: A Finnish manager as a mediator in a multilingual meeting. *Journal of Business Communication, 47,* 505–531.

# Section 4

# Conclusion

*Editors: Sierk Horn, Philippe Lecomte and Susanne Tietze*

# Conclusion

The starting point of this edited collection of contributions was the realisation that language-sensitive research has reached a certain maturity (or, as some would argue, perhaps even a peak) in the international business domain. This, in our eyes, offered the chance to pause and reflect about whether research at the juncture of 'language' and 'management' has had its day, and if not, which direction it could possibly take. In 2017, the three editors organised an interactive workshop (at Ludwigs-Maximilian-University, Munich, Germany) aimed at encouraging business and modern language studies students to adopt a critical awareness of the 'added value' languages and country-specific knowledge can give. We looked at how we can inspire language learners in a time and age where digitalisation offers instant and convenient access to country- or region-specific knowledge. We looked at languages at work and the consequences of talent pools becoming much more diverse in terms of ethnicity or language background. We looked at the dialectics of knowledge creation in the international business (IB) domain and how this impacts how things are done in the corporate world. The workshop created a differentiated and dynamic picture of what languages and, by extension, in-country expertise can do for career development. It also guided the development of the three key themes of this volume: methodological challenges, empirical perspectives and pedagogic innovations. Collectively, they build capacity to tackle the crucial question of what languages can do for the contemporary and future challenges of internationally operating organisations.

Research at the juncture of 'language' and 'management' provides scope for language-sensitive research to inform educational and business practice. The contributions of this volume, individually and collectively, offer much evidence for this. Collectively, the chapters illustrate that the study of language issues in international business and management is not at all running out of steam. Research in this field continues to be vibrant, creative and engaging. No wonder that it has found acceptance amongst international business scholars and finds an increasingly strong voice also in other business and management disciplines.

However, not much has changed in the world of practice in so far as then as now, there is not so much appetite for language-sensitive research amongst practitioners and business schools. Should we be concerned about the lack of impact on the business community and higher education organisations? The answer is 'yes', of course we should, and in particular the chapters in Part 3 about the teaching and underpinning pedagogies of language teaching point to practices that can quite easily be implemented in the classrooms of business schools. Quite often, in business school curricula culture, culture management and cultural communication (or miscommunications) are an established part of what is taught and how diversity as concomitant with globalisation is understood to be mainly (national) cultural diversity. Although much of these approaches are useful, we also want to point to the benefits of espousing language-based approaches as it is the only domain within business management research and pedagogies that has been able to articulate and theorise the dominant role of English as expressive of complexities far beyond the framing of language-as-mere-code. Likewise, language use can be observed directly and offers an immediate trajectory to establish communicative practices in a way that cultural approaches can perhaps not. Thus, we want to break a lance for the continuation for language-based academic practices, but also point to an academic project that requires a more sophisticated dialogue between 'culture' and 'language' and how it is taught and researched within international business and management. In other words, there is, we believe, a dialectical relationship between culture and language (in the Hegelian sense), which is in need of further scrutiny and interrogation. Namely that: (1) there is no access to culture without language; but (2) cultural knowledge highlights the ambiguity and relativity of language and language use, i.e. its potential to be appropriated to all purposes; and (3) only a deeper awareness of culture combined with linguistic reflexivity can restore the clarity of language.

## Reflexivity

An important and potentially unifying approach can be summarised under reflexivity, which is mentioned or discussed in all three parts. Namely, in Part 1 several of the chapters demonstrate how becoming aware of the authors' respective involvement, puzzlement and also their own cultural and language competence or lack thereof made them question their own predispositions to their research and their collaborators and enabled them to dig deeper into data analysis or interrogate the established vocabularies of research philosophies. The impossibility of fixing meaning once and for all (in English) rendered them more sensitive to ongoing interpretations of their data, of which Chapter 2 by Outila, Piekkari and Mihailova is an example as they adopted an editor's proposed translation as appropriate to inform their interpretation of data. In the empirical section, there are examples of authors commenting on the nature of the cross-language collaborations as they inform their engagement with the complexities of the research scene (Chapter 6) or where individuals' abilities to reflect on their own language use and learning is reflected in calls for future research by Tenzer and Pudelko (Chapter 5) and how individuals cope with language asymmetries by developing what Detzen and Löhlein (Chapter 7) refer to as linguistic reflexivity. In Chapter 8, Wilczewski et al., draw on employees' narrative analysis and on the concept of cultural reflexivity to parse learning processes in cross-cultural collaborations.

In Part 3, authors comment on classroom interactions and attitudes toward language learning—this in itself requires a degree of reflective engagement with traditional pedagogic approaches. Here, authors propose the intentional teaching and acquisitions of language skills as mobile and flexible and enabling students to leave their linguistic 'comfort zone' (Chapter 9, Gaibrois and Piekkari) or rethinking the approach to tie a language to a specific country or national culture—with language learning calling for the ability to navigate between cultures and high degrees of sensitivity (Chapter 11, Kassis-Henderson and Cohen), where competence (see Mughan, Chapter 10) can perhaps also include linguistic reflexivity—a competence which is central to the development of cultural sensitivity and the managing and participation in cross-cultural collaborations.

Thus this book offers the notion of linguistic reflexivity to be more strongly, more intentionally and more purposefully incorporated into the exploration of what it means to learn, teach, research and interact in a multilingual world. Reflexivity as an issue within research, and pedagogy is of course quite well established in other business and management fields of inquiry, where it has been defined as "a way of problematising what we know and how we know it, by revealing some of the assumptions on which knowledge is based" (Kelemen & Rumen, 2008, p. 190). Reflexivity can for example include providing information about the author's background or theoretical standpoint or commentary on the socio-political, historical or other aspects within which research and pedagogic projects are founded. Notwithstanding the debates surrounding the use and usefulness of reflexivity (for fuller discussion Johnson & Duberley, 2000), we believe that linguistic reflexivity offers a means to 'break open' some of the hegemonic assumptions about the use of English as the universal language of management knowledge (for fuller discussion about reflexive methodology see Alvesson & Sköldberg, 2009; for fuller discussion in the context of English, management and organisation studies see Steyaert & Janssens, 2013; Tietze, 2018). There is, so we argue, a definite link between hegemonic management practices (including the teaching and publishing of management knowledge and competences) and reflexivity as a way to 'balance out' the influence of such practices in normalising particular ways of being, understanding and responding to a multilingual world. Although reflexivity has not as yet featured all that strongly in the pedagogic and research agendas of language-based management research, there are some earlier pieces which look at hegemony in international research collaborations and which offer reflexivity as a means in response to its influence. In 2008 and 2009 a research collaboration consisting of four senior researchers, two Finnish and two British, reported about the difficulties they had in writing and publishing together. In brief, their analysis (Meriläinen, Tienari, Thomas, & Davies, 2008; Thomas, Tienari, Davies, & Meriläinen, 2009) provides language-based evidence which shows that the Finnish data got sidelined, that asymmetrical relationships between the researchers were founded in language and the normalised position of the English language and its meaning systems. The researchers resolved such unbalanced difference in their collaboration by developing what they call critical reflexivity to bring into sharp relief underlying patterns of thinking that usually remain unquestioned. It is therefore possible in our view to use linguistic reflexivity and to combine it with critical reflection. It then provides a powerful tool to remain thoughtfully involved with the use of English as a pedagogy and knowledge creating means. Linguistic reflexivity provides awareness into one's own language use, competences and preference of use, and critical reflexivity provides insight into the relational aspects of languages, including their status as dominant-central of marginal/peripheral.

A second strand of activity is embedded in the teaching practices and pedagogies employed in particular in business schools when educating and training what can be described as the future generation of global managers. The question arises: How are the findings and insights from research implemented, if at all, within the language teaching curricula and practices of business and management schools? We propose that although there may be pockets of alternate practice, the contemporary teaching of languages is based on assumptions that view languages as 'code', based on a receiver-sender model of communication (Shannon & Weaver, 1949) and that has been challenged by the linguistic turn in social sciences (e.g. Alvesson & Kärreman, 2000) and the development of critical linguistics (e.g. Fowler, Hodge, Kress, & Trew, 1979; Hodge & Kress, 1988; Wodak, 1989) which conceptualises the use of language as 'social practice'. The research in this book, as well as beyond this book, has clearly shown that language/s and their use in context is not a neutral coding and decoding of information, but a situated practice. Girin (1990) uses the notions of indexicality (the ability to point to the elements of the situation) and contextuality (the interpretation patterns and frames necessary to make sense of events) as two concepts to understand language as used in social context. We see these two concepts deriving from linguistics also as complementary to engaging with linguistic reflexivity as they provide pointers to the influence of situational and contextual influences.

Yet, in terms of the pedagogy of language teaching within business schools, the 'code' model still has prevailed to a large extent—beyond the necessities of teaching vocabulary and grammar and even in teaching contexts where the 'social practice' model clearly has a role to play. Its relative dominance is rooted in a variety of interconnected reasons, such as the demands on business schools to provide pragmatic solutions to complexity—teaching languages as a code to address linguistically and culturally complex situations is an expression of this. Likewise, the relative low status of 'languages' in business curricula is alignable to the dominance of the English language, which is seen as a means to standardise communications based sometimes on a native-speaker model of language users. Business English is taught increasingly, and English has become the language of instruction even in countries where English is not the national language. We do not criticise this status of English just for the sake of being critical. Rather, we point here to some of the complexities of multilingual businesses as captured in this edited volume and also in other resources. The realities of multilingual situations are so much more complex and context-contingent as language users respond in different ways to the ever changing and difficult communications they have to engage with. They activate their ability to engage reflectively with the multilingual communicative situations they have to manage, drawing on a large variety of different responses, going from communication avoidance, confrontation or activation, including translanguaging (see Chapter 7, by Detzen and Löhlein). Taking heed of such findings, one wonders whether a combination of teaching languages together with cultural skills based on the development of personal reflexivity may be a productive way forward to make languages a more central part of business schools' curricula. This may be a more appropriate way forward rather than relying on the (misleading) notion that international business is based on monolingual (English) practices and that miscommunications can be explained and addressed by understanding (national) cultural differences.

On the contrary, the chapters in this book show that the real issues faced by internationally operating organisations (as well as many domestic ones) are not of a monolingual nature, but that they are situated, fluid and embedded in language contexts that shift and change sometimes quite radically across a working day or working week. Tietze (2010) proposed to understand the work of international managers as language-based in so far as they have to be able to use and operate in English, but also in other languages. This entails also the notion of international managers being sense-makers and translators, who perpetually align culturally and linguistically different groups and units through their translation work. The integration of translation as a conceptual means and vocabulary has by now taken foot in language-sensitive research. If seen as a situated practice, through which individuals interact in order to construct and negotiate shared meaning (e.g. Ciuk, James, & Sliwa, 2018), there are possible and necessary pedagogic interventions through which cultural and language diversity can be taught and reflected upon in the classroom. In the foreword Denice and Lawrence Welch point to the possibility of 'language deglobalisation', by which they mean that the influence of English may be curtailed due to convenient and accessible machine translation as it becomes integrated in unfolding organisational communications. In this regard, machine translation may become an additional discursive practice through which the linguascapes of multilingual organisations are being negotiated. These are territories that are yet to be explored as some of the main contributions from language-sensitive research have still to be integrated into the mainstream of international business and management research and pedagogy.

What then can we learn from what has been offered in this book? Reflexivity as a means to break open normalised processes of knowledge production, knowledge sharing and dissemination is yet to be fully explored from a linguistic perspective. Specifically, what can be established from this edited volume of chapters is that in terms of research methods, empirical research projects and pedagogic practice, linguistic reflexivity has enabled researchers to question received vocabulary; to analyse data 'differently' and to remain open in terms of emergent meanings; to identify reflexivity as a key competence in learning and cross-cultural collaborations; and to see the classroom as a reflexive space to enable language learners to enjoy language diversity. The notions of indexicality and contextuality can be equally brought to bear on research projects as they can inform pedagogic practice. The contribution of language-sensitive research has been to conceptualise English as in relation with other languages, i.e. to acknowledge the importance of English as a communicative tool, practice and perspective. In this edited book, there is evidence that the field of language-sensitive research has moved on in so far as English is established as an important academic and social practice— yet, it is seen as a practice, rather than the 'super-code' through which everything can be understood and communicated. Taking a speculative glance into the future, one wonders if translatorial reflexivity may be a means and approach to reflect not only on the 'language dominant' (English), the 'language other', but also on the translated outcome and hybrid of multilingual encounters.

In concluding, we want to advocate a different habitus for international business and management research and pedagogy. The notion of habitus goes back to Bourdieu (1977), who defines linguistic habitus as a set of unquestioned dispositions toward languages in society. Bourdieu discusses the symbolic power of language in terms of a linguistic marketplace (1991), defined as an interactive space where even limited proficiency in a certain language or languages offers greater social capital than proficiency in others. In terms of mainstream international business research and pedagogy the most favoured currency is clearly English. The habitus of our field can therefore be described as being a monolingual habitus (Gogolin, 1994). It is built on a set of assumptions about the uniformity of language (and culture), expressed in unrealistic expectations for native-like proficiency in second or foreign languages and research methodologies imperfectly suited to multilingual settings with dominant languages other than English.

The fact that people do not tend to question this status differential between languages means that a certain linguistic habitus is in place. Gogolin (1994) uses the term monolingual habitus, to describe linguistic self-conception that can make a field blind to multilingual, multicultural ways of being in the world and engaging with it. Building on Gogolin's critique of the monolingual habitus, Benson (2013) proposes the term multilingual habitus which transcends the myth of uniformity of languages (and cultures) and that the normality that is produced through the unquestioning and unreflective use of English in our times perpetuates a notion of normality that is dramatically different from the multilingual realities captured, analysed and discussed in this book. We therefore advocate the reflective use of English as a means to share our knowledge through our publications, in classrooms with our students and in our meetings and exchanges. We also believe that adopting a different (multilingual) habitus and how it is embodied and reproduced in practices will remain a challenge. Although the research arm of our community is by now well established and respected, we need to continue to push forward the integration of insights gained into classroom pedagogies and cooperations with business practitioners.

# References

Alvesson, M., & Kärreman, D. (2000). Taking the linguistic turn in organizational research: Challenges, responses, consequences. *The Journal of Applied Behavioral Science, 36*, 136–158.

Alvesson, M., & Sköldberg, K. (2009). *Reflexive methodology: New vistas for qualitative research* (2nd ed.). London: Sage.

Benson, C. (2013). Towards adopting a multilingual habitus in educational development. In K. Kosonen & C. Benson (Eds.), *Language issues in comparative education* (pp. 283–299). Rotterdam: Sense Publisher.

Bourdieu, P. (1977). *Outline of a theory of practice.* Cambridge: Cambridge University Press.

Bourdieu, P. (1991). *Language and symbolic power.* Oxford: Polity Press, Blackwell Publishing Ltd.

Ciuk, S., James, P., & Sliwa, M. (2018). Micropolitical dynamics of interlingual translation process in an MNC subsidiary. *British Journal of Management, 30*(4), 926–942.

Fowler, R., Hodge, B., Kress, G., & Trew, T. (1979). *Language and control*. London: Routledge.

Girin, J. (1990). Problèmes du langage dans les organisations. In J.-F. Chanlat et al. (Eds.), *L'individu dans l'organisation: les dimensions oubliées* (pp. 37–77). Québec: Presses Universitaires de Laval. Collection "Sciences administratives". Paris: et éditions ESKA.

Gogolin, I. (1994). *Der monolingual habitus der multilingualen schule*. Münster and New York: Waxmann Verlag.

Hodges, R., & Kress, G. (1988). *Social semiotics*. Cambridge: Polity Press.

Johnson, P., & Duberley, J. (2000). *Understanding management research: An introduction to epistemology*. London: Sage.

Kelemen, M., & Rumen, N. (2008). *An introduction to critical management research*. London: Sage.

Meriläinen, S., Tienari, J., Thomas, R., & Davies, A. (2008). Hegemonic academic practices: Experiences of publishing from the periphery. *Organization*, *15*(4), 584–597.

Shannon, C. E., & Weaver, W. (1949). *Mathematical theory of communication*. Urbana: University of Illinois Press.

Steyaert, C., & Janssens, M. (2013). Multilingual scholarship and the paradox of translation and languages in organization and management research. *Organization*, *20*(1), 131–142.

Thomas, R., Tienari, J., Davies, A., & Meriläinen, S. (2009). Let's talk about "us": A reflexive account of a cross-cultural research collaboration. *Journal of Management Inquiry*, *18*(4), 313–324.

Tietze, S. (2010). International managers as translation. *European Journal of International Management*, *4*(1–1), 184–199.

Tietze, S. (2018). Multilingual research, monolingual publications: Management scholarship in English only? *European Journal of International Management*, *12*(1–2), 28–45.

Wodak, R. (1989). *Language, power and ideology: Studies in political discourse*. Amsterdam: John Benjamins Publishing Company.

# Index

Note: Page numbers in *italics* indicate figures and in **bold** indicate tables on the corresponding pages.

Printed in the United States
by Baker & Taylor Publisher Services